T0255919

Lecture Notes in Computer Science   10732

Commenced Publication in 1973
Founding and Former Series Editors:
Gerhard Goos, Juris Hartmanis, and Jan van Leeuwen

Editorial Board

David Hutchison
   Lancaster University, Lancaster, UK
Takeo Kanade
   Carnegie Mellon University, Pittsburgh, PA, USA
Josef Kittler
   University of Surrey, Guildford, UK
Jon M. Kleinberg
   Cornell University, Ithaca, NY, USA
Friedemann Mattern
   ETH Zurich, Zurich, Switzerland
John C. Mitchell
   Stanford University, Stanford, CA, USA
Moni Naor
   Weizmann Institute of Science, Rehovot, Israel
C. Pandu Rangan
   Indian Institute of Technology, Madras, India
Bernhard Steffen
   TU Dortmund University, Dortmund, Germany
Demetri Terzopoulos
   University of California, Los Angeles, CA, USA
Doug Tygar
   University of California, Berkeley, CA, USA
Gerhard Weikum
   Max Planck Institute for Informatics, Saarbrücken, Germany

More information about this series at http://www.springer.com/series/7408

Sunita Chandrasekaran · Guido Juckeland (Eds.)

Accelerator Programming Using Directives

4th International Workshop, WACCPD 2017
Held in Conjunction with the International Conference
for High Performance Computing, Networking,
Storage and Analysis, SC 2017
Denver, CO, USA, November 13, 2017
Proceedings

 Springer

Editors
Sunita Chandrasekaran
University of Delaware
Newark, DE
USA

Guido Juckeland
Helmholtz-Zentrum
  Dresden-Rossendorf e.V.
Dresden
Germany

ISSN 0302-9743   ISSN 1611-3349   (electronic)
Lecture Notes in Computer Science
ISBN 978-3-319-74895-5   ISBN 978-3-319-74896-2   (eBook)
https://doi.org/10.1007/978-3-319-74896-2

Library of Congress Control Number: 2018931882

LNCS Sublibrary: SL2 – Programming and Software Engineering

© Springer International Publishing AG, part of Springer Nature 2018
This work is subject to copyright. All rights are reserved by the Publisher, whether the whole or part of the
material is concerned, specifically the rights of translation, reprinting, reuse of illustrations, recitation,
broadcasting, reproduction on microfilms or in any other physical way, and transmission or information
storage and retrieval, electronic adaptation, computer software, or by similar or dissimilar methodology now
known or hereafter developed.
The use of general descriptive names, registered names, trademarks, service marks, etc. in this publication
does not imply, even in the absence of a specific statement, that such names are exempt from the relevant
protective laws and regulations and therefore free for general use.
The publisher, the authors and the editors are safe to assume that the advice and information in this book are
believed to be true and accurate at the date of publication. Neither the publisher nor the authors or the editors
give a warranty, express or implied, with respect to the material contained herein or for any errors or
omissions that may have been made. The publisher remains neutral with regard to jurisdictional claims in
published maps and institutional affiliations.

Printed on acid-free paper

This Springer imprint is published by the registered company Springer International Publishing AG
part of Springer Nature
The registered company address is: Gewerbestrasse 11, 6330 Cham, Switzerland

Preface

Welcome to the proceedings of WACCPD 2017, the 4th Workshop on Accelerator Programming Using Directives (http://waccpd.org/).

In the current pre-exascale era, domain and computational scientists still struggle to adapt large applications or prototype new ideas on the plethora of novel hardware architecture with diverse memory subsystems or cores with different ISAs or accelerators of varied types. The HPC community is in constant need for sophisticated software tools and techniques to port legacy code to these emerging platforms.

Given the complexity in hardware, maintaining a single code base yet achieving performance portable solutions continues to pose a daunting task. Directive-based programming models such as OpenACC and OpenMP have been tackling this issue by offering scientists a high-level approach to accelerate scientific applications and develop solutions that are portable and yet do not compromise on performance or accuracy. Such programming paradigms have facilitated complex heterogeneous systems in order to be classified as first-class citizens for HPC.

This workshop aims to solicit papers that explore innovative language features and their implementations, stories and lessons learnt while using directives to migrate scientific legacy code to parallel processors, state-of-the-art compilation and runtime scheduling techniques, performance optimization and analysis on state-of-the-art hardware etc.

WACCPD has been one of the major forums for bringing together users, developers, as well as the software and tools community to share knowledge and experiences to program emerging complex parallel computing systems.

WACCPD 2017 received 14 submissions out of which nine were accepted for presentation at the workshop and for publication in these proceedings. The Program Committee of the workshop comprised 26 members spanning various university, national labs, and industries. Each paper received at most four reviews. Four papers were accepted directly, while five papers went through a shepherding phase where the authors were asked to revisit and redo the paper based on feedback obtained from reviewers. The authors were given a 15-day window to fix the paper and resubmit for the reviewer to make a decision.

All 14 authors were also strongly encouraged to add source files for reproducibility purposes upon request from reviewers. Ten out of 14 authors were able to add these source files, which the reviewers greatly appreciated.

The program co-chairs invited John E. Stone from UIUC to give a keynote address on "Using Accelerator Directives to Adapt Science Applications for State-of-the-Art HPC Architectures." John is Senior Research Programmer at the Theoretical and Computational Biophysics Group and NIH Center for Macromolecular Modeling and Bioinformatics of the University of Illinois at Urbana-Champaign.

The invited talk was given by Randy Allen, Director of Advanced Research in the Embedded Systems Division of Mentor Graphics. His talk was titled "The Challenges Faced by OpenACC Compilers."

Based on rigorous reviews and ranking scores of all papers reviewed, we arrived at two best paper award recipients this year. They were:

- Takuma Yamaguchi, Kohei Fujita, Tsuyoshi Ichimura, Muneo Hori, Maddegedara Lalith, and Kengo Nakajima (University of Tokyo, Japan).
  "Implicit Low Order Unstructured Finite-Element Multiple Simulation Enhanced by Dense Computation Using OpenACC"
- Khalid Ahmad (University of Utah, USA) and Michael Wolfe (PGI/NVIDIA)
  "Automatic Testing of OpenACC Applications"

Emphasizing the importance of using directives for legacy scientific applications, each presenter was given two recently released textbooks on programming models, one on "Using OpenMP – The Next Step" and the other on "OpenACC for Programmers: Concepts & Strategies." The attendees were given reference guides of both models.

January 2018   Sunita Chandrasekaran
                                                                    Guido Juckeland

Organization

Steering Committee

Barbara Chapman	Stony Brook University, USA
Satoshi Matsuoka	Titech, Japan
Duncan Poole	OpenACC, USA
Thomas Schulthess	CSCS, Switzerland
Oscar Hernandez	ORNL, USA
Kuan-Ching Li	Providence University, Taiwan
Jeff Vetter	ORNL, USA

Program Co-chairs

Sunita Chandrasekaran	University of Delaware, USA
Guido Juckeland	HZDR, Germany

Program Committee

James Beyer	NVIDIA, USA
Henri Callandra	TOTAL, USA
Robert Dietrich	TU Dresden, Germany
Mark Govette	NOAA, USA
Georg Hager	FAU, Germany
Jeff Hammond	Intel, USA
Christian Iwainsky	TU Darmstadt, Germany
Arpith J. Jacob	IBM, USA
Henri Jin	NASA-Ames, USA
Adrian Jackason	EPCC, UK
Wayne Joubert	ORNL, USA
Michael Klemm	Intel, Germany
Jeff Larkin	NVIDIA, USA
Seyong Lee	ORNL, USA
C. J. Newburn	NVIDIA, USA
Antonio J. Pena	BSC, Spain
William Sawyer	CSCS, Switzerland
Thomas Schwinge	MentorGraphics, Germany
Ray Sheppard	Indiana University, USA
Sameer Shende	University of Oregon, USA
Peter Steinbach	Scionics, Germany
Christian Terboven	RWTH Aachen University, Germany

Xiaonan Tian	NVIDIA/PGI, USA
Cheng Wang	Microsoft, USA
Michael Wolfe	PGI, USA

Publicity and Publication Chair

| Sebastian Starke | HZDR, Germany |

Held in conjunction with

SC17: The International Conference for High Performance Computing, Networking, Storage and Analysis
Denver, Colorado,
November 12–18, 2017

Contents

Applications

An Example of Porting PETSc Applications to Heterogeneous Platforms with OpenACC

Pi-Yueh Chuang[1](✉) ⓘ and Fernanda S. Foertter[2] ⓘ

[1] The George Washington University, Washington DC 20052, USA
pychuang@gwu.edu
[2] Oak Ridge National Laboratory, Oak Ridge, TN 37830, USA
foertterfs@ornl.gov

Abstract. In this paper, we document the workflow of our practice to port a PETSc application with OpenACC to a supercomputer, Titan, at Oak Ridge National Laboratory. Our experience shows a few lines of code modifications with OpenACC directives can give us a speedup of 1.34x in a PETSc-based Poisson solver (conjugate gradient method with algebraic multigrid preconditioner). This demonstrates the feasibility of enabling GPU capability in PETSc with OpenACC. We hope our work can serve as a reference to those who are interested in porting their legacy PETSc applications to modern heterogeneous platforms.

Keywords: OpenACC · PETSc · GPU computing

1 Introduction

For over two decades, researchers have been using PETSc (Portable, Extensible Toolkit for Scientific Computation) [1] as an underlying linear algebra library in many large-scale simulation codes (see the list of applications in ref. [2]). While PETSc provides excellent performance on traditional supercomputers (i.e., CPU only), it still lacks satisfying GPU support. In fact, to our best knowledge, PETSc has not had any official release that supports GPU computing. The GPU-enabled version [3] only exists at PETSc's Bitbucket repository [4], which implies it's not yet mature enough for general end users to use. Even with the GPU-enabled version, users may encounter difficulty while trying to use it in their applications, such as compilation or dependency issues. For example,

This manuscript has been co-authored by UT-Battelle, LLC, under contract DE-AC05-00OR22725 with the US Department of Energy (DOE). The US government retains and the publisher, by accepting the article for publication, acknowledges that the US government retains a nonexclusive, paid-up, irrevocable, worldwide license to publish or reproduce the published form of this manuscript, or allow others to do so, for US government purposes. DOE will provide public access to these results of federally sponsored research in accordance with the DOE Public Access Plan (http://energy.gov/downloads/doe-public-access-plan).

© Springer International Publishing AG, part of Springer Nature 2018
S. Chandrasekaran and G. Juckeland (Eds.): WACCPD 2017, LNCS 10732, pp. 3–19, 2018.
https://doi.org/10.1007/978-3-319-74896-2_1

when building GPU-enabled PETSc on Titan [5], the building process will stop and complain that it does not support batch systems. Though there may be workarounds to bypass these issues, end users without strong knowledge in the building process may not be willing to spend extra time just to make PETSc work.

Due to the lagging GPU support in PETSc, developers of PETSc applications need to find other solutions to port their codes to modern heterogeneous platforms (CPU + GPU). Replacing part of PETSc functionalities with GPU libraries is a typical way to do that. For example, in ref. [6, 7], Chuang and Barba replace PETSc's KSP solver with NVIDIA's AmgX solver to access multi-GPU multigrid-preconditioned Krylov solvers. This kind of modifications, however, requires non-trivial code modifications in their original applications. One issue is that many researchers can not afford extra coding time when the code development is not the main topic in their research projects. Another issue is that more code modifications in a mature software imply higher possibility of messing up the whole program and getting into the nightmare of debugging. Hence, researchers may not be willing to spend time on the modifications and just keep running CPU-only codes on modern heterogeneous platforms.

When porting a legacy code to heterogeneous platforms, the balance between coding effort and the performance satisfactory is the top concern. OpenACC stands out for this purpose. Through compiler directives and automatic parallelization, OpenACC provides developers an opportunity to port expensive kernels to GPU without massive code rewriting. That is to say, it provides a possibility of minor code modifications in an exchange for an acceptable performance enhancement.

In this work, we document the workflow of how we, as end users of PETSc, accelerate a PETSc application with OpenACC on Titan at Oak Ridge National Laboratory. The primary goal of this work is to provide a tutorial document to Titan users and encourage them to port their legacy code to GPU. Though the work mainly focuses on Titan, we hope our experience can still serve as a reference to the users of other heterogeneous platforms. The work is not the first OpenACC documentation of linear solvers [8], and it is not the first example of applications using both MPI and OpenACC [9]. We do, however, believe this is the first example of applying OpenACC to PETSc and showing the performance improvement of a PETSc application.

The example code we used is a PETSc-based Poisson solver. Poisson solvers are commonly seen and well-studied in many areas of scientific simulations. Yet it is still a bottleneck in many areas, especially in CFD (computational fluid dynamics). For example, in the simulations of unsteady incompressible fluid flow, solving Poisson equations may take over 90% of the overall computing time [6]. The setting of the linear solver used is preconditioned conjugate gradient method, and the preconditioner is algebraic multigrid preconditioner. The problem size is 27 M unknowns, which fits into the host memory of one Titan computing node.

The result shows that, with few lines of code modification, it's possible to accelerate the Poisson solver with a speedup of 1.34x on a single Titan node. This demonstrates the feasibility of accelerating legacy PETSc application with OpenACC directives. Though it's not the primary focus, we also present strong scaling results which scale up to 64 Titan nodes. Readers can find all necessary material to reproduce the results in the GitHub repository [10].

2   Workflow and System Description

2.1   Workflow

Our workflow is:

Stage (1)   profiling the program at function level with Score-P [11],
Stage (2)   identifying the most expensive kernels and understanding the code,
Stage (3)   inserting OpenACC directives,
Stage (4)   profiling the program with NVProf [12] to show data transfer latency,
Stage (5)   tuning/modifying the program to hide more latency, and
Stage (6)   repeating (4) and (5) until satisfactory performance is obtained.

2.2   System

All works were done on a single computing node on Titan, except the strong scaling test shown in the last section, which scales up to 64 nodes. A single Titan node has 16 AMD CPU cores (Opteron 6274) and 1 NVIDIA K20x GPU. The host memory size is 32 GB. We compiled all codes with the compiler wrapper developed specifically for Titan, and its underlying compiler is PGI 17.5.0. Optimization flags were used. See the Makefile in the GitHub repository.

3   Results and Discussion

3.1   Profiling with Score-P

The source code of PETSc and our Poisson solver were compiled with Score-P instruments in this stage. The result of Score-P profiling shows that, among the top-level functions in the call tree under the `main` function, `KSPSetup` takes about 54% of the overall wall time, and `KSPSolve` 39%. Creation of Laplacian operator (the coefficient matrix), left-, and right-hand side vectors only accounts for the remaining 7%. `KSPSetup` sets up the Krylov solver and the preconditioner, while `KSPSolve` solves the system of linear equations. It is not surprising to see `KSPSetup` takes more time than `KSPSolve` does because algebraic multigrid preconditioners require non-trivial time to generate operators in each grid level.

Figure 1 shows the exclusive time of all functions regardless which levels in the call tree they are in. We can see that the most expensive function, `MatMult_SeqAIJ`, takes only 21% of the overall time. This implies that even if we can accelerate `MatMult_SeqAIJ` with a huge speedup, it won't help the overall performance a lot.

Many simulations, especially in CFD, however, need to call `KSPSolve` many times. For example, each simulation in ref. [13] requires calling `KSPSolve` two hundred thousand times but calling `KSPSetup` only once. Hence, we should focus on `KSPSolve` and neglect `KSPSetup`.

We filter out the functions outside the scope of `KSPSolve` and show the results in Fig. 2. Luckily, `MatMult_SeqAIJ` is still the dominant function, and it now takes over 50% of the run time inside the scope of KSPSolve. If we can accelerate MatMult_SeqAIJ a lot, we should expect to see a non-trivial speedup in KSPSolve and real CFD simulation codes.

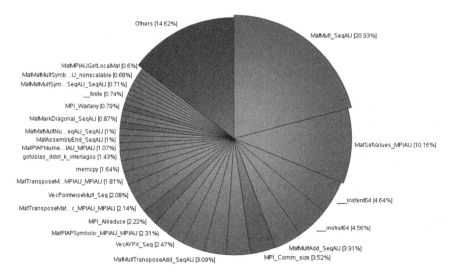

Fig. 1. Accumulated exclusive times of all functions in all levels of call tree

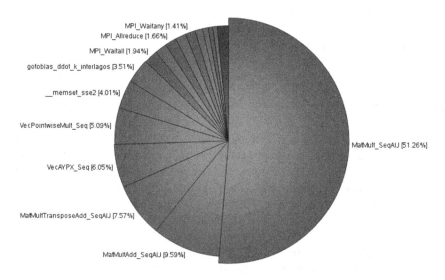

Fig. 2. Acculumated exclusive time of functions inside the scope of KSPSolve

3.2 The Most Expensive Kernel: **MatMult_SeqAIJ**

MatMult_SeqAIJ carries out the multiplication of a sparse matrix and a vector (SpMVM) on a local process with a sequential matrix in AIJ format. AIJ is one of

PETSc's sparse matrix format. Apparently, MPI communication is not involved in this most expensive kernel. This benefits us because we can pretend we are accelerating sequential code with OpenACC and don't bother with MPI issues.

Many lines of code in `MatMult_SeqAIJ` are for conditional compilation and if-condition branches. Only the following lines of code are executed when our Poisson solver calls `MatMult_SeqAIJ` (the line numbers are based on the source files in our GitHub repository):

```
49  for (i=0; i<m; i++) {
50     n              = ii[i+1] - ii[i];
51     aj             = a->j + ii[i];
52     aa             = a->a + ii[i];
53     sum            = 0.0;
54     PetscSparseDensePlusDot(sum,x,aa,aj,n);
55     y[i] = sum;
56  }
```

Code Snippet 1 Original CPU code of `MatMult_SeqAIJ`

From Code Snippet 1, we can see the underlying data layout of AIJ sparse matrix is CSR (compressed sparse row) format. `ii` is the array of compressed row indices; `a->j` is the array of column indices; and `a->a` is the array of non-zero entries. The loop with index `i` loops through all rows. `n` represents the number of nonzeros in the `i`-th row. `aj` and `aa` represent the column indices and values of the nonzeros in the `i`-th row. `PetscSparseDensePlusDot` is a macro (shown in Code Snippet 2) doing the multiplication of `i`-th row and the vector `x`.

```
410  #define PetscSparseDensePlusDot(sum,r,xv,xi,nnz) { \
411      PetscInt __i; \
412      for (__i=0; __i<nnz; __i++) sum += xv[__i] * r[xi[__i]];}
413  #endif
```

Code Snippet 2 Definition of macro `PetscSparseDensePlusDot`

The code shown in Code Snippet 1 includes double loops (after expanding the macro). The outer loop loops through all rows, while the inner loop loops through each non-zero entry in a row. Regardless the competition caused by reading data, each iteration is almost independent to other iterations at the same level, except a reduction operation of `sum` in the end of every iteration of the inner loop.

We ignore the performance issues caused by data-reading competition in this example because this may require redesigning the algorithm, which we try to avoid here. If we consider adding some OpenACC directives to the original code without substantial redesigning, here are two options:

(1) We distribute the outer loop across blocks/gangs and distribute the inner loop with threads/vectors. We will need a reduction clause for the inner loop.
(2) We distribute the outer loop across threads directly, making the inner loop sequential to a CUDA thread.

Note, block/thread and gang/vector are the same concept but different terminology used in CUDA and OpenACC.

Option 1 seems to allow us to launch a huge number of threads, and each thread only has to perform a very simple task at one time, i.e., one multiplication and one addition. NVIDIA GPU favors this kind of massive-simple-task computations. However, one problem is that we are handling sparse matrix, and there are only a few non-zero entries in each row. In other words, the number of iterations of the inner loop may be smaller than the number of threads in a CUDA warp, which is 32. Distributing the inner loops at thread-level may cause a lot of inactive threads in a warp. Given that NVIDIA GPU is warp-based, it means a performance penalty.

In option 2, due to the inner loop becomes sequential to a CUDA thread, there will be no reduction operation required. The loading of one iteration in the outer loop should not be heavy to a CUDA thread because of the small number of iterations in the inner loop. The drawback of this option is that, if we want to maximize the utilization of a GPU, we will need enough total number of threads, and hence enough total number of rows. So, if the matrix is small, this option may not be beneficial.

We choose option 2 here because most of the matrices in this example have many numbers of rows but few nonzeros in each row, i.e., it's extremely sparse. For example, the Laplacian operator is a sparse banded matrix with 27 millions of rows, while there are only up to 7 nonzeros in each row. We believe option 2 best fits this number of rows and the extreme sparsity.

The Laplacian is not the only matrix involved in the SpMVM in our Poisson solver. In the algebraic multigrid preconditioner we used, there is at least one matrix in each grid level involved in SpMVM. These matrices are created by PETSc implicitly. It's not straightforward for end users to know the sparsity and sparse patterns of these implicit matrices, so we cannot be sure about if option 2 still applies. Those matrices, however, are still in CSR layout, which implies a certain degree of sparsity. We hence assume that option 2 is also beneficial for those implicit matrices.

3.3   Four Steps Toward the Final Version of OpenACC Kernel

After several iterations of Stage 4–6, we categorize our progress toward the final OpenACC kernel into 4 steps.

Step 1: inserting basic OpenACC directive
In this step, we insert an OpenACC directive above the outer for loop to automatically parallelize it. Note we also have a directive to tell the compiler that the inner loop is sequential to each CUDA thread:

```
61   # pragma acc kernels loop independent gang vector(32) \
62     copyin(ii[:m+1] , cols[:a->nz], data[:a->nz], x[:xSize]) \
63     copyout(y[:m])
64   for (i=0; i<m; i++) {
65     n          = ii[i+1] - ii[i];
66     aj         = cols + ii[i];
67     aa         = data + ii[i];
68     sum        = 0.0;
69     # pragma acc loop seq reduction(+:sum)
70     PetscSparseDensePlusDot(sum,x,aa,aj,n);
71     y[i] = sum;
72   }
```

Code Snippet 3 OpenACC version of `MatMult_SeqAIJ` *in step 1*

m, `a->nz`, and `xSize` represent the total number of rows, total number of nonzeros, and the length of x array, respectively. `cols` and `data` are two pointers serve as aliases to `a->j` and `a->a`. With these two aliases, we don't have to upload the whole data structure, a, to GPU. a has other members that has nothing to do with CSR layout and are not required for the OpenACC kernel.

The profiling with Score-P shows the OpenACC kernel in this step is slower than the original CPU code. The speedup is about 0.4x compared to the result of the CPU code on a 16-CPU-core Titan node. Figure 3 shows the profiling result with NVProf.

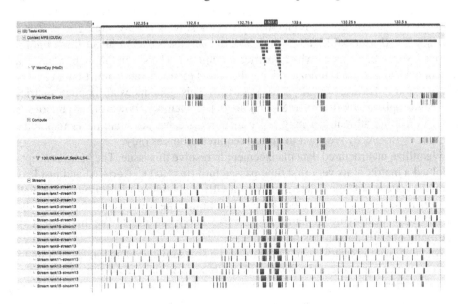

Fig. 3. NVProf result of the OpenACC kernel in the step 1

The light brown and cyan regions represent data movement and kernel execution. Apparently, the kernel takes a long time to upload data from the host to GPU in each call to `MatMult_SeqAIJ`. This is expected because, with this simple OpenACC directive, the kernel uploads the matrix and x array and download the y array whenever it is called. And this is the reason why this OpenACC kernel is much slower than the original CPU code.

An interesting observation is that the GPU doesn't know 16 different processes are running on it. The GPU only sees 16 different streams. And hence it can execute different ranks' GPU kernels concurrently and hide data transfer latency to some degree. We believe this is because of the CUDA Proxy mechanism on Titan. Unfortunately, the size of data is too big, so this surprising concurrent execution cannot hide much latency.

On other machines without CUDA Proxy, like personal desktops or workstations, GPU may still see 16 different processes instead of streams, and the kernel executions may not be concurrent. For those machines, MPS server and the variable CUDA_DEVICE_MAX_CONNECTIONS may be required to enable this kind of concurrent behavior.

Step 2: uploading required data to GPU only once

The code in step 1 takes a long time moving data because it has to upload the matrix and x vector to GPU and download y vector every time it calls MatMult_SeqAIJ. We know, however, the matrices used in SpMVM inside Krylov linear solvers seldom change, at least not in a single solving event (i.e., a single call to KSPSolve in our example). So, the next improvement is to upload those matrices only once, unless it is changed on the host afterward.

The first thought may be to upload required matrices manually. There are, however, many other matrices created implicitly by Krylov solvers and the multigrid preconditioners. As end users of PETSc, we don't have any information about these implicit matrices, so we can't know which matrices to upload. The second thought, then, may be to upload all matrices automatically at the end of matrix creation function. In PETSc, this function is MatAssemblyEnd_SeqAIJ. This guarantees all implicit matrices also being uploaded before MatMult_SeqAIJ. Memory, however, is precious on GPU. Uploading all matrices may waste memory because some are never required in MatMult_SeqAIJ. We want to upload required matrices only.

We utilize unstructured data management to resolve this issue. The basic concept is to upload a matrix at its very first time passed into MatMult_SeqAIJ and just leave it on GPU afterward. We delete a matrix on GPU only when it is destroyed manually by users or automatically by other PETSc functions. The lowest-level function called when PETSc destroying a matrix is MatDestroy_SeqAIJ. We implement the destroying of GPU data in this function.

Another issue is that we can't guarantee the sparse pattern and values of a matrix won't change after being uploaded to GPU. Changes in the sparse pattern require re-allocating memory; changes in values require updating data. Fortunately, in PETSc, every time a sparse matrix changes its data, MatAssemblyEnd_SeqAIJ is called by the end of changing process. We can hence, in this function, re-allocate memory or update data if a matrix already exists on GPU. And if a matrix is purely on CPU, no data manipulations required.

The following are code snippets and some comments of MatMult_SeqAIJ, MatDestroy_SeqAIJ, and MatAssemblyEnd_SeqAIJ. We omit unchanged/ unimportant lines and comments to save space.

MatMult_SeqAIJ :

```
61    # pragma acc enter data copyin(ii[:m+1])
62    # pragma acc enter data copyin(cols[:a->nz])
63    # pragma acc enter data copyin(data[:a->nz])

66    # pragma acc enter data copyin(x[:xSize])

69    # pragma acc kernels loop independent gang vector(32) \
70      present(ii[:m+1], cols[:a->nz], data[:a->nz], x[:xSize]) \
71      copyout(y[:m])
72-80 /* the same for loop as we have in step 1 */

83    # pragma acc exit data delete(x[:xSize])
```

Code Snippet 4 OpenACC version of MatMult_SeqAIJ *in step 2*

We use `enter data` directive and `copyin` clause to upload the data. In recent OpenACC versions, `copyin` will allocate memory and upload data only when the data do not exist on GPU. This behavior ensures we only upload the matrix once at its first time passed into `MatMult_SeqAIJ`. The `present` clause in kernel directive indicates the data should already exist on GPU. Note the x vector in SpMVM normally changes time to time, while the matrix keeps the same. So we don't keep x vector on GPU (the `delete` clause in line 83).

MatDestroy_SeqAIJ:

```
7     # include <openacc.h>

9-19  /* original PETSc's code omitted. Nothing changed */

22    int present[3];

30    present[0] = acc_is_present(ai, (A->rmap->n+1)*sizeof(PetscInt));
31    present[1] = acc_is_present(aj, (a->nz)*sizeof(PetscInt));
32    present[2] = acc_is_present(aa, (a->nz)*sizeof(MatScalar));

35    # pragma acc exit data delete(ai[0:A->rmap->n+1]) if(present[0])
36    # pragma acc exit data delete(aj[0:a->nz]) if(present[1])
37    # pragma acc exit data delete(aa[0:a->nz]) if(present[2])
```

Code Snippet 5 OpenACC version of MatDestroy_SeqAIJ *in step 2*

We use a runtime API, `acc_is_present()`, to check whether data present on GPU, so we have to include the header "`openacc.h`." The clause `if` makes sure that `exit data delete(...)` directives will only be executed when the data present on GPU. Nothing happens in these lines if non-GPU matrices get passed into `MatDestroy_SeqAIJ`.

`MatAssemblyEnd_SeqAIJ:`

7	`# include <openacc.h>`
9-21	`/* Original PETSc source code omitted */`

27
28
29
30
	`present[0] = acc_is_present(ai, (A->rmap->n+1)*sizeof(PetscInt));`
	`present[1] = acc_is_present(aj, (a->nz)*sizeof(PetscInt));`
	`present[2] = acc_is_present(aa, (a->nz)*sizeof(MatScalar));`

34 35	`# pragma acc exit data delete(aj[:a->nz]) if(present[1])` `# pragma acc exit data delete(aa[:a->nz]) if(present[2])`
37-79 80	`/* Original PETSc source code omitted */`

84
85
86
	`# pragma acc update device(ai[0:A->rmap->n+1]) if(present[0])`
	`# pragma acc enter data copyin(aj[0:a->nz]) if(present[1])`
	`# pragma acc enter data copyin(aa[0:a->nz]) if(present[2])`

Code Snippet 6 OpenACC version of `MatAssemblyEnd_SeqAIJ` *in step 2*

If a matrix exists on GPU but is still passed into `MatAssemblyEnd_SeqAIJ`, it means something in the matrix got changed on the host after we last time uploaded it to GPU. Hence, we have to re-allocate memory (if the sparse pattern changed) or update values. When data exist on GPU, we only delete `aj` and `aa` for re-allocating purpose. The length of the array of the compressed row indices, `ai`, is likely to remain the same because changes to sparse patterns won't affect it. But values in `ai` may be changed. We can simply use `update` clause later to update those changed values. Line 84–86 upload updated data if this matrix had GPU data prior being passed into the function. Otherwise, nothing happens in these lines.

Speedup is about 1.34x in `KSPSolve` compared to the result of the CPU code on a 16-CPU-core Titan node. And from Fig. 4, we can see the data moved to GPU during each `MatMult_SeqAIJ` call is less than that in step 1. And now CUDA Proxy on Titan

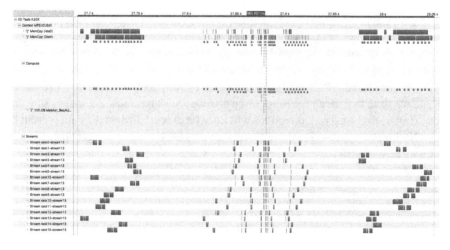

Fig. 4. NVProf result of the OpenACC kernel in the step 2

is doing a good job. Relatively more data latency is hidden by concurrently execute different ranks' GPU tasks.

Step 3: hiding latency with concurrent GPU/CPU executions
So far, during data transfers, the host is idle. If we are sure that the following host code has nothing to do with the data moving to or downloading from GPU, it's safe to execute the following host code at the same time while waiting for data transfer. This should be able to hide some data transfer latency.

The key concept is that, in MatMult_SeqAIJ, when uploading data, we can run partial SpMVM with CPU. We use a while loop to carry out this. In one iteration of the while loop, a row in the matrix multiplies x vector. The while loop will stop when all data finish uploading. Next, the multiplication of remaining rows in the matrix will be handled by the OpenACC kernel, just as in step 1 and step 2.

MatMult_SeqAIJ:

```
64     # pragma acc enter data copyin(ii[:m+1]) async
65     # pragma acc enter data copyin(cols[:a->nz]) async
66     # pragma acc enter data copyin(data[:a->nz]) async

69     # pragma acc enter data copyin(x[:xSize]) async

72     PetscInt offset = 0;
73     while((! acc_async_test_all()) && (offset < m))
74     {
75-80    /* SpMVM of one row and x. The row index is `offset`. */
81       offset += 1;
82     }

85     # pragma acc kernels loop independent gang vector(32) \
86       present(ii[:m+1], cols[:a->nz], data[:a->nz], x[:xSize]) \
87       copyout(y[offset:remain])
88     for (i=offset; i<m; i++) {
89-95    /* SpMVM of a row and x. The row index is `i`. */
96     }

99     # pragma acc exit data delete(x[:xSize]) async
```

Code Snippet 7 OpenACC version of MatMult_SeqAIJ *in step 3*

We add async clause to the directives of data uploading. With async clause, the program will step into the while loop immediately after submitting the data transfer job to default CUDA stream. The while loop executes a single-row SpMVM in each iteration. The condition for the while loop to stop is all jobs on GPU finished. This is done through runtime API acc_async_test_all(). We have to change the starting index of the outer for loop and the y vector in the copyout clause accordingly to offset.

The performance of step 3 is similar to that of step 2 on Titan if we use all 16 CPU cores. But as we will see in the next section (Fig. 7), if we use only one CPU core and one K20x, step 3 is still a little bit faster than step 2. Apparently, the number of rows executed in the while loop is relatively small compared to the overall number of rows. When we use more CPU cores and with CUDA Proxy enabled, the latency hidden in step 3 may be trivial relative to that hidden by CUDA Proxy. In other words, it's still possible to get a slight performance enhancement when using 16 CPU cores in this step if we run it on personal desktops or workstations, which may not have MPS server enabled or have a limited number set in CUDA_MAX_DEVICE_CONNECTIONS.

Step 4: hiding more latency with a block algorithm

In the last step, we try to hide as more latency as possible without heavy code modification. Our strategy is using block algorithm and more CUDA streams on a single MPI rank. Block algorithm divides data into smaller blocks, and each CUDA stream only handles one block. In this way, when one CUDA stream is executing a kernel, another CUDA stream can upload/download data simultaneously. That is, it achieves a better performance by overlapping data transfer and kernels.

One thing to notice is that we are not accelerating serial code with one GPU. We are accelerating an MPI code with only one GPU on a computing node. And as indicated in step 1, with CUDA Proxy on Titan, GPU sees each MPI process as a CUDA stream, and MPI processes' GPU tasks can undergo concurrent execution on that GPU. That is to say, we already had block algorithm to some degree in previous steps. From the perspective of CUDA streams, we already divided the matrix into 16 blocks and had 16 streams per GPU. In this step, what we are trying is just dividing a matrix into more blocks and increasing the overlapping ratio between data transfer and kernel execution.

Using more blocks, however, doesn't always mean better performance. More blocks also mean fewer tasks per thread in a kernel, or even not enough threads to maximize the GPU utilization. Not enough threads to maximize the GPU utilization means a potential overhead, even though CUDA Proxy can execute small kernels concurrently. Furthermore, NVIDIA GPU can handle only one data transfer task in each direction at a time. So, the overall data transfer latency is almost constant regardless the number of streams. And if overall latency is much larger than kernel execution times, the performance won't get improved much even with more blocks. Though this step doesn't guarantee a better performance, it is still worth trying.

MatMult_SeqAIJ:

```
63-82   /* overlap data transfer and host code, as in previous steps. */

85      PetscInt bSize = 32 * 4 * 15 * 512; // block size
86      PetscInt bN = (m - offset) / bSize; // number of blocks

89      for(PetscInt b=0; b<bN; b++)
90      {
92        # pragma acc kernels loop independent gang vector(32) async(b+1) \
93          present(ii[:m+1], cols[:a->nz], data[:a->nz], x[:xSize]) \
94          copyout(y[offset:bSize])
95        for (i=offset; i<(offset+bSize); i++) {
96-103      /* SpMVM of single row and x. The row index is `i`. */
104        }
105        offset += bSize; // offset for the next block
106      }

109     # pragma acc kernels loop independent gang vector(32) async(bN+1) \
110       present(ii[:m+1], cols[:a->nz], data[:a->nz], x[:xSize]) \
111       copyout(y[offset:(m-offset)]) if(offset<m)
112     for (i=offset; i<m; i++) {
113-119   /* SpMVM of single row and x. The row index is `i`. */
120     }
121
123     # pragma acc wait
124
126     # pragma acc exit data delete(x[:xSize]) async
```

Code Snippet 8 OpenACC version of MatMult_SeqAIJ *in step 4*

bSize is the size of each block, in terms of the number of rows. We obtain this optimized number through experiments. We use a new loop to encapsulate the original double-for loop. This loop loops through each block and dispatches each block to a CUDA stream through clause async(b + 1), in which b + 1 is the ID of the stream.

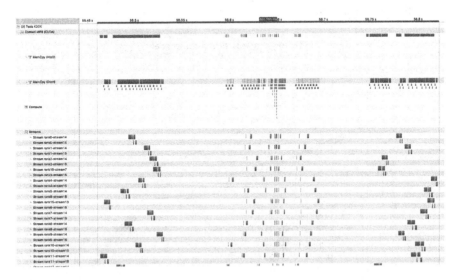

Fig. 5. NVProf result of the OpenACC kernel in step 4. The brown blocks represent latency. The cyan and purple blocks represent the time used by kernel executions. The total length of brown blocks is much longer than the total length of all cyan and purple blocks, which implies the latency is much larger than the time for kernel executions (Color figure online).

There is an extra kernel to deal with remaining rows. This kernel is also dispatched to a stream with ID bN + 1. An `if` clause is added to the second kernel to ensure the kernel will not be launched if there are no remaining rows. A synchronization point is required to guarantee an updated y vector before we use it or delete anything.

Figure 5 shows the NVProf results. As seen, the latency is much larger than the overall time required for kernel executions. So, we can only get very little performance enhancement with more blocks. And also, for small matrix, there is only one block per rank (i.e., only one stream in each MPI rank has jobs), as seen from the middle part in the figure.

The speedup is again close to step 2. However, if we use only one CPU core, we can get a much higher speedup in this step than in step 2, as seen in Fig. 7. This implies that when we use more and more CPU cores and with CUDA Proxy enabled, we are already using block algorithm to hide latency.

4   Speedups and Strong Scaling

Figures 6, 7, 8 and 9 are the speedups of OpenACC kernels in different steps and strong scaling tests. In Fig. 7, the speedup of using a single node shows that with more and more CPU cores used, the performance of step 2 gets closer to that of step 3 and step 4. This may prove that CUDA Proxy helps to hide latency, as we discussed before. In Fig. 6, we observe an abnormal at 8 CPU cores, which is off the linear trends. The reason of this abnormal remains unclear to us. But we believe this may be due to hardware issues and has nothing to do with OpenACC kernels because even original CPU code also shows this abnormal. For the scaling tests of up to 64 computing nodes, there is no apparent difference between step 2 to 4. This again suggests that when we use more CPU

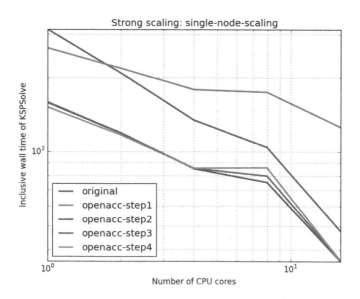

Fig. 6. Strong scaling of using one single node

cores and with CUDA Proxy, we are already using block algorithm to hide latency, and it may not be necessary to have block algorithm inside each MPI process.

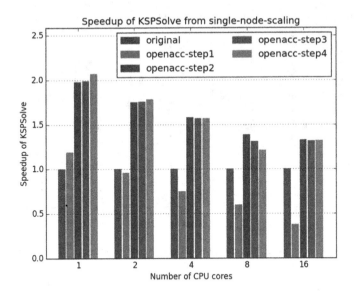

Fig. 7. Speedups of using one single node

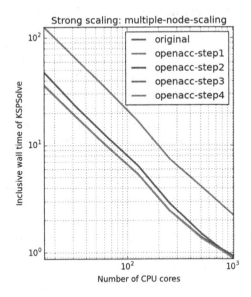

Fig. 8. Strong scaling of using multiple nodes

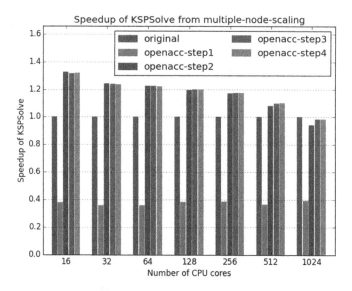

Fig. 9. Speedups of using multiple nodes

5   Conclusion

In this work, we document our practice of porting a PETSc application to Titan, a modern heterogeneous platform. Our experience shows that with OpenACC, we can apply minor code modification to PETSc in an exchange for an acceptable speedup in a Poisson solver, which is a bottleneck in many CFD codes. A thorough understanding of all PETSc source code is unnecessary. We can identify the most expensive kernel through profiling and only work on that piece of source code in PETSc. Hence, this porting effort should not give PETSc users a heavy burden. The results show a 1.34x speedup in a single solving event (a call to `KSPSolve`). We hope this document can serve as a reference to those who are interested in accelerating their legacy PETSc applications with OpenACC.

Our user experience with OpenACC, generally speaking, meets what we expected before starting this work. OpenACC has limited numbers of directives and clauses, yet they are powerful enough under most situations. An issue we encountered during this work does not come from OpenACC itself but comes from the limitation of re-designing the code. When one impression that OpenACC gives to beginners is easy for accelerating legacy CPU code, the fact is that the legacy CPU codes may not have parallel patterns proper for applying OpenACC directly. It's not always like the toy problems in many OpenACC teaching materials that users can simply add directives to existing loops. This potential misunderstanding may, in the end, cause a very wrong estimation of required coding effort before users start to modify their code.

Acknowledgement. This research used resources of the Oak Ridge Leadership Computing Facility at Oak Ridge National Laboratory, which is supported by the Office of Science of the Department of Energy under Contract DE-AC05-00OR22725.

References

1. Balay, S., Abhyankar, S., Adams, M.F., Brown, J., Brune, P., Buschelman, K., Dalcin, L., Eijkhout, V., Gropp, W.D., Kaushik, D., Knepley, M.G., McInnes, L.C., Rupp, K., Smith, B.F., Zampini, S., Zhang, H., Zhang, H.: PETSc Web page (2016). http://www.mcs.anl.gov/petsc
2. PETSc, Applications and Publications. https://www.mcs.anl.gov/petsc/publications/index.html. Accessed 31 Aug 2017
3. Minden, V., Smith, B.F., Knepley, M.G.: Preliminary implementation of PETSc using GPUs. In: Proceedings of the 2010 International Workshop of GPU Solutions to Multiscale Problems in Science and Engineering (2010)
4. PETSc. https://bitbucket.org/petsc/petsc. Accessed 31 Aug 2017
5. OLCF, Titan Cray XK7. https://www.olcf.ornl.gov/computing-resources/titan-cray-xk7/. Accessed 31 Aug 2017
6. Chuang, P.-Y., Barba, L.A.: Using AmgX to Accelerate PETSc-Based CFD Codes, figshare (2017). https://doi.org/10.6084/m9.figshare.5018774.v1
7. Chuang, P.-Y., Barba, L.A.: AmgXWrapper: An interface between PETSc and the NVIDIA AmgX library. J. Open Source Softw. **2**(16), 280 (2017)
8. Larkin, J.: Chapter 2: Profile-guided development with OpenACC. In: Farber, R. (ed.) Parallel Programing with OpenACC. Elsevier (2017)
9. Kraus, J.: Multi-GPU Programming with MPI. In: GTC 2017, San Jose (2017)
10. OLCF, PETSc-OpenACC. https://github.com/olcf/PETSC-OpenACC. Accessed 31 Aug 2017
11. Knüpfer, A., et al.: Score-P: a joint performance measurement run-time infrastructure for periscope, scalasca, TAU, and vampir. In: Brunst, H., Müller, M., Nagel, W., Resch, M. (eds.) Tools for High Performance Computing 2011. Springer, Heidelberg (2012). https://doi.org/10.1007/978-3-642-31476-6_7
12. NVIDIA, Profiler User's Guide. http://docs.nvidia.com/cuda/profiler-users-guide. Accessed 24 Aug 2017
13. Mesnard, O., Barba, L.A.: Reproducible and replicable computational fluid dynamics: it's harder than you think. Comput. Sci. Eng. **19**(4), 44–55 (2017)

Hybrid Fortran: High Productivity GPU Porting Framework Applied to Japanese Weather Prediction Model

Michel Müller[✉] and Takayuki Aoki

Tokyo Institute of Technology, Tokyo, Japan
michel@sim.gsic.titech.ac.jp

Abstract. In this work we use the GPU porting task for the operative Japanese weather prediction model "ASUCA" as an opportunity to examine productivity issues with OpenACC when applied to structured grid problems. We then propose "Hybrid Fortran", an approach that combines the advantages of directive based methods (no rewrite of existing code necessary) with that of stencil DSLs (memory layout is abstracted). This gives the ability to define multiple parallelizations with different granularities in the same code. Without compromising on performance, this approach enables a major reduction in the code changes required to achieve a hybrid GPU/CPU parallelization - as demonstrated with our ASUCA implementation using Hybrid Fortran.

Keywords: HPC · OpenACC · CUDA · GPGPU · OpenMP
Atmospheric · Weather · Parallel programming · Granularity
Memory layout

1 Introduction

With supercomputing shifting towards accelerators, the increasing need for manycore architecture support in software has created a divide between domain scientists who mainly care about modeling, and the supercomputers their applications are required to run on. The high rate of change in both hardware and software creates maintainability issues, especially with codes that are required to run on varying hardware architectures such as multi-core CPU and GPU. The aforementioned divide has widened especially in atmospheric sciences, a field with constant need for model adaptations and high demand for computing resources. Related publications suggest that productivity issues are what is holding back wider accelerator support in this field.

In this work we use the GPU porting task for a Japanese weather prediction model ("ASUCA") as an opportunity to examine productivity issues with the current GPGPU standard "OpenACC" when it is applied to structured grid problems written in Fortran. ASUCA is the main mesoscale weather prediction model developed at the Japan Meteorological Agency. It is used in operation, generating nine-hour-forecasts every hour [10,18].

© Springer International Publishing AG, part of Springer Nature 2018
S. Chandrasekaran and G. Juckeland (Eds.): WACCPD 2017, LNCS 10732, pp. 20–41, 2018.
https://doi.org/10.1007/978-3-319-74896-2_2

We then propose Hybrid Fortran, a solution that is designed to increase productivity when re-targeting structured grid Fortran applications to GPU. It is an improvement over OpenACC in two major aspects:

1. Parallelization granularity is abstracted. This allows the user to have multiple granularities defined in the same codebase, depending on the targeted hardware architecture. This is a crucial advantage in order to implement ASUCA's physical processes on GPU - a code that originally has a very coarse granularity, which is ill-matched for GPUs.
2. Memory layout is abstracted while supporting the already existing user code. More specifically, the layout is reordered at compile-time to match the target architecture, and extended with additional dimensions to match the specified parallelization granularity.

By investigating the necessary code changes with a completed implementation based on Hybrid Fortran we show that this method has enabled high productivity and performance for re-targeting ASUCA to GPU. More than 85% of the hybridized codebase is a one-to-one copy of the original CPU-only code - without counting white-space, code comments and line continuations. An equivalent OpenACC-based solution of ASUCA is estimated to require more than ten thousand additional code lines, or 12.5% of the reference codebase. The new implementation performs up to 4.9x faster when comparing one GPU to one multi-core CPU socket. On a full-scale production run with $1581 \times 1301 \times 58$ grid size and 2 Km resolution, 24 T P100 GPUs are shown to replace more than 50 18-core Broadwell Xeon sockets.

This paper is structured as follows: Sect. 1.1 introduces the application our work focuses on. In Sects. 1.2 and 1.3 we introduce the main difficulties that we face when porting this application to GPU. Section 1.4 outlines the related work in terms of existing methods to solve these difficulties. We then provide a problem summary in Sect. 1.5. In Sects. 2, 3 and 4 we discuss our solution to this problem, the underlying code transformation method, as well as productivity and performance results achieved with this solution, respectively. Finally, in Sect. 5 we draw conclusions and point out future work.

1.1 ASUCA on GPU

The regional scale weather prediction model "ASUCA" is one of the main operational forecast models in Japan [10]. It is developed by the Japan Meteorological Agency (JMA) and used in production since 2014, covering all of Japan as well as relevant ocean areas and surrounding landmasses in East Asia on a rectangular grid with two kilometer resolution, using the finite volume method for the spatial discretization [21].

ASUCA is implemented in Fortran, with multidimensional arrays stored in modules as its main data structure. It is structured as a dynamical core interfacing with physical processes, as commonly seen in other weather models such as WRF [14] and COSMO [1].

Parallelization is applied in the horizontal domain (iterated with I and J loop indices). In order to scale to multiple nodes, ASUCA's grid is decomposed into blocks in the horizontal domain that are scattered across nodes, thus requiring halo communication. OpenMP parallel loop directives are employed as an existing intra-node CPU parallelization. Time discretization is implemented by employing a third order Runge-Kutta scheme, enabling long time steps [24]. Sound and gravity waves are treated separately using a second-order Runge-Kutta scheme to enable a higher time resolution, employing the HEVI scheme (Horizontally explicit - vertically implicit) [21].

ASUCA's dynamical core is a stencil code and thus heavily bounded by memory bandwidth [3, 20]. Since the dynamical core also dominates the runtime, GPUs are an attractive target architecture, with a memory bandwidth that is typically 5 to 7 times higher than Intel Xeon architectures of a similar generation. This work is thus motivated by the task of achieving a GPU port for ASUCA, however with the additional goal of optimizing for minimal code changes in order to achieve better acceptance from the application owner (JMA).

ASUCA is a protected asset of the Japanese government and can not be published at this time - in this paper we thus refer to code snippets to discuss our implementation.

1.2   Parallelization Granularity

Compared to CPUs, GPUs support a very high number of parallel threads while having a very low thread switching overhead - however with the cost of small caches available per thread and a low single-threaded performance. Furthermore, the latency experienced when off-loading code to GPU results in a very high number of threads being optimal, preferably a multiple of the available arithmetic units (i.e. tens of thousands of threads or more). This in turn leads to register pressure being a major factor for the optimization of GPU code, since the number of utilized registers scales linearly with the number of active threads. These characteristics point to an important distinction in the GPGPU programming model: A fine-grained parallelization is strongly preferred or even necessary (as subroutine calls in kernels are required to be inlined, which becomes impractical with deep call graphs).

While ASUCA's original implementation already offers a fine-grained and thus GPU-friendly dynamical core, most of its physical processes use very large kernels and thus coarse granularity. Since each vertical column (K index) can be computed independently for many of the physical processes, these computations are implemented in a single kernel in order to increase cache locality and decrease the amount of context switching and thread synchronization [2,12].

In order to achieve GPU support, a more fine-grained parallelization is thus required for the physical processes. An automated or assisted approach for kernel fission is desirable in order to allow for GPU acceleration while keeping cache locality and low overhead for the CPU case.

1.3 Memory Layout

There are two major aspects in which the memory layout on GPU differs from that on CPU:

Stride-1 Access. On CPU, the memory layout is generally chosen such that the fastest varying dimension is mapped to stride-1 access. GPUs on the other hand require the first parallel dimension to be mapped to stride-1 in order to coalesce the memory operations, since a group of threads is executed in lockstep. In case of ASUCA these are not the same dimensions: K is the fastest varying dimension, yet it is executed sequentially in general (with a few possible exceptions in the dynamical core), while either I or J can be chosen as the first parallel dimension. The original codebase thus employs KIJ memory order. In an unpublished paper submitted for review, we show that KIJ order leads to a 7.7x slowdown on GPU (versus IJK) while IJK ordering leads to a 35% slowdown on CPU (versus KIJ) [15].

Privatization. To create a more fine-grained parallelization for GPU, as discussed in Sect. 1.2, kernel fission is required. This in turn requires thread-local data structures and passed-in data slices to be extended in the parallel domain (IJ). Many scalars thus become 2D-arrays. Many 1D- become 3D-arrays.

Thus, in order to make performance portability possible, the memory layout is required to be changeable and extendable, depending on the target architecture and the parallelization granularity. To achieve this in pure Fortran however, all array specifications and accesses need to be modified and thus specialized for GPU (i.e. code duplication is necessary).

1.4 Related Work

The following works are related to this paper in that they describe alternative or similar methods to achieve a hybrid GPU/CPU capable port for atmospheric models. All of these works have achieved compelling speedups on GPU, this discussion therefore focuses on the productivity aspects.

Stencil Domain-Specific Languages. Domain-specific languages applied to stencil algorithms have been one method to abstract parallelization boiler-plate and memory layout for hybrid GPU/CPU code. For this matter, direct data accesses with loop- or thread indices are abstracted in the point-wise stencil code. This generally requires a complete rewrite of existing code. We take note of the following implementations of weather models using this technique:

- Shimokawabe et al. have completed a research implementation of the ASUCA dynamical core and a portion of its physical processes using their own C++ stencil DSL library [21],

- Fuhrer et al. have implemented the dynamical core of COSMO for operational use at MeteoSwiss, using a purpose-built C++ stencil DSL library for structured grid applications ("STELLA") [6]. The successor project currently enhancing this method is called "GridTools" [5].
- Jumah et al. have proposed a general grid definition and manipulation language (GGDML), an extension to Fortran with applicability to other languages, based on the requirements for three existing models: DYNAMICO, ICON and NICAM. This work is part of the AIMES project [11].

Directive-Based Porting Methods. Directives are used to steer compilers on how to optimize or parallelize already existing code for a specific hardware architecture. Privatization of thread-local data is generally supported in directive-based methods, while storage ordering is not. To switch between multiple parallelization granularities, code duplication is necessary. We are aware of the following implementations of atmospheric models with this method:

- Lapillonne et al. have implemented the relevant physical processes of COSMO for operational use at MeteoSwiss using OpenACC in Fortran [13].
- Govett et al. have ported the dynamical core of the Fortran-based Non-hydrostatic Icosahedral Model (NIM) to GPU, first using their own directive-based transformation tool "F2C-ACC" and later using OpenACC (after critical performance issues and bugs were fixed by the compiler vendors). At the time of this writing we are not aware of a GPU implementation of the NIM physical processes however, an issue that has reduced the potential speedup due to the communication overhead caused by running the physical processes on CPU [7,8].
- Norman et al. have implemented the "Accelerated Model for Climate and Energy" (ACME) for the U.S. DOE using OpenACC. As with ASUCA, ACME's physical processes are problematic for GPU due to their coarse-grained parallelization. GPU-specific code duplication was the only solution found when using OpenACC [16].

Granularity Optimization Methods. Kernel fusion has been the main approach to granularity optimization applied to GPGPU programming we are aware of. We take note of the following related work:

- Wahib and Maruyama have shown the effectiveness of this approach in terms of performance when applied to CUDA C kernels [23].
- Gysi and Hoefler have applied the same approach as well as loop fusion for the aforementioned STELLA stencil DSL library [9].
- Clement et al. are applying kernel fusion and an OpenACC/OpenMP targeted transformation to Fortran code in an ongoing effort as part of the C2SM project (as of yet unpublished[1]).

---

[1] These open-sourced efforts can be found at https://github.com/C2SM-RCM/claw-compiler.

We are not aware of previous or ongoing work regarding kernel fission (and thus support for coarse-grained parallel programming) applied to GPUs.

Memory Layout Abstraction Methods. While stencil DSLs abstract the memory layout, they also require a full rewrite of the point-wise code. The following work allows for the reuse of existing code while keeping the performance portability gains of an abstracted memory layout:

- With the C++ library "Kokkos" (part of the Trilinos project), Edwards et al. have demonstrated that existing point-wise code can be reused even when the underlying data structures are converted to an abstracted memory layout. OpenMP, Pthreads as well as CUDA are provided as backends to the user code for this library. Granularity optimizations are not supported at the time of this writing, neither is Fortran user code [4].
- With a DSL created for the climate model "ICON", Torres et al. have shown that the Fortran syntax can be extended to allow for an abstracted memory layout. A code transformation based on the ROSE compiler [17] is employed towards that goal [22]. Sawyer et al. have subsequently built on this abstraction to port the dynamical core of ICON to GPU using OpenACC directives [19]. We are not aware of any granularity optimizations supported in the ICON DSL.

1.5   Problem Summary

No existing method, that we are aware of, combines memory layout abstraction and a flexible parallelization granularity with the ability to reuse existing Fortran code for GPGPU. In this work we aim at introducing such a method.

2   Hybrid Fortran Language Extension and Code Transformation

Hybrid Fortran has been developed as a method for porting structured grid Fortran applications to GPU. In recognition of the advantages and disadvantages of stencil DSL- and directive-based methods (outlined in Sect. 1.5) we have combined the advantages of both by employing the following characteristics in our approach:

1. it *does abstract* the parallel loops in order to achieve multiple parallelization granularities with the same code,
2. it *does not abstract* the point-wise code (i.e. the loop bodies) - allowing for code reuse,
3. it *does separate* the memory layout as defined in the user code from the layout that is effectively implemented for each architecture.

Hybrid Fortran is an open-source framework and can be accessed together with a library of sample applications[2].

In this Section we discuss how these characteristics have been achieved. Subsection 2.1 describes our approach to parallelization and granularity in Hybrid Fortran, while Subsect. 2.2 discusses and compile-time defined memory layout and device memory handling.

2.1 Parallel Loop Abstraction

Consider the following kernel from JMA's ASUCA reference implementation. As part of the dynamical core it is executed within the second-order Runge-Kutta scheme with high time resolution. It applies lateral and upper damping to ASUCA's grid point values.

Listing 1.1. Lateral and upper damping kernel applied to grid point values.

```
!$OMP PARALLEL DO
  do j = ny_mn, ny_mx
  do i = nx_mn, nx_mx
  do k = nz_mn, nz_mx
    dens_ptb_damp(k,i,j) = &
    & mtratio_bnd * ( dens_ref_f(k,i,j) + dens_ptb_bnd(k,i,j,1) ) &
    & + tratio_bnd * ( dens_ref_f(k,i,j) + dens_ptb_bnd(k,i,j,2) ) &
    & - dens_ref_f(k,i,j)
  end do
  end do
  end do
!$OMP END PARALLEL DO
```

Using Hybrid Fortran we replace the OpenMP directives, as well as the loop instructions to be parallelized, with our parallelization DSL:

Listing 1.2. Lateral and upper damping kernel, modified with Hybrid Fortran.

```
@parallelRegion{ &
& domName(i,j), domSize(nx_mn:nx_mx,ny_mn:ny_mx), &
& startAt(nx_mn,ny_mn), endAt(nx_mx,ny_mx), template(TIGHT_STENCIL) &
& }
do k = nz_mn, nz_mx
  dens_ptb_damp(k,i,j) = &
  & mtratio_bnd * ( dens_ref_f(k,i,j) + dens_ptb_bnd(k,i,j,1) ) &
  & + tratio_bnd * ( dens_ref_f(k,i,j) + dens_ptb_bnd(k,i,j,2) ) &
  & - dens_ref_f(k,i,j)
end do
@end parallelRegion
```

We therefore have an explicit distinction between loops that are treated as parallelizeable (and are thus restricted in their access patterns, i.e. loop carried dependencies are not supported) and loops that are always executed sequentially. The attributes **domName** and **domSize** specify the relevant domain iterators and the domain size relevant to data objects accessed within the parallel region (this relevancy will later be discussed in more detail in Sect. 2.2). The attributes **startAt** and **endAt** explicitly state the region boundaries, which can be a subset

[2] Please refer to https://github.com/muellermichel/Hybrid-Fortran.

of the domain size (however, if omitted, the domain size is also assumed as the region boundary).

For CPU targets, Hybrid Fortran generates an OpenMP code version very similar to the reference code shown in Listing 1.1[3], with multi-core parallelization applied to the outermost loop. For GPU targets it defaults to CUDA Fortran kernels (thus generating all the necessary host- and device code boilerplate and data copy operations) with an option to use OpenACC kernels with CUDA compatible data structures (device pointers)[4]. The attribute **template** specifies a macro suffix used for the generated block size parameters - this allows a central configuration for the block sizes used in an application, rather than leaking this architecture-specific optimization to the user code in each kernel. If omitted, configurable default block sizes are used.

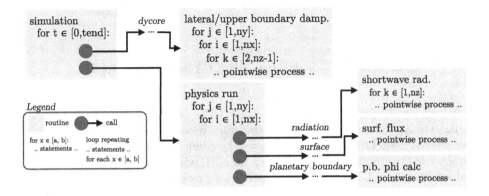

Fig. 1. Simplified code structure of ASUCA.

The main advantage of this parallelization DSL is the following: replacing parallelizeable loops with the @parallelRegion construct allows the user to specify multiple granularities in the same code. Consider ASUCA's code structure, shown in simplified form in Fig. 1. It shows two selected kernels and their embedding in the call graph - the lateral and upper boundary damping already discussed in this section, as well as the physics kernel. Many physical processes are called within this single kernel (of which three sample processes are depicted here). This code therefore has a very coarse granularity, which is problematic on GPU as discussed in Sect. 1.2.

With Hybrid Fortran we can solve this problem as follows: An additional appliesTo attribute in the @parallelRegion statement allows the user to

---

[3] Privatization is the main difference: Hybrid Fortran generated OpenMP code uses "firstprivate" as the default policy with an explicit "shared" clause for all arrays used in the kernel.

[4] OpenACC is mainly used for reduction support - Hybrid Fortran does not automatically generate reduction kernels, however it supports the "reduce" clause, which is forwarded to the generated OpenMP or OpenACC kernels.

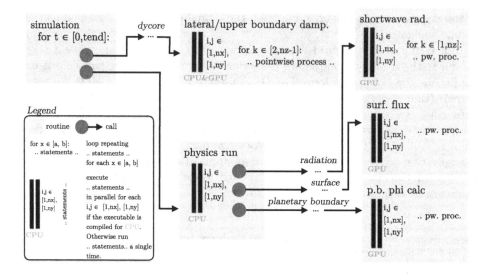

Fig. 2. Simplified code structure of ASUCA using Hybrid Fortran.

selectively apply parallel regions to either CPU or GPU. Applying the parallelization at different granularities therefore becomes possible[5], by enabling user-steered kernel fission. Figure 2 shows the resulting code structure, with the physics run being split into many kernels for GPU while remaining a single coarse grained kernel for CPU. The later Listing 1.4 gives an example of how such a kernel fission works in practice.

2.2 Compile-Time Defined Memory Layout and Device Data Region

As discussed in Sect. 1.3, it is necessary to consider two major aspects for implementing the memory layout: storage order on one hand and the compile-time defined granularity requiring a varying dimensionalities of data objects on the other. Part of Hybrid Fortran is an additional language extension, the @domainDependant construct[6], as a declarative way for the user to specify additional required information concerning data objects. This concerns memory layout as well as device memory operations, which will be discussed in this section.

---

[5] Thus obviating the need for code duplication and/or deep inlining of call trees.

[6] Please note: While this paper follows American English, the Hybrid Fortran language extension has originally been developed following British English, which becomes apparent in the spelling of "domainDependant" (https://en.oxforddictionaries.com/definition/dependant). We consider support for the American English spelling of this directive as part of our future efforts.

Storage Order. Revisiting the code sample from Sect. 2.1, the following Listing shows the specification of the routine implementing the discussed lateral and upper damping kernel:

Listing 1.3. Routine implementing the lateral and upper damping kernel with Hybrid Fortran.

```
subroutine lateral_and_upper_damping()
  use ref, only : dens_ref_f
  use svar, only : dens_ptb_damp
  ! ... further imports omitted
  implicit none

  @domainDependant{ &
    & attribute(autoDom, present), &
    & accPP(AT_TIGHT_STENCIL), domPP(DOM_TIGHT_STENCIL) &
  & }
  dens_ref_f, dens_ptb_damp
  @end domainDependant

  @domainDependant{ &
    & attribute(autoDom, present), &
    & accPP(AT4_TIGHT_STENCIL), domPP(DOM4_TIGHT_STENCIL) &
  & }
  dens_ptb_bnd
  @end domainDependant

  ! ... initialisation of tratio_bnd and mtratio_bnd omitted
  ! ... kernel omitted (already shown in listing 1.2)
end subroutine
```

This shows the specification of the local module data object **dens_ptb_bnd** (density perturbation in the boundary layer) as well as the external module data objects **dens_ref_f** (reference density) and **dens_ptb_damp** (density perturbation in ASUCA grid).

The **autoDom** attribute is used to delegate the dimensions setup to the data object specification parser (which gathers this information in a separate pass from the source modules, here **ref** and **svar**), rather than having the user specify the dimensions explicitly again in the **@domainDependant** construct. The attributes **accPP** and **domPP** are employed to specify the macro names used to implement the dimension ordering for accesses and specification parts, respectively. These macros wrap all dimension lists in access expressions and specifications of respective data objects in the generated code. When **accPP** and **domPP** attributes are omitted, default macro names are used (for a code example after this conversion please refer to Listing 1.6). In case of Listing 1.3 we use explicit macro names for the dynamical core since the default macros are already used with different assumptions for the physical processes (see the paragraph on "Dimensionality Changes" below).

Device Data Region. Similar to OpenACC, in Hybrid Fortran we implement data regions by adding state attributes to data objects. The **present** attribute, shown in Listing 1.3, indicates that the respective objects are located on the device in case of GPU compilation. Analogous **transferHere** attributes are used in the main simulation routine in order to instruct Hybrid Fortran to implement the memory copy operations to- and from the device, once at the beginning and end of the simulation. For dummy variables with specified **intent**, Hybrid Fortran will use the Fortran intent information to determine the correct copy operation[7], which minimizes the potential for bugs in comparison to OpenACC's explicit **copyIn**, **copyOut** and **copy** clauses. Halo region updates, required for every timestep, are implemented explicitly in code sections guarded from CPU compilation.

Dimensionality Changes. Due to the compile-time defined parallelization granularity, discussed in Sect. 2.1, it is necessary to modify the dimensionality of data objects in certain cases in the source generation. This requires hints from the framework user. Consider the following surface flux code snippet:

Listing 1.4. Surface flux code snippet.

```
lt = tile_land
if (tlcvr(lt) > 0.0_r_size) then
  call sf_slab_flx_land_run( &
  ! ... inputs and further tile variables omitted
  & taux_tile_ex(lt), tauy_tile_ex(lt) &
  & )

  u_f(lt) = sqrt(sqrt(taux_tile_ex(lt) ** 2 + tauy_tile_ex(lt) ** 2))
else
  taux_tile_ex(lt) = 0.0_r_size
  tauy_tile_ex(lt) = 0.0_r_size
  ! ... further tile variables omitted
end if
! ... sea tiles code and variable summing omitted
```

Since this process is defined inside the call graph of the physics kernel, as shown in Fig. 1, the relevant 2D- and 3D grid point values are already sliced and passed in as scalars or 1D-arrays, that is, data parallelism is not exposed at this level. Hybrid Fortran allows implementing this as a fine-grained kernel (as outlined in Fig. 2) without modifying the computational user code, as demonstrated in the following snippet:

Listing 1.5. Surface flux code snippet with Hybrid Fortran.

```
@domainDependant{domName(i,j), domSize(nx,ny), attribute(autoDom, present)}
tlcvr, taux_tile_ex, tauy_tile_ex, u_f
@end domainDependant

@parallelRegion{appliesTo(GPU), domName(i,j), domSize(nx,ny)}
lt = tile_land
if (tlcvr(lt) > 0.0_r_size) then
  call sf_slab_flx_land_run( &
  ! ... inputs and further tile variables omitted
  & taux_tile_ex(lt), tauy_tile_ex(lt) &
  & )

  u_f(lt) = sqrt(sqrt(taux_tile_ex(lt) ** 2 + tauy_tile_ex(lt) ** 2))
else
  taux_tile_ex(lt) = 0.0_r_size
  tauy_tile_ex(lt) = 0.0_r_size
```

---

[7] Simple examples of this feature can be found in https://github.com/muellermichel/ Hybrid-Fortran/blob/v1.00rc10/examples/demo/source/example.h90.

```
!  ... further tile variables omitted
end if
!  ... sea tiles code and variable summing omitted
@end parallelRegion
```

Using our parallelization DSL to provide additional dimensionality informa-tion, Hybrid Fortran is able to rewrite this code into a 2D kernel. Dimensions missing from the user code are inserted at the beginning of the dimension lists in access expressions and data object specifications. As an example, the expression u_f(lt) is converted to u_f(AT(i,j,lt)), employing the default ordering macro already mentioned in the paragraph "Storage Order". Dimensions are extended whenever there is a match found for **domName** or **domSize** information between data objects and parallel regions within the same routine *or* in routines called within the call graph of the same routine. It is therefore necessary for Hybrid Fortran to gather global information about the application before implementing each routine.

2.3   Transformed Code

Revisiting Listing 1.5, the following code is generated when applying Hybrid Fortran with the OpenACC backend:

Listing 1.6. Surface flux code snippet after conversion with OpenACC backend.

```
!$acc kernels deviceptr(taux_tile_ex) deviceptr(tauy_tile_ex) &
!$acc& deviceptr(tlcvr) deviceptr(u_f)
!$acc loop independent vector(CUDA_BLOCKSIZE_Y)
outerParallelLoop0: do j=1,ny
!$acc loop independent vector(CUDA_BLOCKSIZE_X)
   do i=1,nx
      ! *** loop body *** :
      lt = tile_land
      if (tlcvr( AT(i,j,lt) )> 0.0_r_size) then
            call sf_slab_flx_land_run(&
                  ! ... inputs and further tile variables omitted
                  & taux_tile_ex( AT(i,j,lt) ), tauy_tile_ex( AT(i,j,lt) ) &
                  & )
         u_f( AT(i,j,lt) )= sqrt(sqrt(taux_tile_ex( AT(i,j,lt) )** 2 + &
               & tauy_tile_ex( AT(i,j,lt) )** 2))
      else
         taux_tile_ex( AT(i,j,lt) )= 0.0_r_size
         tauy_tile_ex( AT(i,j,lt) )= 0.0_r_size
         ! ... further tile variables omitted
      end if
      ! ... sea tiles code and variable summing omitted
   end do
end do outerParallelLoop0
!$acc end kernels
```

Device data is interoperable with the CUDA Fortran backend, thus device pointers are used instead of passing the management to OpenACC. OpenACC directives together with this data type can thus be directly used in the user code as well, i.e. it remains interoperable with device code generated by Hybrid Fortran.

As noted in Sect. 2.2, storage ordering macros (here AT()) are applied to all array access statements. For the thread block setup, the configurable default sizes CUDA_BLOCKSIZE_X/Y are used since no template is specified for the parallel region at hand. Parallel region loops (here for indices i and j are set up explicitly to parallelize. Other loops, such as the loop over k, use a !\$acc loop seq directive to explicitly avoid parallization and give the framework user full expressiveness over the desired granularity.

Applying CUDA Fortran backend to the same user code produces the following host code (here shown together with the routine header and footer):

Listing 1.7. Surface flux host code snippet after conversion with CUDA Fortran backend.

```
subroutine hfd_sf_slab_flx_tile_run ( &
 ! ... inputs omitted
& )
  use cudafor
  type(dim3) :: cugrid , cublock
  integer(4) :: cugridSizeX , cugridSizeY , cugridSizeZ , &
    & cuerror , cuErrorMemcopy
  ! ... other imports and specifications omitted

  cuerror = cudaFuncSetCacheConfig( &
    & hfk0_sf_slab_flx_tile_run , cudaFuncCachePreferL1)
  cuerror = cudaGetLastError()
  if(cuerror .NE. cudaSuccess) then
    ! error logging omitted
    stop 1
  end if
  cugridSizeX = ceiling(real(nx) / real(CUDA_BLOCKSIZE_X))
  cugridSizeY = ceiling(real(ny) / real(CUDA_BLOCKSIZE_Y))
  cugridSizeZ = 1
  cugrid = dim3(cugridSizeX , cugridSizeY , cugridSizeZ)
  cublock = dim3(CUDA_BLOCKSIZE_X, CUDA_BLOCKSIZE_Y, 1)
  call hfk0_sf_slab_flx_tile_run <<< cugrid , cublock >>>( &
    ! ... inputs and further tile variables omitted
    & nx, ny, tile_land , u_f, tlcvr & ! required data objects are
    & taux_tile_ex , tauy_tile_ex &     ! automatically passed to kernel
    & )
  cuerror = cudaThreadSynchronize()
  cuerror = cudaGetLastError()
  if(cuerror .NE. cudaSuccess) then
    ! error logging omitted
    stop 1
  end if
end subroutine
```

The prefix hfd_ is added to host routines that use device data. Hybrid Fortran also duplicates the code for a pure host version of these routines (without a name change in order to remain interoperable with code that is not passed through Hybrid Fortran). In contexts where the data is not residing on the device, such as the setup part of an application, Hybrid Fortran automatically chooses the host version when generating the call statements at compile-time. Code residing within parallel regions is moved within a separated kernel routine (using prefix hfki_ with i representing the kernel number). In case of the surface flux sample shown here, the kernel routine is generated as follows:

Listing 1.8. Surface flux device code snippet after conversion with CUDA Fortran backend.

```
attributes(global) subroutine hfk0_sf_slab_flx_tile_run(&
 !  ... inputs and further tile variables omitted
&, nx, ny, tile_land, u_f, tlcvr &
&, taux_tile_ex, tauy_tile_ex &
& )
use cudafor
use pp_vardef  ! defines r_size
implicit none
real(r_size), device :: u_f(DOM(nx,ny,ntlm))
real(r_size), device :: tlcvr(DOM(nx,ny,ntlm))
real(r_size), device :: taux_tile_ex(DOM(nx,ny,ntlm))
real(r_size), device :: tauy_tile_ex(DOM(nx,ny,ntlm))
integer(4), value :: lt
integer(4), value :: nx
integer(4), value :: ny
integer(4), value :: tile_land
 !  ... other imports and specifications omitted

i = (blockidx%x - 1) * blockDim%x + threadidx%x + 1 - 1
j = (blockidx%y - 1) * blockDim%y + threadidx%y + 1 - 1
if (i .GT. nx .OR. j .GT. ny) then
  return
end if
 ! *** loop body *** :
lt = tile_land
if (tlcvr( AT(i,j,lt) )> 0.0_r_size) then
  call hfd_sf_slab_flx_land_run( &
     !  ... inputs and further tile variables omitted
    taux_tile_ex( AT(i,j,lt) ), tauy_tile_ex( AT(i,j,lt) ) &
    & )
 !  ... rest of loop body already shown in listing 1.6
end subroutine
```

The specification part of these kernels is automatically generated, applying device state information and converting input scalars to pass-by-value[8], among other transformations.

It is notable that CUDA Fortran requires a fairly large amount of boiler plate code for grid setup, iterator setup, host- and device code separation as well as memory- and error handling - Hybrid Fortran allows the user to pass on the responsibility for that to the framework. Compared with the code generated by OpenACC however (assembly-like CUDA C or NVVM intermediate representation), the Hybrid Fortran generated CUDA Fortran code remains easily readable to programmers experienced with CUDA. Experience shows that this is a productivity boost, especially in the debugging and manual performance optimization phase of a project.

Regarding the OpenMP backend, since the surface flux example is parallelized at a much more coarse-grained level for CPU, the generated CPU code for the sample at hand is a one-to-one copy of the user code shown earlier in Listing 1.4. The parallelization is generated at a higher level in the call graph (by use of a parallel region construct with **appliesTo(CPU)** clause) as follows:

---

[8] Reduction kernels are thus not supported with this backend - we use the OpenACC backend selectively for this purpose, see also the discussion in the footnotes to Sect. 2.1.

Listing 1.9. Parallelization of physical processes on CPU.

```
!$OMP PARALLEL DO DEFAULT(firstprivate)
!$OMP& SHARED( ... inputs and outputs omitted ... )
    outerParallelLoop0 : do j=1,ny
    do i=1,nx
      call physics_main(i, j, &
      ! ... inputs and outputs omitted
      & )
    end do
  end do outerParallelLoop0
!$OMP END PARALLEL DO
```

3   Code Transformation Method

In this section we discuss code transformation method involved in implementing Hybrid Fortran's characteristics described earlier. This process is applied transparently for the user, i.e. it is applied automatically by the means of a provided common Makefile[9]. Figure 3 gives an overview of the process and the components involved. We discuss this process in order of execution - each of the following enumerated items corresponds to one transformation phase:

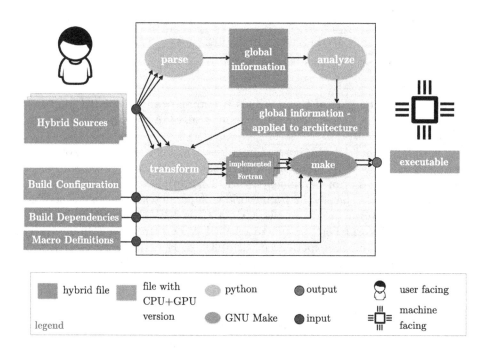

Fig. 3. Hybrid Fortran software components and build workflow.

9 See also the "Getting Started" section in https://github.com/muellermichel/Hybrid-Fortran/blob/v1.00rc10/doc/Documentation.pdf.

1. To simplify the parsing in subsequent phases, Fortran continuation lines are merged.
2. Facilitating later phases, the application's call graph and parallel region directives are parsed globally ("parse" phase in Fig. 3).
3. Using the appliesTo information in kernels and the call graph, the position of each routine in relation to kernels is computed. Possible positions are "has kernel(s) in its caller graph", "contains a kernel itself" and "is called inside a kernel" ("analyze" phase in Fig. 3).
4. In two passes, module data object specifications are parsed and then linked against all routines with imports of such objects, together with the locally defined objects.
5. A global application model is generated, with model classes representing the modules, routines and code regions. This model can be regarded as a target hardware independent intermediate representation.
6. Each routine object is assigned an implementation class depending on the target architecture[10]. For each coding pattern, a separate class method of the implementation class is called by the model objects - e.g. CUDA parallelization boilerplate is generated. Using the previously gathered global kernel positioning and data object dimension information, data objects are transformed according to the behavior discussed in Sect. 2.2. Implementation class methods return strings that are concatenated by the model objects into source files ("transform" phase in Fig. 3).
7. Code lines are split using Fortran line continuations in order to adhere to line limits imposed by Fortran compilers.
8. Macros generated by Hybrid Fortran (to implement storage reordering and configurable block sizes) are processed by using the GNU compiler toolchain. Subsequently, a user specified compiler and linker is employed in order to create the CPU and GPU executables. A common makefile is provided with the framework, however the build dependency graph is user-provided in the format of makefile rules[11] ("make" phase in Fig. 3).

This process makes it possible to have a unified source input and create executables targeted for either multi-core CPU or many-core GPU.

4   Productivity- and Performance Results

In this section we discuss the productivity- and performance results that have been achieved when applying Hybrid Fortran to weather prediction models.

At the time of this writing an additional paper has been submitted for review, in which the following results are discussed: Hybrid Fortran has been applied

---

[10] Hybrid Fortran allows the user to switch between varying backend implementations per routine, such as OpenACC and CUDA Fortran - the user specified information as well as the defaults given by the build system call thus steers this implementation class.

[11] Alternatively, a dependency generator script can be configured as well.

to both dynamical core and physical processes of ASUCA. This implementation (here referred to as "Hybrid ASUCA") consists of 338 kernels and covers almost all modules required for an operative weather prediction, with convection being the main exception due to development time constraints. Communication between host and device has been eliminated with the exception of setup, output and halo exchange. On a $301 \times 301 \times 58$ grid with real weather data, a 4.9x speedup has been achieved when comparing the Hybrid Fortran port on four Tesla K20x versus the JMA provided reference implementation on four 6-core Westmere Xeon X5670 (TSUBAME 2.5). The same setup executes at a speedup of 3x when comparing a single Tesla P100 versus a single 18-core Broadwell Xeon E5-2695 v4 (Reedbush-H). On a full-scale production run with $1581 \times 1301 \times 58$ grid size and 2 Km resolution, 24 T P100 GPUs are shown to replace more than 50 18-core Broadwell Xeon sockets [15].

In order to further examine the performance of Hybrid Fortran kernels and compare them to OpenACC and OpenMP user codes, a performance model has been constructed for a reduced weather application. The Hybrid Fortran implementation with unified code performs on par or better than OpenACC- and OpenMP- implementations separately optimized for GPU and CPU, respectively. In this application, whose runtime is dominated by the memory bandwidth used for a seven point stencil diffusion kernel, the Hybrid Fortran GPU version performs 25% better than the no-cache-model on Tesla K20x. It achieves 36% of the theoretical limit given by a perfect-cache-model. The CPU version performs 56% better than the no-cache-model and achieves 67% of the theoretical limit on Westmere Xeon X5670 [15].

To examine the productivity of our solution we have analyzed the code and compare it against the reference implementation[12]. The high-level results of this analysis is shown in Fig. 4. In order to gain GPU support in addition to the already existing multi-core and multi-node parallelization, the code has grown by less than 4% in total, from 155k lines of code to 161k. Sanitizing the two code versions (removing white space, comments and merging continued lines), the code has grown by 12%, from 91k to 102k lines of code. 95% of the sanitized reference code is used as-is in the new implementation, while 5% or approximately 5k lines of code is replaced with approximately 15k new code lines.

Code changes and additions have the largest impact in terms of productivity. We have analyzed the additional 15k lines of code in more detail. Figure 5 shows a breakdown of these changes and compares them to an estimate of what would be required with an OpenACC-based implementation. The following methodology has been used for this analysis:

1. for the parallelization- and data layout DSL line count we have used information parsed for Hybrid ASUCA, as well as the OpenACC backend available

---

[12] Since the input to this analysis is the closed source ASUCA codebase, full reproducibility cannot be provided in this context. However the intermediate data, the method employed to gather this data as well as a sample input is provided and documented in https://github.com/muellermichel/hybrid-asuca-productivity-evidence/blob/master/asuca_productivity.xlsx.

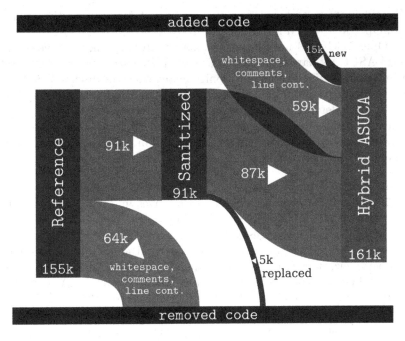

Fig. 4. Flow of code lines from reference implementation to Hybrid ASUCA by number of lines of code.

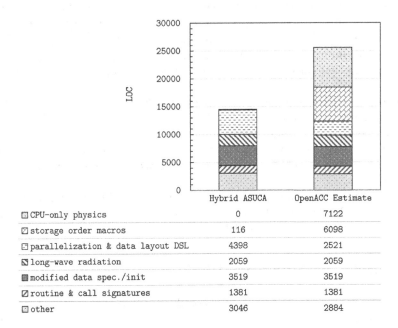

	Hybrid ASUCA	OpenACC Estimate
CPU-only physics	0	7122
storage order macros	116	6098
parallelization & data layout DSL	4398	2521
long-wave radiation	2059	2059
modified data spec./init	3519	3519
routine & call signatures	1381	1381
other	3046	2884

Fig. 5. New code required for Hybrid ASUCA vs. estimate of equivalent OpenACC implementation (LOC stands for "lines of code").

in Hybrid Fortran, to acquire an accurate count for the directives required for an OpenACC-based implementation,

2. since OpenACC does not offer a granularity abstraction, we have used the Hybrid ASUCA's parsed global application information to arrive at a set of routines that require a kernel positioning change (see the discussion in Sect. 3) - the resulting code lines require duplication for the CPU in an equivalent OpenACC implementation (shown as "CPU-only physics" in Fig. 5),

3. we have used the OpenACC backend in Hybrid Fortran to count the lines of code where storage order macros are introduced in order to achieve a compile-time defined data layout.

"Parallelization & data layout DSL" refers to the number of code lines for @parallelRegion and @domainDependant directives in case of Hybrid Fortran, and OpenACC !$acc directivies in case of OpenACC. Hybrid Fortran replaces the requirement for code changes to implement a varying data layout ("storage order macros", 6098 lines of code, "LOC") as well as a code duplication for multiple parallelizations with varying granularities ("CPU-only physics", 7122 LOC) with a higher number of DSL code lines compared to OpenACC (4398 vs. 2521 LOC). "Modified data specifications/initializations" (3519 LOC) as well as "routine & call signature" (1381 LOC) refers to changes applied to the setup of data and call parameter lists, respectively. These changes are necessary due to device code limitations and optimizations and are largely required for both the Hybrid Fortran version as well as a potential OpenACC solution, so we use the result from Hybrid ASUCA as an estimate for what would be required with OpenACC. Finally, one physics module concerning long-wave radiation (2059 LOC), has been replaced with a version that uses less local memory per thread (a factor of 10 improvement in that regard) to make it more GPU-friendly. We again estimate that an OpenACC version would have approximately the same code size.

This result shows that an equivalent OpenACC implementation of ASUCA can be estimated to require approximately 11k LOC in additional changes compared to the Hybrid Fortran-based implementation. When comparing to the sanitized reference codebase, an OpenACC user code would require approximately 28% of code lines to be changed or added, while Hybrid Fortran currently requires 16%.

In addition to the results regarding ASUCA presented here, a library of small applications and kernel samples has been created to demonstrate Hybrid Fortran general applicability to data parallel code[13].

5   Conclusion and Future Work

With this work we have shown that it is possible for large structured grid Fortran applications to

---

[13] Please refer to https://github.com/muellermichel/Hybrid-Fortran/blob/v1.00rc10/examples/Overview.md for an overview of the available samples and their results.

1. achieve a GPU implementation without rewriting major parts of the computational code,
2. abstract the memory layout and
3. allow for multiple parallelization granularities.

With our proposed method, a regional scale weather prediction model of significant importance to Japan's national weather service has been ported to GPU, showing a speedup of up to 4.9x on single GPU compared to a single Xeon socket. When scaling up to 24 T P100, less than half the number of GPUs is required compared to contemporary Xeon CPU sockets to achieve the same result. Approximately 95% of the existing codebase has been reused for this implementation and our implementation has grown by less than 4% in total, even though it is now supporting GPU as well as CPU. Through a library of results, the general applicability of our framework to data parallel Fortran code has been shown.

Considering that much of the changes still required in the user code are "mechanical" in nature, we expect additional productivity gains to be possible from further automation. We strive to achieve a solution where a Hybrid Fortran-based transformation can be applied to large structured grid applications wholesale with minimal input required by the user.

Acknowledgments. This work has been supported by the Japan Science and Technology Agency (JST) Core Research of Evolutional Science and Technology (CREST) research program "Highly Productive, High Performance Application Frameworks for Post Peta-scale Computing", by KAKENHI Grant-in-Aid for Scientific Research (S) 26220002 from the Ministry of Education, Culture, Sports, Science and Technology (MEXT) of Japan, by "Joint Usage/Research Center" for Interdisciplinary Large-scale Information Infrastructures (JHPCN)" and "High Performance Computing Infrastructure (HPCI)" as well as by the "Advanced Computation and I/O Methods for Earth-System Simulations" (AIMES) project running under the German-Japanese priority program "Software for Exascale Computing" (SPPEXA). The authors thank the Japan Meteorological Agency for their extensive support, Tokyo University and the Global Scientific Information and Computing Center at Tokyo Institute of Technology for the use of their supercomputers Reedbush-H and TSUBAME 2.5.

References

1. Cumming, B., Osuna, C., Gysi, T., Bianco, M., Lapillonne, X., Fuhrer, O., Schulthess, T.C.: A review of the challenges and results of refactoring the community climate code COSMO for hybrid Cray HPC systems. In: Proceedings of Cray User Group (2013)
2. Douglas, C.C., Hu, J., Kowarschik, M., Rüde, U., Weiß, C.: Cache optimization for structured and unstructured grid multigrid. Electron. Trans. Numer. Anal. **10**, 21–40 (2000)
3. Dursun, H., Nomura, K.I., Wang, W., Kunaseth, M., Peng, L., Seymour, R., Kalia, R.K., Nakano, A., Vashishta, P.: In-core optimization of high-order stencil computations. In: PDPTA, pp. 533–538 (2009)

4. Edwards, H.C., Trott, C.R., Sunderland, D.: Kokkos: enabling manycore performance portability through polymorphic memory access patterns. J. Parallel Distrib. Comput. **74**(12), 3202–3216 (2014). Domain-specific languages and high-level frameworks for high-performance computing

5. Fuhrer, O.: Grid tools: towards a library for hardware oblivious implementation of stencil based codes (2014). http://www.pasc-ch.org/projects/2013-2016/grid-tools. Accessed 13 July 2017

6. Fuhrer, O., Osuna, C., Lapillonne, X., Gysi, T., Cumming, B., Bianco, M., Arteaga, A., Schulthess, T.C.: Towards a performance portable, architecture agnostic implementation strategy for weather and climate models. Supercomputing Front. Innovations **1**(1), 45–62 (2014)

7. Govett, M., Middlecoff, J., Henderson, T.: Directive-based parallelization of the NIM weather model for GPUs. In: 2014 First Workshop on Accelerator Programming using Directives (WACCPD), pp. 55–61. IEEE (2014)

8. Govett, M., Rosinski, J., Middlecoff, J., Henderson, T., Lee, J., MacDonald, A., Wang, N., Madden, P., Schramm, J., Duarte, A.: Parallelization and performance of the NIM weather model on CPU, GPU and MIC processors. Bulletin of the American Meteorological Society (2017)

9. Gysi, T., Hoefler, T.: Integrating STELLA & MODESTO: definition and optimization of complex stencil programs (2017)

10. Ishida, J., Muroi, C., Kawano, K., Kitamura, Y.: Development of a new nonhydrostatic model ASUCA at JMA. CAS/JSC WGNE Res. Activities Atmos. Oceanic Model. **40**, 0511–0512 (2010)

11. Jumah, N., Kunkel, J., Zängl, G., Yashiro, H., Dubos, T., Meurdesoif, Y.: GGDML: icosahedral models language extensions (2017)

12. Kwiatkowski, J.: Evaluation of parallel programs by measurement of its granularity. In: Wyrzykowski, R., Dongarra, J., Paprzycki, M., Waśniewski, J. (eds.) PPAM 2001. LNCS, vol. 2328, pp. 145–153. Springer, Heidelberg (2002). https://doi.org/10.1007/3-540-48086-2_16

13. Lapillonne, X., Fuhrer, O.: Using compiler directives to port large scientific applications to GPUs: an example from atmospheric science. Parallel Process. Lett. **24**(01), 1450003 (2014)

14. Mielikainen, J., Huang, B., Huang, A.: Using Intel Xeon Phi to accelerate the WRF TEMF planetary boundary layer scheme. In: SPIE Sensing Technology + Applications, p. 91240T. International Society for Optics and Photonics (2014)

15. Müller, M., Aoki, T.: New high performance GPGPU code transformation framework applied to large production weather prediction code (2017, to be published in ACM TOPC)

16. Norman, M.R., Mametjanov, A., Taylor, M.: Exascale programming approaches for the accelerated model for climate and energy (2017)

17. Quinlan, D.: ROSE: compiler support for object-oriented frameworks. Parallel Process. Lett. **10**(02n03), 215–226 (2000)

18. Sakamoto, M., Ishida, J., Kawano, K., Matsubayashi, K., Aranami, K., Hara, T., Kusabiraki, H., Muroi, C., Kitamura, Y.: Development of yin-yang grid global model using a new dynamical core ASUCA (2014)

19. Sawyer, W., Zaengl, G., Linardakis, L.: Towards a multi-node OpenACC implementation of the ICON model. In: EGU General Assembly Conference Abstracts, vol. 16 (2014)

20. Shimokawabe, T., Aoki, T., Muroi, C., Ishida, J., Kawano, K., Endo, T., Nukada, A., Maruyama, N., Matsuoka, S.: An 80-fold speedup, 15.0 TFlops full GPU acceleration of non-hydrostatic weather model ASUCA production code. In: Proceedings of the 2010 ACM/IEEE International Conference for High Performance Computing, Networking, Storage and Analysis, pp. 1–11. IEEE Computer Society (2010)

21. Shimokawabe, T., Aoki, T., Onodera, N.: High-productivity framework on GPU-rich supercomputers for operational weather prediction code ASUCA. In: Proceedings of the International Conference for High Performance Computing, Networking, Storage and Analysis, SC 2014, pp. 251–261. IEEE Press, Piscataway (2014). https://doi.org/10.1109/SC.2014.26

22. Torres, R., Linardakis, L., Kunkel, J., Ludwig, T.: ICON DSL: A domain-specific language for climate modeling. In: International Conference for High Performance Computing, Networking, Storage and Analysis, Denver, CO (2013)

23. Wahib, M., Maruyama, N.: Scalable kernel fusion for memory-bound GPU applications. In: Proceedings of the International Conference for High Performance Computing, Networking, Storage and Analysis, SC 2014, pp. 191–202. IEEE Press, Piscataway (2014). https://doi.org/10.1109/SC.2014.21

24. Wicker, L.J., Skamarock, W.C.: Time-splitting methods for elastic models using forward time schemes. Mon. Weather Rev. **130**(8), 2088–2097 (2002)

Implicit Low-Order Unstructured Finite-Element Multiple Simulation Enhanced by Dense Computation Using OpenACC

Takuma Yamaguchi[1]([✉]) [iD], Kohei Fujita[1,2], Tsuyoshi Ichimura[1,2],
Muneo Hori[1,2], Maddegedara Lalith[1,2], and Kengo Nakajima[3]

[1] Department of Civil Engineering, Earthquake Research Institute,
The University of Tokyo, 1-1-1 Yayoi, Bunkyo, Tokyo, Japan
{yamaguchi,fujita,ichimura,hori,lalith}@eri.u-tokyo.ac.jp
[2] Advanced Institute for Computational Science, RIKEN, Kobe, Japan
[3] Information Technology Center, The University of Tokyo,
2-11-16 Yayoi, Bunkyo, Tokyo, Japan
nakajima@cc.u-tokyo.ac.jp

Abstract. In this paper, we develop a low-order three-dimensional finite-element solver for fast multiple-case crust deformation computation on GPU-based systems. Based on a high-performance solver designed for massively parallel CPU-based systems, we modify the algorithm to reduce random data access, and then insert OpenACC directives. By developing algorithm appropriate for each computer architecture, we enable to exhibit higher performance. The developed solver on ten Reedbush-H nodes (20 P100 GPUs) attained speedup of 14.2 times from the original solver on 20 K computer nodes. On the newest Volta generation V100 GPUs, the solver attained a further 2.52 times speedup with respect to P100 GPUs. As a demonstrative example, we computed 368 cases of crustal deformation analyses of northeast Japan with 400 million degrees of freedom. The total procedure of algorithm modification and porting implementation took only two weeks; we can see that high performance improvement was achieved with low development cost. With the developed solver, we can expect improvement in reliability of crust-deformation analyses by many-case analyses on a wide range of GPU-based systems.

1 Introduction

Simulations reflecting the physical phenomena of earthquake disasters are useful for gaining knowledge on earthquake disaster processes and improve estimation accuracy for future earthquakes. As the target domain of earthquake disaster simulations is heterogeneous and involves complex geometry, large-scale implicit three-dimensional (3D) finite-element analysis using low-order unstructured elements is suitable. In such simulations, most of the computing cost is spent in solving a large system of linear equations. Thus, we have been developing fast solver algorithms for CPU-based systems; our solvers GAMERA and GOJIRA

© Springer International Publishing AG, part of Springer Nature 2018
S. Chandrasekaran and G. Juckeland (Eds.): WACCPD 2017, LNCS 10732, pp. 42–59, 2018.
https://doi.org/10.1007/978-3-319-74896-2_3

running on the massively parallel CPU-based K computer system [1] were nominated as Gordon Bell Prize finalists in SC14 and SC15 [2,3]. Furthermore, we ported this solver to GPU environments using OpenACC [4], which was presented at the Workshop on Accelerator Programming Using Directives (WACCPD) 2016 [5]. This enabled further acceleration and use on wider computing environments with low additional development cost.

Although very challenging, forecasting of the time, position, and magnitude of an earthquake is one of the major goals in earthquake science and disaster mitigation. One promising means of such forecasting could be physics-based forecasting that uses GPS observation data of crust-deformation and many-case analyses to estimate plate boundary states via inverse analyses. In these analyses, many cases of 3D finite-element simulations for each slip distribution are required. Thus, the required computing cost increases significantly when compared with single case finite-element simulations. To deal with the increased computational costs, an algorithm that is specialized for crust-deformation analysis has been developed based on GAMERA [6]. This solver enabled 2.18 times speedup on crust-deformation problems on the K computer when compared with GAMERA. Porting this solver to GPU-based systems using OpenACC can be expected to result in further speedup of crust-deformation analysis with small development cost. On the other hand, GPUs are known to involve large memory access latencies for random accesses, and in addition, standard finite-element applications tend to be memory bandwidth bound. Thus, simple porting of the CPU code is not sufficient to utilize the high computing capability of GPUs. Thus, we change the computational order of calculation such that random memory access can be reduced when porting the solver to GPUs. To show the effectiveness of the solver on the newest architecture, we measure performance on the Pascal [7] and Volta [8] generation GPUs. As the Volta GPUs have less memory throughput per floating-point computation capability, we expect higher effectiveness of our method on these GPUs. As a demonstration of the developed method, we estimate slip distribution during the 2011 Tohoku-oki earthquake.

The remainder of the paper is as follows. Section 2 summarizes the CPU-based finite-element solver developed in [6] for the K computer. Section 3 explains the algorithm changes and the use of OpenACC for acceleration of the solver on GPUs. Section 4 explains the performance of the developed solver on the newest Volta GPUs and recent Pascal GPUs. Section 5 shows an application example using the developed solver on a Tohoku-oki earthquake problem. Section 6 summarizes the paper.

2   Finite-Element Earthquake Simulation Designed for the K Computer

As the time scale of crust-deformation due to faulting is a few hours to a few days, we can regard the target crust (including the lithosphere and the asthenosphere) as a linear elastic solid. Here we analyze the static elastic response at the surface given a slip distribution at the fault plane. This follows the governing equations below:

$$\epsilon_{ij} = \frac{1}{2}\left(\frac{\partial u_i}{\partial x_j} + \frac{\partial u_j}{\partial x_i}\right), \tag{1a}$$

$$\sigma_{ij} = C_{ijkl}\epsilon_{kl}, \tag{1b}$$

$$\frac{\partial \sigma_{ij}}{\partial x_j} = 0. \tag{1c}$$

Here, ϵ_{ij} is the elastic strain, u_i is the displacement, C_{ijkl} is the elastic coefficient tensor, and σ_{ij} is the stress. By discretizing the governing equation using second ordered tetrahedral elements, we obtain

$$\mathbf{Ku} = \mathbf{f}, \tag{2}$$

where $\mathbf{K}$, $\mathbf{u}$, and $\mathbf{f}$ are the global stiffness matrix, displacement vector, and force vector, respectively. We can compute the response of the crust structure model by setting the boundary condition based on the given slip at the fault using the split-node technique [9].

Most of the cost in finite-element analysis involves solving Eq. (2). Since the finite-element model of crust structure can have as many as billions of degrees of freedom, a fast and scalable solver capable of utilizing large supercomputer systems is required. Thus, we have designed an algorithm that attains high convergence of an iterative solver with low computation and communication cost with a small memory footprint for use on the K computer system [6]. The algorithm of this CPU-based solver is shown in Algorithm 1. Below, we summarize the key concepts used in the solver.

Adaptive Conjugate Gradient method [10]: In a standard preconditioner in the conjugate gradient method, a fixed matrix $\mathbf{M}^{-1}$ that is close to the inverse of $\mathbf{K}$ is used to improve the convergence of the iterative solver (i.e., $\mathbf{r} = \mathbf{M}^{-1}\mathbf{z}$). In the adaptive conjugate gradient method, the equation $\mathbf{Kz} = \mathbf{r}$ is roughly solved instead of using a fixed matrix $(\mathbf{M}^{-1})$, which in turn opens up room for improvement of the solver. Here, lines 8–17 of Algorithm 1(a) correspond to the adaptive preconditioner, and a conjugate gradient method with 3 × 3 block Jacobi preconditioner is used for the inner loop solvers (Algorithm 1(b)). From here on, we refer to the iterations for solving the preconditioning equation as the inner loop, and the iterations of the original solver as the outer loop. The inner loops are terminated based on the maximum number of iterations and error tolerance.

Mixed Precision Arithmetic: Although double-precision variables are required for accurate calculation of the outer loop, the inner loops are required only to be solved roughly. Thus, we use single-precision variables in the inner loops (denoted with bars in Algorithm 1). By setting suitable thresholds in the inner solvers, we can shift computation cost from the outer loop to the inner loops, enabling double-precision results computed mostly with single-precision computation. This halves the memory footprint, memory transfer size, and communication size, and doubles the apparent cache size.

Algorithm 1. The iterative solver is calculated to obtain a converged solution of $\mathbf{Ku} = \mathbf{f}$ using an initial solution, $\mathbf{u}$, with a threshold of $\|\mathbf{Ku} - \mathbf{f}\|^2/\|\mathbf{f}\|^2 \leq \epsilon$. The input variables are: $\mathbf{u}, \mathbf{f}, \mathbf{K}, \overline{\mathbf{K}}, \overline{\mathbf{K}}_1, \overline{\mathbf{A}}_2, \overline{\mathbf{P}}_{1-2}, \epsilon, \overline{\epsilon}_{0-2}$, and N_{0-2}. The other variables are temporal. $\overline{\mathbf{P}}_{1-2}$ are mapping matrices from the coarser model to the finer model. $diag[\ ]$, ϵ, and N indicate a 3×3 block Jacobi of $[\ ]$, tolerance for relative error, and maximum number of iterations, respectively. $(^{\,-})$ represents the single-precision variables, while the others represent the double-precision variables.

(a) Outer loop

1: set $\overline{\mathbf{M}}_0 \Leftarrow diag[\overline{\mathbf{K}}]$
2: set $\overline{\mathbf{M}}_1 \Leftarrow diag[\overline{\mathbf{K}}_1]$
3: set $\overline{\mathbf{M}}_2 \Leftarrow diag[\overline{\mathbf{A}}_2]$
4: $\mathbf{r} \Leftarrow \sum_i \mathbf{K}_e^i \mathbf{u}_e^i$
5: $\mathbf{r} \Leftarrow \mathbf{f} - \mathbf{r}$
6: $\beta \Leftarrow 0$
7: $i \Leftarrow 1$
8: **while** $\|\mathbf{r}\|^2/\|\mathbf{f}\|^2 > \epsilon$ **do**
9:     $\overline{\mathbf{r}} \Leftarrow \mathbf{r}$
10:     $\overline{\mathbf{u}} \Leftarrow \overline{\mathbf{M}}_0^{-1} \overline{\mathbf{r}}$
11:     $\overline{\mathbf{r}}_1 \Leftarrow \overline{\mathbf{P}}_1^T \overline{\mathbf{r}}, \ \overline{\mathbf{u}}_1 \Leftarrow \overline{\mathbf{P}}_1^T \overline{\mathbf{u}}$
12:     $\overline{\mathbf{r}}_2 \Leftarrow \overline{\mathbf{P}}_2^T \overline{\mathbf{r}}_1, \ \overline{\mathbf{u}}_2 \Leftarrow \overline{\mathbf{P}}_2^T \overline{\mathbf{u}}_1$
13:     solve $\overline{\mathbf{u}}_2 = \overline{\mathbf{A}}_2^{-1} \overline{\mathbf{r}}_2$ using **(b)** with $\overline{\epsilon}_2$ and N_2
        inner loop level 2
14:     $\overline{\mathbf{u}}_1 \Leftarrow \overline{\mathbf{P}}_2 \overline{\mathbf{u}}_2$
15:     solve $\overline{\mathbf{u}}_1 = \overline{\mathbf{K}}_1^{-1} \overline{\mathbf{r}}_1$ using **(b)** with $\overline{\epsilon}_1$ and N_1
        inner loop level 1
16:     $\overline{\mathbf{u}} \Leftarrow \overline{\mathbf{P}}_1 \overline{\mathbf{u}}_1$
17:     solve $\overline{\mathbf{u}} = \overline{\mathbf{K}}^{-1} \overline{\mathbf{r}}$ using **(b)** with $\overline{\epsilon}_0$ and N_0
        inner loop level 0
18:     $\mathbf{u} \Leftarrow \overline{\mathbf{u}}$
19:     **if** $i > 1$ **then**
20:         $\gamma \Leftarrow (\mathbf{z}, \mathbf{q})$
21:         $\beta \Leftarrow \gamma/\rho$
22:     **end if**
23:     $\mathbf{p} \Leftarrow \mathbf{z} + \beta \mathbf{p}$
24:     $\mathbf{q} \Leftarrow \sum_i \mathbf{K}_e^i \mathbf{p}_e^i$
25:     $\rho \Leftarrow (\mathbf{z}, \mathbf{r})$
26:     $\gamma \Leftarrow (\mathbf{p}, \mathbf{q})$
27:     $\alpha \Leftarrow \rho/\gamma$
28:     $\mathbf{r} \Leftarrow \mathbf{r} - \alpha \mathbf{q}$
29:     $\mathbf{u} \Leftarrow \mathbf{u} + \alpha \mathbf{p}$
30:     $i \Leftarrow i + 1$
31: **end while**

(b) Inner loop

1: $\overline{\mathbf{e}} \Leftarrow \overline{\mathbf{K}}(\text{or}\overline{\mathbf{A}})\overline{\mathbf{u}}$
2: $\overline{\mathbf{e}} \Leftarrow \overline{\mathbf{r}} - \overline{\mathbf{e}}$
3: $\overline{\beta} \Leftarrow 0$
4: $i \Leftarrow 1$
5: **while** $\|\overline{\mathbf{e}}\|^2/\|\overline{\mathbf{r}}\|^2 > \overline{\epsilon}$
    and $i < N$ **do**
6:     $\overline{\mathbf{z}} \Leftarrow \overline{\mathbf{M}}^{-1}\overline{\mathbf{e}}$
7:     $\overline{\rho}_a \Leftarrow (\overline{\mathbf{z}}, \overline{\mathbf{e}})$
8:     **if** $i > 1$ **then**
9:         $\overline{\beta} \Leftarrow \overline{\rho}_a/\overline{\rho}_b$
10:    **end if**
11:    $\overline{\mathbf{p}} \Leftarrow \overline{\mathbf{z}} + \overline{\beta}\overline{\mathbf{p}}$
12:    $\overline{\mathbf{q}} \Leftarrow \overline{\mathbf{K}}(\text{or}\overline{\mathbf{A}})\overline{\mathbf{p}}$
13:    $\overline{\gamma} \Leftarrow (\overline{\mathbf{p}}, \overline{\mathbf{q}})$
14:    $\overline{\alpha} \Leftarrow \overline{\rho}_a/\overline{\gamma}$
15:    $\overline{\rho}_b \Leftarrow \overline{\rho}_a$
16:    $\overline{\mathbf{e}} \Leftarrow \overline{\mathbf{e}} - \overline{\alpha}\overline{\mathbf{q}}$
17:    $\overline{\mathbf{u}} \Leftarrow \overline{\mathbf{u}} + \overline{\alpha}\overline{\mathbf{p}}$
18:    $i \Leftarrow i + 1$
19: **end while**

Geometric/Algebraic Multi-grid method: We use a multi-grid [11] for improving the convergence of the inner loops. As the target problem is discretized with second-order tetrahedral elements, we first use a geometric multi-grid to coarsen the problem. Here, we use the same mesh but without edge nodes to construct the first-order tetrahedral element coarse grid, and we use the solution on this coarsened grid as the initial solution for the second-order inner loop. From here on, we refer to the model with second-order elements as inner loop level 0, and the model with first-order elements as inner loop level 1. As the degrees of freedom of the first-order model is smaller than that of the second-order model, we can expect speedup. In the case of static crust-deformation problems, we can expect further speedup from further coarsening of the grids. Here, we coarsen the first-order tetrahedral grid using the algebraic multi-grid method such that low-frequency components of the solution can be resolved quickly using a conjugate gradient solver. The degrees of freedom of this grid becomes further smaller, leading to further reduction in computing cost. From here on, we refer to this as inner loop level 2.

Element-by-Element method [12]: The most costly part of the solver consists of sparse matrix-vector products that are called in each iteration of the inner and outer conjugate gradient solvers. Here we use the element-by-element (EBE) method for computing sparse matrix-vector products. In the EBE method, matrix-vector products are calculated by summing element-wise matrix-vector products as

$$\mathbf{f} = \sum_i \mathbf{Q}_i \mathbf{K}_i \mathbf{Q}_i^T \mathbf{u}. \tag{3}$$

Here, $\mathbf{K}_i$ indicate the element stiffness matrix and $\mathbf{Q}_i$ indicates the mapping matrix between local and global node numbers. Instead of storing the element stiffness matrix in memory, it is computed every time a matrix-vector product is computed using nodal coordinates and material properties. As $\mathbf{u}$ and coordinate information are read many times during the computation of Eq. (3), it can be stored on cache. This enables shifting the memory bandwidth load to an arithmetic load in sparse matrix-vector multiplication. This is especially effective when targeting recent architectures with high arithmetic capability per memory bandwidth capability. In addition to the reduction in memory transfer, we can also expect improvement in load balance by allocating the same number of elements per core. In the CPU-based implementation, multi-coloring and SIMD buffering is used to attain high performance on multi-core SIMD-based CPUs. This EBE computation is applied to the outer loop, inner loop level 0, and inner loop level 1. As the matrix for inner loop level 2 is algebraically generated and thus EBE method cannot be applied, we read the global matrix from memory stored in 3×3 block compressed row storage format. As the model for inner loop 2 is significantly smaller than the original second-order tetrahedral model, the memory footprint for storing level 2 models is expected to be small.

In summary, the method above is designed to reduce computation cost and data transfer size with good load balancing through the combination of several methods. Such properties are also expected to be beneficial for GPUs as well. In the next section, we explain porting of this solver using OpenACC and measure its performance.

3   Proposed Solver for GPUs Using OpenACC

Compared with CPUs, GPUs have relatively smaller cache sizes and tend to be latency bound for computation with random data access. Therefore, algorithm and implementation to attain optimal performance in GPU differ from the base algorithm for CPU-based computers. We modify the solver algorithm such that random memory access is reduced, and we port this modified algorithm solver to GPUs using OpenACC. Subsequently, we first explain the algorithm modification and then the details of porting with OpenACC.

3.1   Modification of Algorithm for GPUs

We first update the solver algorithm to suit the GPU architecture. The target application requires solving many systems of equations with the same stiffness matrix but different right-hand side input vectors. Thereby, we improve performance by conducting multiple computations simultaneously. Since the performance of the most costly EBE kernel is bound by loading and storing of data, we can expect significant performance improvement by reducing the irregularity of memory accesses. Based on this idea, we solve multiple systems of equations simultaneously by multiplying the same element stiffness matrix to multiple vectors at the same time. This approach enables coalesced memory access for the number of vectors, leading to a shorter time to solution than repeating multiplication of a matrix and a single vector multiple times. In this paper, we solve 16 systems of equations in parallel ($\mathbf{K}\left[\mathbf{u}_1, \mathbf{u}_2, ..., \mathbf{u}_{16}\right]^T = \left[\mathbf{f}_1, \mathbf{f}_2, ..., \mathbf{f}_{16}\right]^T$). This modification changes all of the computational loops into nested loops, with the inner loop having a loop length of 16. The maximum values for the errors in the 16 residual vectors are used for judging the convergence of each loop.

3.2   Introduction of OpenACC

We introduce OpenACC to the modified algorithm. Here, the solver part is ported to GPUs to reduce the application runtime. For high performance, we first need to maintain data transfer at a minimum and then conduct all computation on the GPUs.

Control of Data Transfer. Unless explicitly specified otherwise, OpenACC automatically transfers all data necessary for GPU computation between the host memory and the GPU device memory every time a kernel is called. This data transfer seriously degrades performance; thus, we insert directives to control the data transfer. In the solver, data transfer is necessary only for MPI communication and checking the convergence of each loop. We use the `present` option in the `data` directive of OpenACC for other parts of the solver to eliminate unnecessary data transfer. For the MPI communication part, we use GPU Direct, which enables MPI communication without routing through the host memory system. This is enabled by inserting OpenACC directives before and after MPI communication that declares the use of device memory.

Porting of Each Kernel. Next we port each kernel by using the `loop` directives with suitable options. Figure 1 shows a porting example of the EBE kernel with multiple vectors in Fortran. Each of the kernels in the solver has a nested loop with an inner loop length of 16. The length of the inner loop is not large; thus, we collapse these nested loops by adding `collapse` options in the `loop` directives. In the current specification of OpenACC, target loops must be adjacent to each other for collapsing loops. Thus, parts of the kernel must be computed redundantly (e.g., the node connectivity array is read redundantly in Fig. 1); however, collapsing of the loops enables coalesced memory accesses for the vectors leading to higher computing performance. In GPU computation, SIMT computation is applied automatically; thus we do not have to designate parallel code explicitly as in SIMD computation in CPUs. We insert `atomic` directives for adding thread-wise temporal variables to the resulting vector. Our previous study has shown that atomic operations attain higher performance than reordering the elements to avoid a data race using the coloring method [5], because atomic operations can retain data locality of nodal data (i.e., **u** and nodal coordinate information) and thus utilize the L2 cache more efficiently.

Although other calculations, such as multiplication, addition, and subtraction of vectors, can also be computed on GPUs by adding `loop` directives, we must take care when porting the inner product kernel with multiple vectors. In the case of inner vector products with a single vector, we can directly port the CPU code by inserting the `reduction` option in `loop` directives. However, the reduction option in OpenACC is available for scalars but not for arrays. Thus, the innermost loop cannot be parallelized directly in the present specification of OpenACC. Thereby, we allocate scalars corresponding to each of the multiple vectors and compute the reduction of these scalars in a single loop (Fig. 2). In this case, memory access becomes strided, possibly leading to performance decrease when compared with the single vector type inner product kernel. Adding collapse options with reduction options for arrays in OpenACC that enable contiguous memory access might be beneficial in this case.

Examining the parameters in OpenACC defining parallelism of computation is important for exhibiting high performance. In OpenACC, three hierarchies of `gang`, `worker` and `vector` determine the granularity of parallelization. The parameter `gang` corresponds to a thread block in an NVIDIA GPU, and `vector` corresponds to a thread. For instance, in EBE kernels, we must assign one thread per element to attain their optimal performances on GPUs. Without any instructions, threads can be unintendedly mapped; thus these two options, gang and vector, must be inserted in appropriate places explicitly. The length of `vector`,

```
1    !$acc parallel loop collapse(2)
2    do i_ele = 1, n_element
3    do i_vec = 1, n_block
4
5    cny1 = connect(1, i_ele)
6    cny2 = connect(2, i_ele)
7       :
8    cny10 = connect(10, i_ele)
9
10   u0101 = u(i_vec, 1, cny1)
11   u0102 = u(i_vec, 2, cny1)
12   u0103 = u(i_vec, 3, cny1)
13   u0201 = u(i_vec, 1, cny2)
14      :
15   u1003 = u(i_vec, 3, cny10)
16
17   Ku01 = ...
18   Ku02 = ...
19      :
20   Ku30 = ...
21
22   !$acc atomic
23   r(i_vec, 1, cny1) = r(i_vec, 1, cny1) + Ku01
24   !$acc atomic
25   r(i_vec, 2, cny1) = r(i_vec, 2, cny1) + Ku02
26      :
27   !$acc atomic
28   r(i_vec, 3, cny10) = r(i_vec, 3, cny10) + Ku30
29   enddo
30   enddo
31   !$acc end parallel
```

```
1    !$acc parallel loop
2    !$acc& reduction(+:tmp1,tmp2,...,tmp16)
3    do i_node = 1, n_node
4    tmp1 = tmp1 + (a(1, 1, i_node)*b(1, 1, i_node)
5              + a(1, 2, i_node)*b(1, 2, i_node)
6              + a(1, 3, i_node)*b(1, 3, i_node))
7              * dupli(i_node)
8    tmp2 = tmp2 + (a(2, 1, i_node)*b(2, 1, i_node)
9              + a(2, 2, i_node)*b(2, 2, i_node)
10             + a(2, 3, i_node)*b(2, 3, i_node))
11             * dupli(i_node)
12      :
13   tmp16 = tmp16 + (a(16, 1, i_node)*b(16, 1, i_node)
14             + a(16, 2, i_node)*b(16, 2, i_node)
15             + a(16, 3, i_node)*b(16, 3, i_node))
16             * dupli(i_node)
17   enddo
18   !$acc end parallel
```

Fig. 1. EBE kernel for multiple vectors on GPUs.

Fig. 2. Vector inner product kernel for multiple vectors on GPUs.

which corresponds to the block size in NVIDIA GPUs, is automatically determined by the compiler. In most cases, these parameters have little impact on performance; however, we searched for optimal parameters for core kernels in the solver to attain optimal performance. For EBE kernels, in which the usage of registers rather than the block size has the largest impact on the number of working threads, we can set their lengths of vector to 32. This saves the need for synchronization in the block among different warps; thus this parameter is expected to be the most optimal one.

4   Performance Measurements

In this section, we show the effectiveness of the developed solver through performance measurements.

We first compare the performance of the ported solver on NVIDIA P100 GPUs with that of the base solver on the K computer. Here we use Reedbush-H of the Information Technology Center, The University of Tokyo for a computation environment with P100 GPUs [13]. The K computer is a massively parallel CPU-based supercomputer system at the Advanced Institute of Computational Science, RIKEN. The computation environments are summarized in Table 1. We continue to compute until the residual error in outer loop goes below 10^{-8}. The maximum iteration and tolerance thresholds for inner loops greatly affect

Table 1. Comparison of hardware capabilities of K computer and Reedbush-H.

	K computer	Reedbush-H (Tesla P100)
# of nodes	20	10
CPU/node	1 × eight-core SPARC64 VIIIfx	2 × eighteen-core Intel Xeon E5-2695 v4
Accelerator/node	-	2 × NVIDIA P100
# of MPI processes/node	1	2
hardware peak DP FLOPS /process	128 GFLOPS	5.30 TFLOPS (GPU only)
Bandwidth/process	64 GB/s	732 GB/s (GPU only)
Interconnect	Tofu (4 lanes × 5 GB/s in both directions)	PCIe Gen3 × 16 + NVLink (20 GB/s) × 2 + InfiniBand FDR 4 × 2
Compiler	Fujitsu Fortran Driver Version 1.2.0	PGI compiler 17.5
Compiler option	-Kfast,openmp,parallel,ocl	-ta=tesla:cc60,loadcache:L1 -acc -Mipa=fast -fastsse -O3
MPI	custom MPI	OpenMPI 1.10.7

the convergence of the outer loop and whole computation time. In this paper, these parameters are empirically configured as in Table 2 so that the computation time for the whole solver is reduced. For performance measurement, we use a finite-element model with 125,177,217 degrees of freedom and 30,720,000 second-order tetrahedral elements. The material properties of the two-layered model are shown in Table 3. The computation time in the conjugate gradient loop is shown in Fig. 3. From the figure, we can see that the base solver attains 21.5% of peak FLOPS on the K computer system, which is very high performance for a low-order finite-element solver. Compared to this highly tuned CPU solver implementation, we confirmed that direct porting of the original solver without algorithm changes enabled 5.0 times speedup. By using the proposed method solving 16 vectors simultaneously in GPUs, the solver was accelerated further by 2.82 times per vector from the directly ported solver. This leads to

Table 2. Error tolerance $\bar{\epsilon}_{0-2}$ and maximum iteration N_{0-2} used for our solver for solving measurement models and application problems.

Inner loop	Error tolerance	Maximum iteration
level 0	0.1	30
level 1	0.05	300
level 2	0.025	3,000

Table 3. Material properties of performance measurement models. V_p, V_s, and ρ indicate primary wave velocity, secondary wave velocity, and density, respectively.

Layer	V_p (m/s)	V_s (m/s)	ρ (kg/m^3)
1	1,600	400	1,850
2	5,800	3,000	2,700

14.2 times speedup with respect to the base solver on the K computer. For comparison, we measured the computation time using 16 vectors on the K computer. As shown in Fig. 3, we attained 1.48 times speedup with regard to the original solver using single vector. Considering the speedup ratio is 2.82 between using 16 vectors and single vector on Reedbush-H, we can confirm that we have attained higher performance in P100 GPUs by introduction of dense computation, which is more effective for GPU computation. The speedup ratio in using 16 vectors is 9.6 between Reedbush-H and K computer. In standard finite-element solvers using sparse matrix storage formats, the expected speedup will be near the peak memory bandwidth ratio, which is 11.4 times in this case. However, for practical cases, the computation includes random accesses that severely degrade GPU performance; thus the speedup ratio is assumed to get much less than the peak bandwidth ratio. Thus, we can see that the 9.6 times speedup attained is reasonable performance. This speedup ratio is mainly due to the introduction of

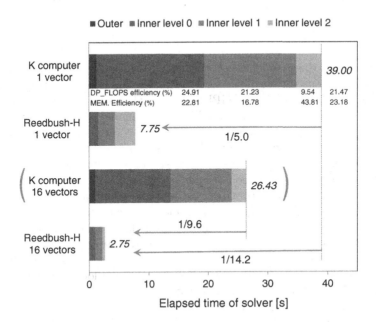

Fig. 3. Performance comparison of the entire solver. Here, the computation time when using 16 vectors is divided by 16 and converted per vector.

EBE multiplication, which has changed global memory bandwidth bound computation into cache memory bandwidth bound. We examine the cause of the performance improvement by checking the speedup of each kernel in Table 4. As the sparse matrix-vector product in inner loop level 2 is bound by reading the global matrix from memory, the total computation time is nearly constant regardless of the number of vectors multiplied. Thus, the efficiency of computation is significantly improved when 16 vectors are multiplied simultaneously. The reduction in random memory access in EBE kernels leads to performance improvement by 1.6–1.7 times. Although the performance of the inner vector product kernel decreased as a result of strided memory access, the acceleration of sparse matrix-vector products and EBE computation has a profound effect leading to performance improvement of the entire solver.

Table 4. Performance of main kernels in Reedbush-H.

Kernel	Elapsed time per vector (s)		Speedup
	1 vector	16 vectors	
SpMV ($\overline{\mathbf{A}}_2\overline{\mathbf{u}}_2$)	1.465	0.091	16.10
2nd order EBE ($\mathbf{Ku}$)	0.044	0.025	1.78
2nd order EBE ($\overline{\mathbf{K}}\overline{\mathbf{u}}$)	0.687	0.401	1.71
1st order EBE ($\overline{\mathbf{K}}_1\overline{\mathbf{u}}_1$)	0.948	0.584	1.62
Inner product ($\overline{\mathbf{p}} \cdot \overline{\mathbf{q}}$)	0.213	0.522	0.41
Total time of the solver	7.75	2.75	2.82

We next check the parallelization efficiency by measuring weak scaling. Here, we measure the elapsed time of the solver using the full Reedbush-H system with 240 P100 GPUs. The number of GPUs, degrees of freedom, and the number of elements of the models are shown in Table 5. Here, model No.1 is the same model as used in the performance comparison with the K computer. To assure that the convergence characteristics of the models are similar, we compared the number of iterations required for convergence of a standard conjugate gradient solver with a 3 × 3 block Jacobi preconditioner (from here on referred to as PCGE). PCGE corresponds to Algorithm 1(a) without the adaptive conjugate gradient preconditioner part (lines 8–17). From Table 5, we can see that the number of iterations in PCGE is nearly constant, and thus this model set is suitable for measuring weak scaling. Figure 4 shows the elapsed time of the developed solver and the total number of iterations required for convergence. Although there are slight fluctuations in the number of iterations of the inner loops, the computation time is roughly constant up to the full system.

Finally, we check the effectiveness of the developed solver on the latest Volta GPU architecture. Here, we compare performance of four Reedbush-H nodes with eight P100 GPUs, a DGX-1 with eight P100 GPUs, and a DGX-1 with eight V100 GPUs [14] (Table 6). The target model size is 38,617,017 degrees

Table 5. Model configuration for weak scaling in Reedbush-H.

Model	# of GPUs	Degrees of freedom (DOF)	DOF per GPU	# of elements	PCGE iterations
No.1	20	125,177,217	6,258,861	30,720,000	4,928
No.2	40	249,640,977	6,241,024	61,440,000	4,943
No.3	80	496,736,817	6,209,210	122,880,000	4,901
No.4	160	992,038,737	6,200,242	245,760,000	4,905
No.5	240	1,484,953,857	6,187,308	368,640,000	4,877

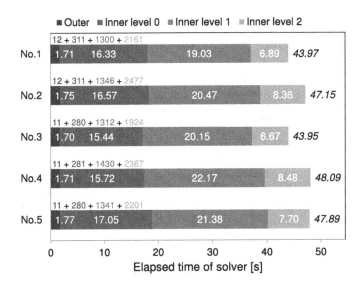

Fig. 4. Performance in weak scaling. The numbers of iterations for the outer loop, inner loop level 0, inner loop level 1, and inner loop level 2 are written in the insets.

of freedom and 9,440,240 tetrahedral elements, almost filling the 16 GB device memory of the eight P100 and V100 GPUs on each system. From Fig. 5, we can see that the elapsed time has decreased from 19.2 s to 17.3 s when DGX-1 (P100) is used. This performance difference may be attributed to the inter-node InfiniBand communication between the four Reedbush-H nodes in contrast to the intra-node communication inside a single DGX-1. In the comparison of the P100 and V100 versions of DGX-1, the elapsed time has decreased from 17.3 s to 6.86 s. This corresponds to 2.52 times speedup, higher than the 1.23 times increase in hardware peak memory bandwidth. Architectural improvements for caches contribute to this speedup ratio. Volta GPU has 128 kB of combined L1 cache/shared memory per SM and 6 MB of L2 cache per GPU, which are 5.3 times and 1.5 times larger than L1 and L2 cache of Pascal GPU, respectively. In the solver, random memory accesses in sparse matrix-vector multiplications is one of bottlenecks. Larger cache size in V100 GPU is thought to reduce memory

Table 6. Comparison of hardware capabilities of Reedbush-H, P100 DGX-1, and V100 DGX-1. Latest compilers available in each environment are used.

	Reedbush-H (P100)	DGX-1 (P100)	DGX-1 (V100)
# of nodes	4	1	1
CPU/node	2 × eighteen-core Intel Xeon E5-2695 v4	2 × twenty-core Intel Xeon E5-2698 v4	2 × twenty-core Intel Xeon E5-2698 v4
Accelerators/node	2 × NVIDIA P100	8 × NVIDIA P100	8 × NVIDIA V100
MPI processes/node	2	8	8
GPU memory size/process	16 GB	16 GB	16 GB
GPU peak DP FLOPS/process	5.3 TFLOPS	5.3 TFLOPS	7.5 TFLOPS
GPU memory bandwidth/process	732 GB/s	732 GB/s	900 GB/s
Interconnect	InfiniBand FDR 4 × 2 + PCIe Gen3 × 16 + NVLink	InfiniBand EDR × 4 + NVLink	InfiniBand EDR × 4 + NVLink
Compiler	PGI compiler 17.5	PGI compiler 17.9	PGI compiler 17.9
Compiler option	-ta=tesla:cc60 -ta=loadcache:L1 -acc -Mipa=fast -fastsse -O3	-ta=tesla:cc60 -ta=loadcache:L1 -acc -Mipa=fast -fastsse -O3	-ta=tesla:cc70 -ta=loadcache:L1 -acc -Mipa=fast -fastsse -O3
MPI	OpenMPI 1.10.7	OpenMPI 1.10.7	OpenMPI 1.10.7

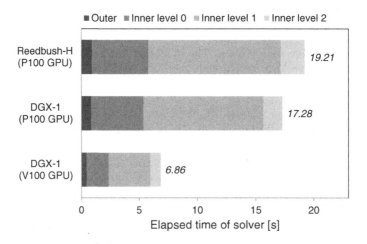

Fig. 5. Performance comparison of the entire solver on Reedbush-H, DGX-1 (P100), and DGX-1 (V100).

bandwidth demand and improve performance of these kernels, including atomic addition part. Thereby it is inferred that these improvements in the hardware result in a speedup ratio more than the peak memory bandwidth ratio or the double-precision peak performance ratio.

5   Application Example

In this section, we demonstrate the use of the developed solver by estimating the coseismic fault slip distribution in the 2011 Tohoku-oki earthquake. This estimation is important for considering earthquake generation processes. Previous studies [15,16] have shown that approximation in the geometry of the crust significantly changes the slip distribution. Thus, conducting crustal deformation analysis reflecting local geometry is required.

First, we describe the method used to estimate the coseismic fault slip distribution following a previous study [17]. The assumed fault plane is divided into n small unit faults, and the fault slip is expanded using these unit faults as bases:

$$\mathbf{x} = \sum_{i=1}^{n} a_i \phi_i, \tag{4}$$

where $\mathbf{x}$ is the fault slip distribution vector, a_i is the coefficient for the ith unit fault slip, and ϕ_i is the distribution vector of the ith unit fault slip. We assume that observation data are available on the crustal surface at m points, and that the coseismic crustal deformation can be regarded as a linear elastic deformation. Using Green's function g_{ji} (i.e., surface response on observation point j for unit fault slip ϕ_i), yields the following estimation of the slip distribution:

$$\begin{pmatrix} \mathbf{G} \\ \alpha\mathbf{L} \end{pmatrix} \mathbf{a} = \begin{pmatrix} \mathbf{d} \\ \mathbf{0} \end{pmatrix}, \tag{5}$$

where $\mathbf{G}$ is an $m \times n$ matrix with components g_{ji}, and $\mathbf{d}$ is an m dimensional vector of crustal deformation data on observation point j. $\mathbf{L}$ is a smoothing matrix introduced because $\mathbf{G}$ is generally ill-posed. α is a weighting factor defined using the L-curve method [18]. These Green's functions are obtained by computing surface responses against n unit fault slips. In typical problems, n is of the order 10^2–10^3; thus, we must conduct crustal deformation computation more than 10^2 times. When we use finite-element models with 10^8 degrees of freedom required for reflecting the geometry of the crust, this simulation leads to huge computational cost. In this analysis, multiple crustal deformation computations are performed for the same finite-element model; thereby, use of the developed solver is expected to lead to high speedup.

The four-layered 792 km × 1,192 km × 400 km target area is shown in Fig. 6. Modeling this area with a resolution of 1,000 m leads to a finite-element model consisting of 409,649,580 degrees of freedom and 100,494,786 tetrahedral elements (Fig. 7). We use the x, y, and z components of GEONET, the x and y

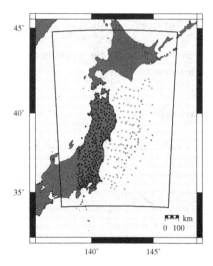

Fig. 6. Target region of the application example (black line). The black, blue, and red points indicate the positions for GEONET, GPS-A, and S-net, respectively. (Color figure online)

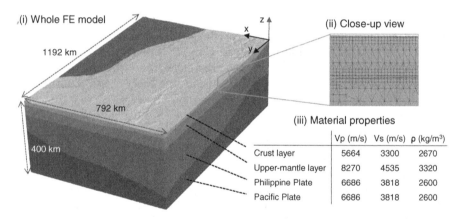

(i) Whole FE model

1192 km

792 km

400 km

(ii) Close-up view

(iii) Material properties

	Vp (m/s)	Vs (m/s)	ρ (kg/m³)
Crust layer	5664	3300	2670
Upper-mantle layer	8270	4535	3320
Philippine Plate	6686	3818	2600
Pacific Plate	6686	3818	2600

Fig. 7. Finite-element model used for the application example.

components of GPS-A, and the z component of S-net for the observed crust-deformation data. The locations of the 184 input unit fault slips are shown in Fig. 8. For each point, Green's functions with unit B-spline function fault slips (Fig. 9) are computed in the dip and strike directions. Thus, the total number of Green's functions becomes $n = 184 \times 2 = 368$. We used 32 nodes of Reedbush-H and obtained 368 Green's functions by conducting 23 sets of crustal deformation computations with 16 vectors. Figure 10 shows the estimated slip distribution obtained by solving Eq. (5) using the computed Green's functions and observed data, a result consistent with previous studies [17].

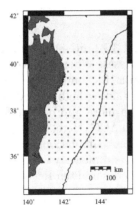

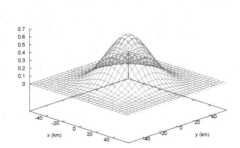

Fig. 8. Location of the centers of the unit fault slips.

Fig. 9. Distribution of unit fault slip.

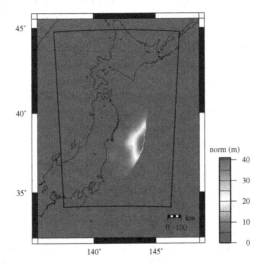

Fig. 10. Estimated coseismic slip distribution.

The computation time for solving systems of linear equations was 828 s for 368 crustal deformation computations. This computation is 29.2 times better in performance (5.11 times larger problem × solved 5.71 times faster) than previous studies on smaller computational environments in [5] with eight K40 GPUs, which conducted 360 crustal deformation computations with 80 million degrees of freedom in 4,731 s. From here we can see that the developed solver enabled reduction in computation time for a practical problem. In the future, we plan to use this method to optimize the crustal structure based on 10^6 cases of Monte Carlo crustal deformation computations with varying geometries and material properties.

6   Concluding Remarks

In this paper, we accelerated a low-order unstructured 3D finite-element solver targeting multiple large-scale crustal deformation analyses. When we introduce accelerators, it is important to redesign the algorithm as its computer architecture greatly changes. Based on a CPU-based solver attaining high performance on the K computer, we developed the solver algorithm more appropriate for a GPU architecture and then ported the code using OpenACC. Here, we changed the algorithm such that multiple cases of finite-element simulations are conducted simultaneously thereby reducing random access and memory transfer per simulation case. When the runtime on 20 K computer nodes and ten Reedbush-H nodes (20 P100 GPUs) were compared, the directly ported solver attained 5.0 times speedup, and the ported solver with modification to the algorithm attained 14.2 times speedup. We confirm that this modification is important to exhibit high performance in P100 GPUs and more effective for GPU-based Reedbush-H than for CPU-based K computer. The developed solver is also highly effective on the Volta GPU architecture; we confirmed 2.52 times speedup with respect to eight P100 GPUs to eight V100 GPUs. This acceleration enabled 368 crustal deformation computations targeting northeast Japan with 400 million degrees of freedom in 828 s on 32 Reedbush-H nodes, which is significantly faster than in the previous study. The entire procedure of algorithm modification and OpenACC directive insertion was completed within two weeks; hence, we can see that high-performance gain can be attained with low development cost by using a suitable porting strategy. Fast computations realized by the developed method are expected to be useful for quality assurance of earthquake simulations in the future.

Acknowledgments. We thank Mr. Craig Toepfer (NVIDIA) and Mr. Yukihiko Hirano (NVIDIA) for the generous support and performance analyses concerning the use of NVIDIA DGX-1 (Volta V100 GPU) and NVIDIA DGX-1 (Pascal P100 GPU) environment. Part of the results were obtained using the K computer at the RIKEN Advanced Institute for Computational Science (Proposal numbers: hp160221, hp160160, 160157, and hp170249). This work was supported by Post K computer project (priority issue 3: Development of Integrated Simulation Systems for Hazard and Disaster Induced by Earthquake and Tsunami), Japan Society for the Promotion of Science (KAKENHI Grant Numbers 15K18110, 26249066, 25220908, and 17K14719) and FOCUS Establishing Supercomputing Center of Excellence.

References

1. Miyazaki, H., Kusano, Y., Shinjou, N., Shoji, F., Yokokawa, M., Watanabe, T.: Overview of the K computer system. FUJITSU Sci. Tech. J. **48**(3), 302–309 (2012)
2. Ichimura, T., Fujita, K., Tanaka, S., Hori, M., Maddegedara, L., Shizawa, Y., Kobayashi, H.: Physics-based urban earthquake simulation enhanced by 10.7 blndof x 30 K time-step unstructured fe non-linear seismic wave simulation. In: Proceedings of the International Conference on High Performance Computing, Networking, Storage and Analysis, pp. 15–26 (2014)

3. Ichimura, T., Fujita, K., Quinay, P.E.B., Maddegedara, L., Hori, M., Tanaka, S., Shizawa, Y., Kobayashi, H., Minami, K.: Implicit nonlinear wave simulation with 1.08t dof and 0.270t unstructured finite elements to enhance comprehensive earthquake simulation. In: Proceedings of the International Conference on High Performance Computing, Networking, Storage and Analysis, pp. 1–12 (2015)

4. OpenACC. http://www.openacc.org

5. Fujita, K., Yamaguchi, T., Ichimura, T., Hori, M., Maddegedara, L.: Acceleration of element-by-element kernel in unstructured implicit low-order finite-element earthquake simulation using openacc on pascal gpus. In: Proceedings of the Third International Workshop on Accelerator Programming Using Directives, pp. 1–12 (2016)

6. Fujita, K., Ichimura, T., Koyama, K., Inoue, H., Hori, M., Maddegedara, L.: Fast and scalable low-order implicit unstructured finite-element solver for earth's crust deformation problem. In: Proceedings of the Platform for Advanced Scientific Computing Conference, pp. 11–20 (2017)

7. NVIDIA Pascal GPU. http://www.nvidia.com/object/tesla-p100.html

8. NVIDIA Volta GPU. http://www.nvidia.com/en-us/data-center/tesla-v100

9. Melosh, H.J., Raefsky, A.: A simple and efficient method for introducing faults into finite element computations. Bull. Seismol. Soc. Am. **71**(5), 1391–1400 (1981)

10. Golub, G.H., Ye, Q.: Inexact conjugate gradient method with inner-outer iteration. SIAM J. Sci. Comput. **21**(4), 1305–1320 (1997)

11. Brandt, A.: Multi-level adaptive solutions to boundary-value problems. Math. Comput. **31**(138), 333–390 (1977)

12. Winget, J.M., Hughes, T.J.R.: Solution algorithms for nonlinear transient heat conduction analysis employing element-by-element iterative strategies. Comput. Methods Appl. Mech. Eng. **52**, 711–815 (1985)

13. Reedbush-H. http://www.cc.u-tokyo.ac.jp/system/reedbush/Reedbush-EN.pdf

14. NVIDIA DGX-1. http://www.nvidia.com/dgx1

15. Masterlark, T.: Finite element model predictions of static deformation from dislocation sources in a subduction zone: sensitivities to homogeneous, isotropic, poisson-solid, and half-space assumptions. J. Geophys. Res. **108**(B11), 2540 (2003)

16. Hughes, K.L., Masterlark, T., Mooney, W.D.: Poroelastic stress-triggering of the 2005 m8.7 nias earthquake by the 2004 m9.2 sumatra-andaman earthquake. Earth planet. Sci. Lett. **293**, 289–299 (2010)

17. Agata, R., Ichimura, T., Hirahara, K., Hyodo, M., Hori, T., Hori, M.: Robust and portable capacity computing method for many finite element analyses of a high-fidelity crustal structure model aimed for coseismic slip estimation. Comput. Geosci. **94**, 121–130 (2016)

18. Hansen, P.C.: Analysis of discrete ill-posed problems by means of the l-curve. SIAM Rev. **34**(4), 561–580 (1992)

Runtime Environments

The Design and Implementation of OpenMP 4.5 and OpenACC Backends for the RAJA C++ Performance Portability Layer

William Killian[1,2,3]([✉]), Tom Scogland[1], Adam Kunen[1], and John Cavazos[3]

[1] Lawrence Livermore National Laboratory, Livermore, CA 94550, USA
{killian4,scogland1,kunen1}@llnl.gov
[2] Millersville University of Pennsylvania, Millersville, PA 17551, USA
[3] University of Delaware, Newark, DE 19716, USA
cavazos@udel.edu

Abstract. Portability abstraction layers such as RAJA enable users to quickly change how a loop nest is executed with minimal modifications to high-level source code. Directive-based programming models such as OpenMP and OpenACC provide easy-to-use annotations on for-loops and regions which change the execution pattern of user code. Directive-based language backends for RAJA have previously been limited to few options due to multiplicative clauses creating version explosion. In this work, we introduce an updated implementation of two directive-based backends which helps mitigate the aforementioned version explosion problem by leveraging the C++ type system and template meta-programming concepts. We implement partial OpenMP 4.5 and OpenACC backends for the RAJA portability layer which can apply loop transformations and specify how loops should be executed. We evaluate our approach by analyzing compilation and runtime overhead for both backends using PGI 17.7 and IBM clang (OpenMP 4.5) on a collection of computation kernels.

Keywords: Directive-based programming model
Performance portability · Abstraction layer · Code generation

1 Introduction

Directives provide a simple mechanism for annotating source code which provides additional hints to a compiler. OpenMP [12] was one of the first standardized models to leverage directive-based program transformations. Such models enable a user to annotate a region or `for`-loop which allows the compiler to deduce additional information about the program. Compilers with OpenMP support are able to emit parallelized code from source code which had no original notion of being parallelizable.

Due to the increasing demand of heterogeneous computing, OpenACC [11] emerged as a directive-based programming model targeting accelerators including GPUs. OpenACC tends to prefer a more descriptive annotation model where

© Springer International Publishing AG, part of Springer Nature 2018
S. Chandrasekaran and G. Juckeland (Eds.): WACCPD 2017, LNCS 10732, pp. 63–82, 2018.
https://doi.org/10.1007/978-3-319-74896-2_4

a user may not need to explicitly state *how* a loop should be executed. Instead, the user indicates to the compiler that a loop *can* be parallelized. On the other hand, OpenMP leans toward a more prescriptive annotation model where a user must clearly state how a loop should be executed. The OpenMP standards committee released OpenMP 4.0 and 4.5 which enabled and improved upon [13] heterogeneous targets. Both programming models are interesting in the scope of this research due to (1) their directive-based approach of parallelization, (2) cross architecture support, and (3) targeting heterogeneous systems.

Performance Portability Layers make a limited set of assumptions about programs and allow a user to represent a program as an embedded domain specific language. Although this language has reduced usage compared to a general-purpose programming model, the portability layer is able to make additional assumptions about a user's code and apply high- and low-level source code transformations. This is incredibly useful when a user may wish to explore an unknown optimizations search space or compare/contrast multiple programming models.

There are many portability layers in active and maintained development. Thrust [1] is a C++ library which enables users to easily target GPUs and multi-core CPUs without needing to know CUDA [10], NVIDIA's proprietary programming language for targeting GPUs. Agency [9] is a relatively new portability layer which leverages C++ templates to drive parallel programming. The primary difference between Agency and Thrust lies with the level of abstraction – Agency provides much more fine-grained control over *how* and *where* to execute.

Kokkos [2] is another C++ library with an interest in unifying data parallelism and memory access patterns. Kokkos is capable of restructuring data at compile time with their generic *View* concept which helps improve performance across different target architectures, such as CPUs, GPUs, and many-core architectures. Kokkos also provides many different execution policies to end users, giving them enough flexibility to experiment with competing programming models (e.g. OpenMP 4.5 and CUDA).

More recently, the C++ Standards Committee (WG21) approved parallel Standard Template Library functions as part of the Parallelism TS [5]. They augmented many of the algorithms found under `algorithm` and `numeric` to include *execution policy* types. The standard defines three types: `seq` (sequential, ordered), `par_seq` (parallelized but in sequenced order), and `par_useq` (parallelized, unsequenced ordering) [6]. Vendors are also able to provide their own execution policies. Intel [4], SYCL [8], and HPX [7] were the first entities to release feature-complete versions of the Parallelism TS publicly.

The Khronos group has also come out with SYCL, a C++ single-source heterogeneous programming model for OpenCL [8]. SYCL provides a cross-platform API which enables code to be written in C++ and target any OpenCL device.

RAJA [3] is another C++ library which provides many different types of *execution policies*. One advantage to RAJA over other portability layers is the support for a variety of backends, ranging from sequential, SIMD, and OpenMP on CPU architectures to CUDA, OpenMP 4.5, and (with this research)

OpenACC on GPU architectures. In this research we extend our OpenMP backend and propose an initial OpenACC backend implementation. We outline the concepts and key structures of RAJA in Sect. 2. Then we introduce our type framework for creating execution policies in Sect. 3. We then outline the specializations required for OpenMP 4.5 and OpenACC in Sects. 4 and 5. Finally, we evaluate the overhead in terms of (1) compilation time and (2) execution time. We leverage a collection of kernels, both hand written and automatically generated RAJA versions, to evaluate the overhead in using a portability abstraction layer outlined in Sect. 6.

2   RAJA

RAJA can be reduced to three relevant concepts for the scope of this research. These three concepts define the expected interfaces, types, and pre- and post-conditions when library writers and users leverage RAJA to generate target code from a portable interface.

Execution Policy. First, an execution policy in RAJA tells the compiler which code path to follow and expand when expanding on loop and loop nests. RAJA provides many different backend targets, including sequential, OpenMP, SIMD, CUDA, and OpenACC implementations. Depending on the type of execution policy, the code which is conditionally enabled may change. Execution policies ultimately drive the required code transformations and generation necessary to provide a user with the expected behavior of specifying a given policy.

Callable. Second, a callable is a lambda function or a function which is invocable with a specified number of arguments. The *Callable* is also known as the loop body of a loop nest within the scope of RAJA. The callable must not be *mutable*. Depending on the target backend, the *Callable* may need additional attributes specified, such as __host__ __device__ attribute indicators for CUDA.

RandomAccessContainer. Third, a random-access container defines an *iteration space* for a given range of elements. The functional requirements of a RandomAccessContainer are:

- must have begin() and end() which each return *RandomAccessIterator*s to the underlying type
- must have size() to indicate the size of the container
- the underlying type (decltype(*container.begin())) must be convertible to a specified *Callable* lambda function.

2.1   Basic Execution Policies

The most basic executor in RAJA is a simple for-loop executor in the current thread. No code transformations or directives are emitted in this base case. Instead, RAJA will just create a for-loop which iterates over the *RandomAccessContainer* specified in the forall call and invoke the *Callable* function with the underlying value of each element contained within the *RandomAccessContainer*. More complex executors may augment or change the code path to include the emission of directives or other code. Section 3.3 outlines the specialization of `forall` for arbitrary execution policies.

2.2 `RAJA::NestedPolicy` and Loop Transformations

RAJA provides a powerful loop transformation construct, `forallN`. `forallN` is similar to `forall`, but enables the user to specify loop transformations for nested loops such as permutation and tiling. Any combinations of permutations and tiles can be applied. The `NestedPolicy` type is composed with an `ExecList` followed by any number of `Tile` clauses. `ExecList` describes the execution policy to apply to each loop nest. `Tile` clauses can specify a `TileList` to apply tiles of specified sizes to each loop. Permutations can also be specified with a `Permute` clause. Multiple `Tile` clauses can be applied to a single loop nest, making it feasible to optimize for outer- and inner-cache data access patterns. An example `NestedPolicy` is shown in Listing 1.

```
using Policy = NestedPolicy<
  ExecList<
    omp_collapse_nowait_exec,
    simd_exec,
    omp_collapse_nowait_exec>,
  OMP_Parallel<
      Tile<TileList<
        tile_none,
        tile_fixed<8>,
        tile_fixed<32>>,
      Permute<idx_seq<1,2,0>>>>>;
```

Listing 1: Sample `NestedPolicy` for use within `RAJA::forallN`. Note that multiple tiling policies may be specified in addition to outer "wrap" policies which can create regions of code. Loops may also be permuted to an arbitrary ordering, and, provided backend support, loops may also be collapsed

RAJA provides specializations for `omp_for_nowait_exec` policies that are next to one another. After any permutation of loops is applied, RAJA will look for any number of adjacent `omp_collapse_nowait_exec` policies. If two or more `collapse` policies are directly adjacent, a single *#pragma omp for collapse(N)* directive is emitted above the N next loops.

3 Embedding Directives in the C++ Type System

In general, most execution-based directives are applied to `for`-loops. RAJA provides the `forall` and `forallN` loop constructs to specify an execution policy on a single loop or loop nest. The most challenging component of this research is embedding the required directive information in a C++ type to apply *template specialization* with careful consideration of SFINAE[1]. To tackle this embedding problem, we make the following translations:

- All supported directives have a functional mapping to a single type; not all clauses and options are supported.
- OpenACC/OpenMP `parallel` and OpenMP 4.5 `target` enclose *regions*, or structured code blocks.
- OpenACC `loop`, OpenMP 4.5 `teams distribute`, and OpenMP `for` constructs are *variadic* – zero or more clauses may be added to one of these constructs.

The construction of a type system for a directive-based programming language can be described with the following steps:

1. Define all valid constructs, directives, and clauses as *policy tags*
2. Construct explicit types for each construct, directive, and clause
   - When defining a *construct* that encloses a region, an `inner` type must be defined. The appropriate region code shall be emitted and the inner policy will then be invoked.
   - When defining a *construct* or *directive* which may have clauses optionally specified, the new type must accept a variadic number of template argument types and inherit from all specified variadic template arguments.
   - Clauses with value-based options, e.g. `num_gangs`, must be defined with a uniquely-identifiable `static constexpr int` member variable.
3. Implement all specializations for the backend planned for support

Below, we highlight a trivial case of supporting OpenMP 3.x `parallel` for with an optionally specified `schedule` clause.

3.1   Defining Policy Tags for a Backend

Tags are defined within a nested `tags` namespace for the supported backend. For the case of an `OpenMP` policy, we will make use of the `omp` namespace. Listing 2 shows the definitions of various tags used to build OpenMP policies. There are two primary types of tags. The first – region-based tags – describe tags which are used to define a region containing another policy. The second type of tag, construct- and clause-based tags, describe all other valid policy tags present for a given backend (e.g. OpenMP). The aggregation of these tags within a single C++ type is how we specialize `forall` for a backend implementation.

---

[1] Substitution Failure Is Not An Error – the C++ standard states that substitution failure shall not result in a compiler error unless no valid substitutions are found.

```
namespace omp::tags {
  // region-based tags
  struct Parallel {};
  struct BarrierAfter {};
  // ... BarrierBefore, etc.
  // construct- and clause-based tags
  struct For {};
  struct Static {};
  // ... Guided, Dynamic
}
```

Listing 2: Defining tag types for the OpenMP 3.x **parallel** for clause

3.2 Constructing Explicit Execution Policy Types

Once the policy tags are defined, we construct our explicit types for directives and clauses. Each of these explicit types defines a component of a *policy*. A *policy* defines how the code should be analyzed by a generator or specialization. Within the scope of RAJA, a policy must define (1) a type (e.g. *sequential, OpenMP*) and (2) a platform (e.g. *undefined, cpu, gpu*). The type is useful for determining whether a constructed policy is valid. The platform information is used by the optional data integration layer to automatically perform data transfer. In Listing 3 we show the definitions of a `PolicyBase` type used to construct subsequent execution policies.

```
enum class Policy { seq, simd, cuda, openmp, target_openmp, openacc };
enum class Platform { undefined, cpu, gpu };

template <Policy Pol, Platform P, typename... Args>
struct PolicyBaseT : public Args... {
  static constexpr Policy policy    = Pol;
  static constexpr Platform platform = P;
};

// specific policy alias type for all OpenMP policies
namespace omp {
template <typename... Args>
using policy = PolicyBaseT<Policy::openmp, Platform::undefined, Args...>;
}
```

Listing 3: Base policy types and platforms used to construct additional policies in RAJA. Note that the specialized OpenMP type alias has no defined platform to permit reuse between OpenMP 3.x and OpenMP 4.5 target offload execution policies.

Region-like directives (e.g. omp **parallel** in OpenMP 3.x) define a code block to enclose. A generic region policy must represent a code region within the type system. We accomplish this by defining an *inner policy* type. This *inner policy* type indicates how the code within the region should execute with another execution policy. Listing 4 shows the construction of a Parallel policy within the omp namespace. Once the parallel execution policy is defined, it can be used in conjunction with other policies to drive source code transformations at compile time.

```
namespace omp {
template <typename Inner>
struct Parallel : policy<tags::Parallel> {
  using inner = Inner;
};
}
```

Listing 4: Construction of an OpenMP 3.x parallel region policy

Other directives, such as omp for define how an immediately-following for-loop should be distributed within the current parallel region. Additional clauses can change the execution behavior of the for-loop, specifically schedule and nowait. Listing 5 shows how a for-loop directive is constructed. Specifying additional options for an OpenMP for execution policy is not required, but a policy clause still must indicate any required information through the type system. The specialization of the schedule(static,N) clause is shown in Listing 6. In addition to a template argument specifying the static chunk size, a static constexpr int member variable with a uniquely identifiable name is defined as an accessor for the template argument value. Additional clauses, including guided and dynamic scheduling clauses, are omitted for brevity.

```
template <typename... Options>
struct For : policy<tags::For>, Options... {};
```

Listing 5: Construction of an OpenMP for policy with template arguments. Note that the Options are variadically inherited to encode the underlying policy a "parent" to the current policy.

3.3   Implement forall Specializations

Once all directives and clauses are defined, we can implement RAJA::forall specializations with *aggregate* policies. An aggregate policy is a fully-defined policy which should be made available to end users. RAJA provides a few aggregate policies for OpenMP 3.x, e.g. omp_parallel_for, omp_parallel_for_nowait, OMP_Parallel. An aggregate policy can be viewed as a type alias to a nesting of policy directives and clauses. Listing 7 shows a subset of aggregate policies implemented for the RAJA OpenMP 3.x backend.

```
template <unsigned int N>
struct Static : policy<tags::Static>  {
  static constexpr unsigned int static_chunk_size = N;
};
```

Listing 6: Definition of an OpenMP static schedule clause for an OpenMP for directive. Since the static schedule has no other options besides the chunk size, there is no additional inheritance besides the policy definition.

```
using omp_for_exec = omp::BarrierAfter<omp::For<>>;

template <unsigned int N>
using omp_static_exec = omp::BarrierAfter<omp::For<omp::Static<N>>>;

using omp_for_nowait_exec = omp::For<>;

template <unsigned int N>
using omp_static_nowait_exec = omp::For<omp::Static<N>>;

template <typename Inner>
using omp_parallel_exec = omp::Parallel<Inner>;

using omp_parallel_for_exec = omp_parallel_exec<omp_for_exec>;

template <unsigned int N>
using omp_parallel_static_exec = omp_parallel_exec<omp_static_exec<N>>;
```

Listing 7: Aggregate policy definitions for the RAJA OpenMP 3.x backend. Note that the default `for` execution policy is `nowait` and all aggregate policies are type aliases; no new types are introduced.

We implement corresponding `RAJA::forall` specializations for each defined aggregate policy. Given the type hierarchy of an aggregate policy, we can determine all enclosed directives and clauses in the following manner:

1. α is the set of all possible directives/clauses valid for the current backend.
2. ϵ is the set of directives/clauses required for a `forall` specialization.
3. β is the set of directives/clauses present in a given execution policy.
4. Ensure $\beta \cup \epsilon = \beta$.
5. Ensure $\beta \cup (\alpha \setminus \epsilon) = \emptyset$.
6. Use SFINAE-safe conditional visibility of the `forall` specialization by restricting visibility of the specialization, ϵ, to policies equivalent to β.

We show an example type hierarchy of an OpenMP Parallel for directive with a fixed, static schedule in Fig. 1. Furthermore, when we collapse the type hierarchy into a flat view, depicted in Fig. 2, we can easily check the constraints to determine the most specialized valid execution.

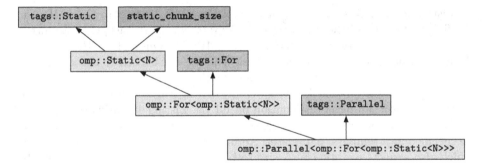

Fig. 1. The full type hierarchy of an instantiated `omp parallel for schedule(static, N)` policy. Red indicates a `static constexpr int` member variable, green indicates a *tag* type, and yellow represents a *policy* type. (Color figure online)

Fig. 2. The flattened type hierarchy of an instantiated `omp parallel for schedule(static, N)` policy. The specialization is easy to deduce from the specified tags (shown in green). Any attributes needed by the specialization can be accessed with *field names* (shown in red). (Color figure online)

This constraint satisfaction can easily be implemented in C++ by counting the occurrences of β in both α and ϵ and ensuring they are the same. The `exact<T...>` metafunction provides an alias to `std::enable_if<T...>::type` if and only if the constraint is met. An additional layer of dispatch to the generic `forall` interface exists to generalize to a given backend. Listing 8 shows a subset of `forall` specialization for the OpenMP 3.x backend as well as the `forall` dispatch to an OpenMP policy type.

4   Case Study: OpenMP 4.5

In addition to supporting `parallel for` and other clauses from the OpenMP 3.x standard, we extend RAJA to support a number of OpenMP 4.5 directives and clauses. From a design perspective, we chose to extend the OpenMP implementation as follows:

1. Extend the tags to include `Target`, `Teams`, and `Distribute`
2. Define aggregate policies for `TargetTeamsDistribute`, `TargetTeams DistributeParallelFor`, and `TargetTeamsDistributeParallelStatic`
3. Define a dispatch overload for `forall` with all OpenMP 4.5 policies
4. Define built-in policies for some OpenMP 4.5 policies: `OMP_Target` (for `forallN`), `omp_target_teams_distribute_parallel_for`, and a few others.

Listing 9 highlights the augmentation of OpenMP 3.x tags to OpenMP 4.5. We first include all of the tags under the `omp::tags` namespace, then we introduce the additional tags required by OpenMP 4.5. Once all of the tags are defined, we need to construct the *tag list*. The *tag list* is used to determine the most specialized and valid version of an execution policy.

Once all tags are defined, we can create the aggregate policies to allow for proper OpenMP 4.5 team distribution on GPUs. Listing 10 shows the creation of the aggregate policies. Each aggregate policy requires the number of teams to be specified at a template parameter. Additionally, there is one aggregate policy which also expects a static chunk size to be specified as an additional template parameter. By configuring the sizes as template parameters, we can ensure (1) the specialization can be encoded into a C++ custom data type and (2) the compiler is aware of the sizes at compile time.

Finally, once all aggregate policies are created, we can implement the `forall` overloads within the OpenMP 4.5 backend. Listing 11 shows the overload for one of the aggregate policies and the dispatch code expecting a policy and potentially invoking the OpenMP 4.5 policy.

5   Case Study: OpenACC

OpenACC provides a different set of directives, constructs, and clauses for RAJA to consider with code generation. First, OpenACC allows two different types of region constructs: `parallel` and `kernels`. `parallel` is more synonymous with the OpenMP 4.5 `parallel` construct while `kernels` provides a much higher-level annotation of a loop nest. The compiler is ultimately able to make many more decisions regarding code optimization and transformation when given a `kernels` construct compared with a `parallel` construct. The increased number of clauses present in OpenACC also mandate additional tag definitions as depicted in Listing 12. Like other backends, some tags are only valid in certain contexts. Therefore, a program is illformed if a user specifies an invalid policy construction.

Listing 13 shows definitions for a subset of OpenACC aggregate policies. `Parallel` and `Kernels` are scope-based policies which do not generate any loop iteration code. Policies such as `NumGangs` and `VectorLength` require template parameters indicating their size but will always be additional clauses specified for the scope-based policies. Likewise, `Independent`, `Gang`, and `Worker` policies have no template arguments but must be specified as additional clauses for a `Loop` construct.

Ultimately, the grammar defined by the OpenACC standard is adhered to through the established constraints of our type system. Only valid execution policies have specializations implemented. Listing 14 shows a subset of specializations defined in our OpenACC backend. It is important to note that the number of specializations we need is a function of the configuration parameters which can either exist or not exist for a given construct. Since `Kernels` can have any number of three clauses specified (`NumGangs`, `NumWorkers`, `VectorLength`), we must implement 8 versions of kernels. Likewise, the `Loop` construct can have any number of four clauses specified (`Independent`, `Gang`, `Worker`, `Vector`), resulting in 16 versions required.

6   Evaluation

Our evaluation system is a CORAL Early Access System which has two IBM POWER 8 processors and four NVIDIA P100 GPUs with NVLINK. The processor, a 10-core IBM POWER 8+, has a core frequency of 4.0GHz. Two processors are on each node and is coupled with 256 GB of DDR3 RAM. Only one NVIDIA P100 (SMX variant) was used for consistent experimentation. For all of our tests we restrict execution to GPU device 0 and leverage unified memory for data allocation and offload. When using the proposed OpenACC backend, we compile our test set with PGI Compiler 17.7[2]. With the OpenMP 4.5 backend, we compile our test set with IBM's version of clang with OpenMP 4.5 support. Both of these compilers and supporting libraries leverage CUDA 8.0.61.

6.1   Test Set

We used a collection of various kernels which highlight different access patterns (dense linear algebra, stencils, and reductions of k-dimensions to $k - 1$ dimensions). One limitation of our evaluation is the absence of any reductions. To this end, RAJA cannot provide support for directive-based reductions because the variable name is required within a directive reduction clause. Because of this limitation, inclusion of directive-based reductions is out of scope for this research – it is impossible to generate the directives with library-only solutions (e.g. RAJA). RAJA does have support for reductions, but it is achieved using allocated arrays and specialized kernels and combiners. OpenMP 4.5 reducers are implemented and are currently being used, but we wanted to focus on execution policies instead of reducers.

Shown above is the test set we end up comparing compiler overhead of RAJA-based versions to directive-based implemented versions. There is a larger "tuning" space for OpenACC versions due to the expanded clause options for `loop` directives compared to the clause options available for `parallel for` and `teams distribute` directives.

6.2   Goals and Non-Goals

It is our goal in this evaluation section to highlight:

- Compare the compile-time overhead of leveraging meta-programming concepts and C++ templates to drive code generation to directive-based approaches

---

[2] This work was not feasible until the release of V17.7 in early August which added support for lambdas and no-copy captures.

Kernel	Description	OpenACC	OpenMP
Jacobi1D	1-D Stencil	64	16
Jacobi2D	2-D Stencil	256	64
Heat3D	3-D Heat Equation	1024	256
MatMul	Matrix Multiplication	1024	256
MatVec	Matrix-Vector Multiplication	256	64
VecAdd	Vector Addition	64	16
Tensor2	Synthetic tensor contraction (2D to 1D)	256	64
Tensor3	Synthetic tensor contraction (3D to 2D)	1024	256
Tensor4	Synthetic tensor contraction (4D to 3D)	4096	1024

– Compare the code generation of RAJA-fied loop nests to hand-written directive-based loop nests

In no way to we intend to highlight the following:

– Compare the two compilers' performance on the same kernel directly
– Compare OpenACC to OpenMP 4.5 in terms of:
  • Compilation time
  • Compilation resources (RAM, page faults, etc.)
  • Code generation
  • Execution time
– Identify bottlenecks of toolchains without vendors' knowledge of the problem
– Determine any limitations of drivers, software, hardware, or runtimes.

6.3   Compilation Overhead

For each kernel we show the compilation overhead. We used a wall clock timer to measure the total amount of time it took to compile each set of kernels with a given compiler. In the following Table 1 we highlight (1) the kernel name, (2) the average compilation overhead when compiling the various versions of the kernel, and (3) the backend used. The overhead is computed by taking the difference in compilation times over the directive-based compilation time. The average overhead with the OpenACC backend is 95.07% while the average overhead with the OpenMP backend is 38.78%.

There are somewhat significant changes between our original kernels and RAJA kernels. First, The original kernels are essentially C functions. The first change that the RAJA versions make is converting from traditional for-loops to RAJA *Iterables* and lambda expressions. A simple two-nested for-loop would go from zero template instantiations to at least three (two for each *Iterable* and one for the execution policy). When the code passes through the compiler for code generation and specialization, the execution policy will dictate overload visibility from substitution failure. In the case of a RAJA *forall* construct, we will attempt to specialize for each possible backend (sequential, SIMD, OpenMP, OpenACC,

Table 1. Compilation overhead of test programs using a directive-based RAJA backend instead of manually-specified directives

Kernel	OpenACC	OpenMP
Jacobi1D	17.50%	8.75%
Jacobi2D	50.24%	20.42%
Heat3D	74.40%	30.91%
MatMul	80.28%	31.24%
MatVec	45.41%	16.47%
VecAdd	15.20%	6.24%
Tensor2	48.94%	17.57%
Tensor3	72.85%	27.53%
Tensor4	120.74%	59.29%
Average	*95.07%*	*38.78%*

OpenMP, TBB, CUDA, etc.). Determining the code path would require traversing through all possible backends results in over 8 resolution attempts. Once a policy is determined, then the per-backend specializations are evaluated and the correct version is visited for code emission. The *Iterable* must also be validated which adds two additional overload resolution checks per nest level. The current RAJA *forallN* nested loop construct will construct at least 5 additional types per nest level. On a three-nested loop, at least 18 type constructions and 110 overload resolution attempts will be made with an OpenACC execution policy. For OpenMP 4.5 the overload resolution number reduces down to 62. Comparing this to the zero type constructions and no overload resolutions from the original kernel versions provides some additional insight as to where the compilation overhead comes from.

6.4   Runtime Overhead

Next, we show the runtime overhead for each kernel. We used a timer to measure the total amount of time it took to execute the kernel *on the GPU* with each set of kernels and a given compiler. In the following Table 2 we highlight (1) the kernel name, (2) the average execution overhead when executing the various versions of the kernel, and (3) the backend used. The average overhead with the OpenACC backend is 1.66% while the average overhead with the OpenMP backend is 1.69%. This overhead differs greatly from the compilation overhead, suggesting that although compilation takes significantly longer, the emitted code performs about the same as the plain directives. One of the underlying goals of performance portability layers, such as RAJA, is to minimize the execution overhead.

Table 2. Runtime overhead of test programs using a directive-based RAJA backend instead of manually-specified directives

Kernel	OpenACC	OpenMP
Jacobi1D	2.52%	1.94%
Jacobi2D	1.25%	1.14%
Heat3D	1.08%	1.19%
MatMul	0.96%	1.01%
MatVec	1.13%	1.38%
VecAdd	0.21%	0.38%
Tensor2	0.98%	1.21%
Tensor3	1.34%	1.44%
Tensor4	2.18%	2.14%
Average	*1.66%*	*1.69%*

7 Future Work and Conclusion

In this research we propose a backend design and implementation which provides a subset of OpenMP 4.5 and OpenACC to users of the RAJA portability layer. We address concerns related to template specialization and overloading, version explosion, compilation overhead, and runtime overhead. We highlight the various components of our implementation including execution policy dispatch, specialization for regions, and aggregation for various clause combinations found within OpenMP and OpenACC.

We show that with the OpenMP 4.5 backend compiled with the IBM clang we observe – on average – a 40% slowdown in compilation time but only a 1.69% slowdown in execution time compared to directive-only based implementations of the test programs. When using the OpenACC backend compiled with PGI 17.7 we observe – on average – a 95% slowdown in compilation time but only a 1.66% slowdown in execution time compared to directive-only based implementation of the test programs. We attribute most of the compilation slowdown to the compiler needing to (1) instantiate many more templates compared to the directive-based solutions and (2) perform template overload resolution to find the most specific and valid version of policies. We plan to continue this research by:

- Augmenting our current reduction implementation for OpenMP 4.5 and extending it to the OpenACC backend
- Add more directives and clauses to the backends, specifically some of the `if()` constructs being added with OpenMP 5.0. This would help reduce the total number of specializations required
- Reduce the number of template instantiations necessary by simplifying the check for the most specific policy

– Expand our results to include reductions and other high-level source code
transformations (collapsing for OpenACC and OpenMP 4.5, tiling for
OpenACC)

```cpp
namespace omp {
// all tags for the given backend shall be listed in tag_list
using tag_list = list<tags::Parallel, tags::Static,
  tags::BarrierAfter, tags::For>;

template <typename Exec, typename Iterable,
  typename Body, typename TagList>
exact<Exec, TagList, tags::For, tags::Static>
forall_impl(const Exec &&, Iterable && iter, Body && body) {
  auto size = iter.size();
  #pragma omp for schedule(static, Exec::static_chunk_size)
  for (decltype(size) i = 0; i < size; ++i)
    body(*(iter.begin() + i));
}

template <typename Exec, typename Iterable,
  typename Body, typename TagList>
exact<Exec, TagList, tags::Parallel>
forall_impl(const Exec &&, Iterable && iter, Body && body) {
  #pragma omp parallel
  {
    forall(typename Exec::inner(),
      std::forward<Iterable>(iter), std::forward<Body>(body));
  }
}

template <typename Exec, typename Iterable,
  typename Body, typename TagList>
exact<Exec, TagList, tags::BarrierAfter>
forall_impl(const Exec &&, Iterable && iter, Body && body) {
  forall(typename Exec::inner(),
    std::forward<Iterable>(iter), std::forward<Body>(body));
  #pragma omp barrier
}

// dispatch to target omp policy
template <typename Exec, typename Iterable, typename Body>
typename std::enable_if<Exec::policy == Policy::openmp>::type
forall(const Exec &&p, Iterable && iter, Body && body) {
  omp::forall_impl<Exec, omp::tag_list>(
    std::forward<const Exec>(p),
    std::forward<Iterable>(iter),
    std::forward<Body>(body));
}
```

Listing 8: forall implementations for a subset of OpenMP 3.x specializations.

```
namespace target_omp {
namespace tags {
// include all tags from namespace omp::tags
using namespace omp::tags;
struct Target {};
struct Teams {};
struct Distribute {};
} // end namespace tags

using tag_list =
  list<tags::Target, tags::Teams, tags::Distribute, tags::Parallel,
       tags::Static, tags::BarrierAfter, tags::BarrierBefore, tags::For>;
} // end namespace target_omp
```

Listing 9: Tag definitions for OpenMP 4.5. Reuse of tags from OpenMP 3.x reduces the overall implementation size with minimal cost.

```
namespace target_omp {
template <typename... Args>
using policy = PolicyBaseT<Policy::target_openmp, Platform::undefined, Args...>;

using omp::BarrierAfter;
using omp::BarrierBefore;
using omp::For;
using omp::Parallel;
using omp::Static;

template <unsigned int N>
struct TargetTeamsDistribute : policy<tags::Target, tags::Teams, tags::Distribute> {
  constexpr static unsigned int num_teams = N;
};

template <unsigned int N>
struct TargetTeamsDistributeParallelFor
    : policy<tags::Target, tags::Teams, tags::Distribute, tags::Parallel, tags::For> {
  constexpr static unsigned int num_teams = N;
};

template <unsigned int N, unsigned int M>
struct TargetTeamsDistributeParallelStatic
    : policy<tags::Target, tags::Teams, tags::Distribute, tags::Parallel,
             tags::For, tags::Static> {
  constexpr static unsigned int num_teams = N;
  constexpr static unsigned int static_chunk_size = M;
};
} // end namespace target_omp
```

Listing 10: Aggregate policy definitions for OpenMP 4.5. In addition to all OpenMP 3.x policies, three new policies are added to aid with target offload

```
namespace target_omp {
template <typename Exec, typename Iterable,
  typename Body, typename TagList>
exact<Exec, TagList, tags::Target, tags::Teams,
  tags::Distribute, tags::Parallel, tags::For>
forall_impl(const Exec &&, Iterable && iter, Body && body) {
  auto size = iter.size();
  #pragma omp target teams distribute parallel for \
    num_teams(Exec::num_teams)
  for (decltype(size) i = 0; i < size; ++i) {
    body(*(iter.begin() + i));
  }
}
} // end namespace target_omp

template <typename Exec, typename Iterable, typename Body>
typename std::enable_if<Exec::policy == Policy::target_openmp>::type
forall(const Exec &&p, Iterable && iter, Body && body) {
  target_openmp::forall_impl<Exec, omp::tag_list>(
    std::forward<const Exec>(p),
    std::forward<Iterable>(iter),
    std::forward<Body>(body));
}
```

Listing 11: A `forall` specialization shown for OpenMP 4.5. Note that the second function performs tagged dispatch of a policy to an OpenMP 4.5 policy if the type matches.

```
namespace openacc {
namespace tags {
struct Parallel {};
struct Kernels {};
struct Loop {};
struct Independent {};
struct Gang {};
struct Worker {};
struct Vector {};
struct NumGangs {};
struct NumWorkers {};
struct VectorLength {};
} // end namespace tags

using tag_list =
  list<tags::Parallel, tags::Kernels, tags::Loop, tags::Independent,
       tags::Gang, tags::Worker, tags::Vector, tags::NumGangs,
       tags::NumWorkers, tags::VectorLength>;
} // end namespace openacc
```

Listing 12: Tag definitions for OpenACC. Note the difference between `Gang` and `NumGangs` – the former indicates a clause on a `loop` construct while the latter specifies the number of gangs on a `parallel` or `kernels` construct.

```
namespace openacc {
template <typename... Args>
using policy = PolicyBaseT<Policy::openacc, Platform::gpu, Args...>;

template <unsigned int N>
struct NumGangs : policy<tags::NumGangs> {
  static constexpr unsigned int num_gangs = N;
};

template <typename Inner>
struct Parallel : policy<tags::Parallel>, Inner {
  using inner = Inner;
};

struct Independent : policy<tags::Independent> {};

template <typename ... Options>
struct Loop : policy<tags::Loop>, Options... {};

} // end namespace openacc
```

Listing 13: A subset of aggregate policy definitions for OpenACC. The user can directly construct their own RAJA OpenACC type policy or leverage one of the policies RAJA provides.

```
namespace openacc {
template <typename Exec, typename Iterable,
  typename Body, typename TagList>
exact<Exec, TagList, tags::Parallel, tags::NumGangs>
forall_impl(const Exec &&, Iterable && iter, Body && body) {
  #pragma acc parallel num_gangs(Exec::num_gangs)
    forall(Exec::inner(),
      std::forward<Iterable>(iter),
      std::forward<Body>(body));
}


template <typename Exec, typename Iterable,
  typename Body, typename TagList>
exact<Exec, TagList, tags::Kernels, tags::NumGangs, tags::VectorLength>
forall_impl(const Exec &&, Iterable && iter, Body && body) {
  #pragma acc kernels num_gangs(Exec::num_gangs) \
      vector_length(Exec::vector_length)
    forall(Exec::inner(),
      std::forward<Iterable>(iter),
      std::forward<Body>(body));
}

// A total of 8 specializations are required for each of tags::Parallel
// and tags::Kernel. Only one is shown for each above.

template <typename Exec, typename Iterable,
  typename Body, typename TagList>
exact<Exec, TagList, tags::Loop, tags::Independent, tags::Vector>
forall_impl(const Exec &&, Iterable && iter, Body && body) {
  auto size = iter.size();
  #pragma acc loop independent vector
  for (decltype(size) i = 0; i < size; ++i) {
    body(*(iter.begin() + i));
  }
}

// A total of 16 specializations are required for tags::Loop
// Only one is shown above.

} // end namespace openacc
```

Listing 14: `forall` specializations for OpenACC. Note we must provide specializations for any number of **kernels** or **parallel** constructs with the {**num_gangs**, **num_workers**, **vector_length**} clauses either (1) being specified or (2) omitted. The same must be done for **loop** constructs with {**independent**,**gang**,**worker**,**vector**}. We do not show the OpenACC policy dispatch overload for brevity.

References

1. Bell, N., Hoberock, J.: Thrust: a productivity-oriented library for CUDA. In: GPU Computing Gems (2011)
2. Edwards, H.C., Trott, C.R., Sunderland, D.: Kokkos: enabling manycore performance portability through polymorphic memory access patterns. J. Parallel Distrib. Comput. **74**(12), 3175–3272 (2014)
3. Hornung, R.D., Keasler, J.A.: The RAJA portability layer: overview and status. No. LLNL-TR-661403. Lawrence Livermore National Laboratory (LLNL), Livermore, CA (2014)
4. Intel Corporation: Getting Started with Parallel STL, March 2017. https://software.intel.com/en-us/get-started-with-pstl
5. ISO/IEC: Programming Languages - Technical Specification for C++ Extensions for Parallelism, May 2015. http://www.open-std.org/jtc1/sc22/wg21/docs/papers/2015/n4507.pdf
6. ISO/IEC: Working Draft, Standard for Programming Language C++, July 2017. http://www.open-std.org/jtc1/sc22/wg21/docs/papers/2017/n4687.pdf
7. Kaiser, H., et al.: HPX: a task based programming model in a global address space. In: Proceedings of the 8th International Conference on Partitioned Global Address Space Programming Models. ACM (2014)
8. Khronos OpenCL Working Group: SYCL Provisional Specification Version 2.2, February 2016. https://www.khronos.org/registry/SYCL/specs/sycl-2.2.pdf
9. NVIDIA Corporation: Agency 0.1.0 (2016). https://agency-library.github.io/0.1.0/index.html
10. NVIDIA Corporation: NVIDIA CUDA Compute Unified Device Architecture Programming Guide, June 2017. http://docs.nvidia.com/cuda/cuda-c-programming-guide/index.html
11. OpenACC Standard Committee: The OpenACC Application Programming Interface Version 2.5, October 2015. https://www.openacc.org/sites/default/files/inline-files/OpenACC_2pt5.pdf
12. OpenMP Architecture Review Board: OpenMP Application Program Interface Version 3.0, May 2008. http://www.openmp.org/mp-documents/spec30.pdf
13. OpenMP Architecture Review Board: OpenMP Application Program Interface Version 4.5, November 2015. http://www.openmp.org/wp-content/uploads/openmp-4.5.pdf
14. Stone, J.E., Gohara, D., Shi, G.: OpenCL: a parallel programming standard for heterogeneous computing systems. Comput. Sci. Eng. **12**(3), 66–73 (2010). IEEE

Enabling GPU Support for the COMPSs-Mobile Framework

Francesc Lordan[1,2]([✉]) [ID], Rosa M. Badia[1,3] [ID], and Wen-Mei Hwu[4]

[1] Department of Computer Sciences, Barcelona Supercomputing Center (BSC-CNS),
Barcelona, Spain
{francesc.lordan,rosa.m.badia}@bsc.es
[2] Department of Computer Architecture,
Universitat Politècnica de Catalunya (UPC), Barcelona, Spain
[3] Spanish National Research Council (CSIC),
Artificial Intelligence Research Institute, Barcelona, Spain
[4] Coordinated Science Lab, University of Illinois, Urbana-Champaign (UIUC),
Urbana-Champaign, IL, USA

Abstract. Using the GPUs embedded in mobile devices allows for increasing the performance of the applications running on them while reducing the energy consumption of their execution. This article presents a task-based solution for adaptative, collaborative heterogeneous computing on mobile cloud environments. To implement our proposal, we extend the COMPSs-Mobile framework – an implementation of the COMPSs programming model for building mobile applications that offload part of the computation to the Cloud – to support offloading computation to GPUs through OpenCL. To evaluate our solution, we subject the prototype to three benchmark applications representing different application patterns.

Keywords: Programming model · Heterogeneous computing
Collaborative computing · GPGPU · OpenCL
Mobile cloud computing · Android

1 Introduction

Graphical Processing Units (GPUs) employ SIMT architecture to achieve higher instruction execution rates compared to multi-core CPUs while saving energy through simpler control logic. During the last decade, heterogeneous systems combining multi-core CPU, GPU, and other accelerators have become ubiquitous thanks to the general-purpose computing on GPU (GPGPU) frameworks. Even some system-on-chips (SoCs) already have integrated them on the same die; for instance, the Qualcomm Snapdragon and the NIVIDA Tegra. Both target mobile devices where energy efficiency is a major issue and CPU computing power, highly constrained.

© Springer International Publishing AG, part of Springer Nature 2018
S. Chandrasekaran and G. Juckeland (Eds.): WACCPD 2017, LNCS 10732, pp. 83–102, 2018.
https://doi.org/10.1007/978-3-319-74896-2_5

The most widely used programming models for developing applications for GPGPU are OpenCL [9] and CUDA [14]. Both present the hardware as a parallel platform allowing programmers to be agnostic to the actual parallel capabilities of the underlying hardware. On the one hand, these frameworks offer a multi-platform programming language to describe the computation to perform on the computing device; and, on the other hand, they provide an API to handle the parallel platform (launching computations, managing memory, and querying actual hardware details for high-performance purposes).

In this article, we propose a solution to enable applications running on a mobile device to exploit the heterogeneous resources of a distributed system. The internal computing devices within the mobile (CPU, GPU and other accelerators) and external resources in the Cloud (either nearby cloudlets or VM instances hosted on Cloud providers such as Amazon) collaborate to shorten the execution time, reduce the energy footprint and improve the user experience. For that purpose, we based our work on COMPSs-Mobile [11], an implementation of the COMPSs [12] programming model specifically designed for Mobile Cloud environments.

COMPSs is a task-based programming model that automatically exploits the parallelism inherent in an application. Developers code in a sequential fashion, being totally unaware of the underlying infrastructure and without using any specific API. At execution time, a runtime system detects the tasks that compose the application and orchestrates their execution on the available resources (local computing devices or remote nodes) guaranteeing the sequential consistency of the application.

Given that CUDA is a proprietary platform exclusive for devices equipped with the Tegra SoC – considering only embedded devices –, we opted for building our prototype on OpenCL: an open standard widely adopted by processor manufacturers, and thus, by a wide range of users. However, the proposed architecture does not lose any generality, and CUDA support could be easily added.

The contribution presented in this work consists on enabling COMPSs-Mobile applications to benefit from the computing resources within the mobile device other than the cores of CPU. For that purpose, we extend the COMPSs programming model to allow developers to declare the availability of OpenCL kernels that implement a task. Regarding the COMPSs-Mobile system, we revisit the policy to assign computing resources to each task, so it considers offloading parts of the computation to any embedded OpenCL device. To ease the interaction of the runtime system with the devices, we construct a generic computing platform leveraging on OpenCL. This platform orchestrates the execution of tasks on a settable OpenCL device; it submits the necessary commands to execute the corresponding kernels and manage the content of the memory of the device for kernels to operate on correct values. Thus, our solution hides from the programmer all the parallel platform management details (no need of invoking the API of the GPGPU framework) while the application user profits from their use. Finally, we conducted several tests to evaluate the behavior of the resulting prototype in different situations and measure the potential benefits of our proposal on Android applications.

The article goes on presenting the related work in Sect. 2. Section 3 introduces the extended COMPSs programming model, while Sect. 4 gives insights on the runtime implementation to support the execution of tasks on GPGPU devices. In Sect. 5, we describe the applications used for evaluating the performance of the solution and present the obtained results. Finally, to wrap up the article, we expose the conclusions and future directions of our research in Sect. 6.

2 Related Work

To the best of our knowledge, COMPSs-Mobile is the first framework targeting mobile devices to bring together adaptative, heterogeneous computing and computation offloading to the Cloud.

Regarding adaptative heterogeneous computing on mobile devices, Android already provides a natively integrated framework for running computationally intensive tasks at high performance: RenderScript [2]. Programming with a C99-derived language, developers write code portable across the computing devices available on the SoC. At execution time, the RenderScript toolkit parallelizes the work considering the availability of the resources (load balancing) and manages the memory. Although RenderScript achieves performances similar to OpenCL or CUDA, it can not exploit remote resources.

Beyond mobile computing, there exist other programming models/languages aiming to ease the development of task-based applications with GPU support. OmpSs [7] and StarPU [3] are two programming models that leverage on OpenMP pragmas to declare either CPU or GPU task implementations. Conversely, PaRSEC [4] allows programmers to describe the application as a DAG compactly represented in a format called JDF. For each task, JDF indicates the execution space, the parallel partitioning of the data, how the method operates on the parameters and the method to call to execute the task (allowing one CPU implementation and one for the GPU).

Regarding automatic computation offloading to Cloud resources from mobile devices, there exist several other frameworks that consider CPU task offloading. Some examples are AlfredO [16], Cuckoo [8], MAUI [6], CloneCloud [5] and ThinkAir [10]. However, they only consider CPU code offloading; developers need to deal explicitly with GPGPU frameworks to exploit the computing power of GPUs and manually balance the load across the computing devices.

Although COMPSs-Mobile does not currently offload GPU code to remote nodes, other frameworks already have implemented it. To exploit GPGPUs on mobile devices without a GPU, Ratering et al. [15] propose using virtual OpenCL devices as the interface to compute clouds. For CUDA-enabled applications, rCUDA [17] takes a driver-split approach where the driver manages all the necessary details to execute the kernels on the local or remote GPU. A complete framework for computation offloading is the result of the RAPID [13] EU project, which allows CPU and GPU code offloading; however, none of the proposed offloading frameworks automatically deals with load balancing.

3   Programming Model

COMP Superscalar (COMPSs) is a framework that aims to ease the development and execution of parallel applications atop distributed infrastructures. The core of the framework is the COMPSs Programming Model (PM) which abstracts away the parallelization and distribution concerns by offering a sequential, infrastructure-agnostic way of programming. The PM considers applications as composites of invocations to pieces of software whose execution is to be orchestrated aiming to exploit the parallelism inherent in the application. These computations are encapsulated as methods, called Core Elements (CEs).

During application development, programmers write their code in a sequential fashion with no references to any COMPSs-specific API or the underlying infrastructure. At execution time, calls to CE methods are transparently replaced by asynchronous tasks whose execution is to be orchestrated by the runtime system. To define CE methods, developers create an interface, called Core Element Interface (CEI), where they declare those methods along with some meta-data in the form of directives. To pick a method as a CE, the programmer annotates the method declaration on the CEI with *@Method* indicating the class containing the method implementation. The code snippet in Fig. 1 reproduces a simple example of a COMPSs application. Figure 1(a) shows the sequential code of the application which runs N simulations and selects the best one. The CEI presented in Fig. 1(b) selects two methods to become a CE: *runSimulation* and *getBest*.

For the runtime system to determine the dependencies between CE invocations, developers specify how each CE operates on the accessed data (its parameters) by adding (*@Parameter*) directive indicating the parameter type – which can be automatically inferred at execution time – and directionality (in, out, inout). The *runSimulation* CE is a void method with no parameters that updates the content of the callee instance with the result of the simulation considering its initial value; therefore, the only datum on which the method operates is the callee. COMPSs considers the object from which the method is invoked as an implicit *INOUT* access. Conversely, *getBest* is a static method which compares two *Sim* objects and returns the one whose simulation obtained a better performance. Consequently, the developer declares the CE on the CEI with two *IN* parameters.

```
public Sim checkSimulation(int N) {
    Sim best = null;
    for (int i=0; i < N; i++) {
        Sim s = new Sim();
        s.prepareSimultation(...);
        s.runSimulation();
        best = Sim.getBest(best, s);
    }
    return best;
}
```

```
public interface SampleCEI {
    @Method(declaringClass="Sim")
    void runSimulation();

    @Method(declaringClass = "Sim")
    Sim getBest(
        @Parameter(direction = IN)
        Sim s1,
        @Parameter(direction = IN)
        Sim s2
    );
}
```

(a) Application main code   (b) Core Element Interface

Fig. 1. Sample application code written in Java

Often, several algorithms exist to achieve the same functionality with different requirements and complexity; for instance, the MergeSort and RadixSort algorithms sort a set. COMPSs supports these cases, but all the versions of the same CE need to be homonymous – *sort* – and share parameters and access patterns. To declare multiple versions for a CE, the programmer adds as many *@Method* directives as different versions and in each one indicates the implementing class as shown in the code snippet in Fig. 2. The runtime creates a new task for the CE regardless the called method and selects the implementation to run according to the running host and input data characteristics.

```
@Method (declaringClass = "containing.package.RadixSort")
@Method (declaringClass = "containing.package.MergeSort")
void sort (
    @Parameter(direction = INOUT)
    int[] values
);
```

Fig. 2. Sort method CE declaration with two possible versions implemented in Radix-Sort and MergeSort classes respectively.

3.1 Extension for GPU Support

Likewise, different versions can target different computing architectures; programmers can implement the same CE to run on a CPU core or GPU threads. To indicate OpenCL implementations of a method, programmers annotate the method declaration with *@OpenCL*. In this case, instead of pointing out the class implementing the method, programmers indicate the file (attached as an application resource) containing the OpenCL code of the kernel.

As with native language implementations, the runtime determines which version is to run and makes all the management to enable its execution. In the case of an OpenCL implementation, this includes the copy of input values into the GPU memory, the kernel invocation, the monitoring of the execution, and the collection of output values.

Unlike CPU-oriented languages, where programmers describe the computation to run on a single core, the sequential code in OpenCL and CUDA runs concurrently on several execution threads known as work-items. For each work-item to operate on a specific subset of the input/output data, they are uniquely identified according to the coordinates within a 3D grid. Developers are to specify the number of work-items through the dimensions of this grid (*global_work_size*) and the offset (*global_work_offset*) used to calculate the global ID of the work-item regarding the original coordinates. Besides, the library partitions the grid in several work-groups whose dimensions are defined as another 3D grid (*local_work_size*). Each work-item within a work-group has a local ID, and programmers can synchronize the progress of the work-items within a work-group. For the COMPSs runtime system to invoke the kernel automatically, developers indicate these three values on the CEI by adding three attributes to the @*OpenCL* directive. However, the actual value of these variables – specially *global_work_size* – may depend on the input values or its size. For that purpose, COMPSs allows simple algebraic expressions using the values and dimensions of the parameters as variables. To refer to a parameter, the developer uses the keyword *par* along with its index – starting by 0 –; for instance, *par0* would refer to the first parameter of the invocation; *par1*, to the second one; and so on so forth. If the parameter is a number, COMPSs can use its value; if the parameter is an array, it can use the value of one of its positions or its length. For multi-dimensional arrays, developers can refer to the length of any of its dimensions using the dimensional identifiers x, y and z respectively to indicate the first, second and third dimension. The default value for *global_work_offset* is (0, 0,... 0) and *NULL* for the *local_work_size*, in which case the OpenCL implementation determines how to break the global work-items into appropriate workgroup instances.

Another important characteristic of OpenCL is that kernels do not return values. To work around the constraint that OpenCL kernels must be void functions, COMPSs assumes the return value, if any, to be the last parameter of the kernel; therefore, the kernel implementations of a CE with return value have an additional parameter compared to the native language implementations. As opposed to native methods, where the return value is created within the method code, the memory space for the return value of OpenCL implementations needs to be allocated prior the invocation of the kernel. The runtime is to manage the allocation of result values automatically when it decides to run an OpenCL kernel. Again, the amount of memory to allocate depends on each CE and, likely, on the input values; therefore, programmers need to specify the number of elements within each dimension of the return value with an algebraic expression. The actual number of bytes is inferred according to the return type of the declaration.

Figure 3 depicts an example of a COMPSs application performing a matrix multiplication. The actual computation of the operation is encapsulated within a CE, *multiply*, implemented either as a regular method and an OpenCL kernel. Note that, while the Java version has two parameters (A and B) and returns value, the OpenCL implementation is a void method with three parameters (a, b and c).

4   Runtime Support Implementation

To parallelize and distribute the computation, COMPSs-Mobile replaces the CE invocations by asynchronous tasks whose execution is orchestrated by the runtime toolkit. Also, accesses to data generated on remote nodes need to fetch the value. To instrument the application, COMPSs-Mobile extends the Android application building process and adds an extra step: Parallelization. For code instrumentation, the framework leverages on Javassist [1] to replace the original Java bytecode with an instrumented version. Thus, when the user runs the application, the instrumented calls are executed and invoke the runtime toolkit.

```
package es.bsc.compss.matmul;

public class Matmul {
    public static void main(String[] args) {
        int[][] A;
        int[][] B;
        int[][] C;
        ...
        C = multiply(A, B);
        ...
    }

    public static int[][] multiply(int[][] A, int[][] B) {
        // Matrix multiplication code
        // C = AB
        ...
        return C;
    }
}
```

(a) Application Java code

```
__kernel void multiply (
    __global const int *a,
    __global const int *b,
    __global int *c)
{
    //Matrix multiplication code
    // C = AB
    ...
}
```

(b) OpenCL code in matmul.cl

```
public interface CEI {
    @OpenCL(kernel="matmul.cl", globalWorkSize="par0.x,par1.y", resultSize="par0.x,par1.y")
    @Method(declaringClass="es.bsc.compss.matmul.Matmul")
    int[][] multiply (
        @Parameter(direction = IN)
        int[][] A,
        @Parameter(direction = IN)
        int[][] B
    );
}
```

(c) Core Element Interface

Fig. 3. Example of a matrix multiplication with two implementations: one in OpenCL and one as a regular method.

4.1 COMPSs-Mobile Runtime Architecture

The main purpose of the toolkit is to orchestrate the execution of CE invocations (tasks) to fully exploit the available computing resources (local devices or remote nodes) while guaranteeing sequential consistency. Since several applications can share computing resources and data values, the runtime library consists of two parts.

On the one hand, the application-private part of the runtime controls those aspects of the execution related to the application. In other words, it detects CE invocations and creates new asynchronous tasks, monitors the private values they access (objects) and hosts the execution of the tasks. On the other hand, the orchestrator is in charge of handling all those aspects of the execution that might affect several applications; namely, accesses to shared data (files) and managing the usage of the available computing devices. While each COMPSs-Mobile application instantiates the application-private part of the runtime, there is only one single instance of the former deployed in an Android device running as an Android service on a separate process.

The *Analyzer* processes tasks upon their detection; private and public data registers identify the accessed data values and assign a unique ID to the corresponding version. These IDs allow the runtime to detect and enforce data dependencies among tasks. After that, tasks move forward to the *Executor* for their execution. To decide which resources should host the execution, the runtime relies on the concept of *Computing Platform*: a logical grouping of computing resources capable of running tasks. The decision is made by the *Decision Engine (DE)*, which is unaware of the actual computing devices supporting the platform nor the details of their interaction. The *DE* polls each of the available platforms – configured by the user beforehand – for a forecast of the expected end time, energy consumption and economic cost of the execution. According to a configurable heuristic, the *DE* picks the best platform to run the task and requests its execution. The selected platform is responsible for monitoring the data dependencies of the task and scheduling both the execution of the task on its resources and the obtaining and preparation of any necessary value. To achieve these duties, each platform can turn to different strategies: centralizing the management on the orchestrator process, centralizing it in a remote resource or distributed across multiple resources. Regardless the approach followed to solve the scheduling, all platforms delegate the execution of tasks on a *Platform Backend* hosted off the orchestrator. For platforms handling local resources, the backend runs on the application-private part of the runtime since both the application code and any possible object are private elements of the application. Otherwise, the backend is a service running on a remote node.

In order to support data value delivery, each process hosts a common data repository, the *Data Manager (DM)*. The *DM* is asynchronous; either *Computing Platforms*, *Platform Backends* or the instrumented code of the application subscribe to the existence or value of datums (using the unique ID assigned by the *Analyzer*), and the *DM* notifies all the subscribers upon the publication of the value. The local instance of the *DM* is responsible for handling the fetching of requested values if they are located in a different process.

Figure 4 contains a diagram of the runtime architecture.

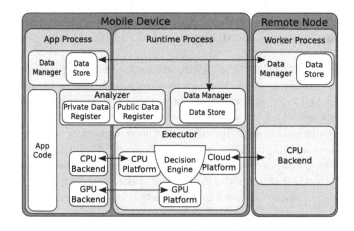

Fig. 4. Runtime system architecture

4.2   OpenCL Platform

In order to enable the execution of tasks on GPU devices, we implemented a *Computing Platform* with its corresponding OpenCL *Platform Backend* running on the application process. Each such platform maps to one computing device of an OpenCL platform, whose names are provided by the users when setting up the available platforms.

Upon the submission of a new task execution, the platform subscribes to the existence of all the input values and continues to monitor the status update from the *DM* until the task is dependency-free. To properly manage the lifecycle of several concurrent tasks, the platform has an event-based *Task Scheduler* that leverages on the out-of-order mode of OpenCL. The out-of-order mode allows OpenCL users to enqueue commands with no specific order of execution; users explicitly enforce order constraints across commands using events that OpenCL returns upon the command submission. Once the last dependency is satisfied, the platform orders its backend to fetch all the input values in a remote location through the *DM* and run the kernel.

Once the *DM* in the application process has all the input values loaded on the host memory, the backend needs to copy the input values from the host memory to the memory of the GPU device before launching the kernel on the GPU. For that purpose, it creates a memory buffer for each parameter and enqueues buffer copies for every value read by the kernel. Immediately after that, it enqueues the kernel invocation depending on the ordered copies to enforce the completion of the copies before the kernel executes. For each parameter updated during the kernel execution, the backend enqueues a memory copy command depending on the kernel execution to retrieve the new value. For detecting the end of the kernel and collecting all the outputs, the backend subscribes a listener for the kernel execution event and one for each value-to-read. Once it finishes, the backend stores the results on the local *DM*.

To better exploit locality, the backend monitors the content of the device memory. By keeping track of the buffer containing each data value and the writing event, the backend can discover the existence of another buffer with the value. Using the existing buffer as a parameter of the kernel and enforcing its execution to wait upon the corresponding writing event, the scheduler avoids the overhead of creating and filling a new buffer. Hence, the backend notices the existence of those values computed on the device when the producing kernel invocation is enqueued and internally bypasses the existence notification of the *DM* to hand over the scheduling of the kernel to OpenCL.

We expect COMPSs-Mobile applications to have a high degree of parallelism and a sufficient number of coarse-grain tasks so that data transfers (from the remote nodes and to the GPU memory) can overlap with the execution of other tasks. When generating a forecast of completion time for tasks, the runtime considers the execution time and the wait for resources (memory allocation for result values happens during this waiting period, and the actual transfer time is negligible). Cost is only related to the number of bytes transferred from remote nodes. The energy model considers the consumption during the execution and the energy spent on transfers from remote nodes; transfers from and to the device memory are also negligible. The platform uses the statistical data from the profiling of previous executions to predict the forecasts.

5   Performance Evaluation

To validate our proposal, we ported three applications to Android following the COMPSs programming model: Digits Recognition (DR), Bézier Surface (BS) and Canny Edge Detection (CED). DR is a Convolutional Neural Network trained to recognize digits out of hand-written numbers. The algorithm applies eight processing steps to a set of images. We merge the processing of all the images on each step within a task; thus, the application becomes a sequence of tasks. BS is a mathematical spline that interpolates a surface given a set of control points. The application splits the output surface, and each task computes the result values within a chunk independently of each other. Finally, CED is an image-processing algorithm for edge detection where each frame goes through a four-stage process (Gaussian filter, Sobel filter, non-maximum suppression and hysteresis) each one encapsulated within a CE. We apply the algorithm to 30 frames of 354×626 pixels producing a workload composed of 30 parallel chains of four tasks. We selected these applications and implementations because of the diversity of patterns presented by their workloads as shown in Fig. 5.

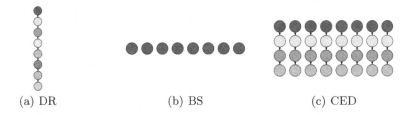

(a) DR   (b) BS   (c) CED

Fig. 5. Applications' dependency graphs

The experiments to evaluate the behavior of our prototype run on a OnePlus One smartphone equipped with a Qualcomm SnapDragon 801 processor (a Krait 400 quad-core CPU at 2.5 GHz and an Adreno 330 GPU). We appraise different configurations using two Computing Platforms operating on the local resources: the CPU Platform using the cores of the CPU (varying the number of available ones) and the OpenCL Platform leveraging on the Adreno device.

5.1   OpenCL Platform Performance

The first test aims to check the proper behavior of the OpenCL platform and evaluate the impact of the implemented optimizations. For that purpose, we executed the three applications considering six possible scenarios: CPU,

GPU, R1CPU, R4CPU, RGPU, RGPUO. The CPU and GPU scenarios execute an Android-native version of the application; while CPU runs the application sequentially on the CPU, GPU naively[1] offloads the computation to the GPU through OpenCL. On the remaining four scenarios, the developer codes the application following the COMPSs programming model and the final user sets up the runtime to force the runtime to execute on a specific computing platform. On R1CPU and R4CPU, the runtime uses only the CPU platform exploiting one and four cores respectively. On RGPU and RGPUO, the runtime offloads all the tasks to the GPU through the OpenCL platform. The former disables all the optimizations obtaining a behavior similar to the GPU scenario, while the latter enables all the optimizations (reusing memory buffers and overlapping transfers with other kernel executions).

For each scenario, we measured the execution time and its energy consumption. Within the execution time, we distinguish the amount time spent on the execution of tasks (*Tasks*) from the overhead surrounding the computation (*Overhead*). This experiment focuses on isolating the part of this overhead corresponding to transfers between main and devices memories (*Ov. Mem.*) to evaluate the benefits of the optimizations implemented on the GPU backend. Regarding the energy consumption, we only separate the energy used for computing the tasks (*Tasks*) from the energy consumed by the whole system including the screen (*System*).

Digits Recognition. Charts in Fig. 6 depict the results obtained from processing 512 images with the Digits Recognition application. It is plain to see that GPU allows a significant improvement both on time and energy regardless of using COMPSs. Comparing CPU to GPU scenarios, the execution time shrinks from 18,516 ms to 4,358 ms (23.53%) – 1,531 ms of which correspond to memory transfers –; and the energy consumption, from 36.48 J to 8.68 J (27.8%). R1CPU and R4CPU present a behavior similar to the CPU case since the application has no task-level parallelism; however, on both cases, the runtime incurs a negligible overhead (31 ms and 0.02 J) caused by the inter-process communication among the runtime components. Likewise, the overhead appears on both scenarios where the runtime uses the GPU. Besides this overhead, the application performs as on GPU when the platform optimizations are disabled. When enabled, the runtime reuses the memory values generated by one task as the input of the succeeding one; thus allows to reduce the overhead of data copies from and to the device memory from 1,531 ms to 5 ms. The optimizations implemented for the management of the device memory allow COMPSs-Mobile to speed up the execution of the application on GPUs even when they have no task level parallelism. Despite the improvement on the execution time, these optimizations have a low impact on the energy consumption (0.56 J) since the source of the most significant part of it is the actual computation of the kernels.

---

[1] OpenCL commands are synchronous, and all the input and output data is copied to and from the device memory on every kernel execution.

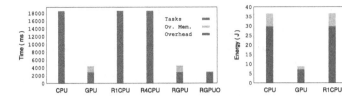

Fig. 6. Execution time (left) and energy consumption (right) obtained from the Digits Recognition runs

Bézier Surface. Interpolling a surface of 1024×1024 points using 256×256 blocks with the Bézier Surface application presents results similar to DR as shown in Fig. 7. Although GPU computes the tasks 2.99 times faster than the CPU (2,672 ms vs. 7,984 ms), the memory transfers overhead (337 ms) slows down the application. It only achieves a 2.65x lower execution time (3,009 ms) and a 50.45% reduction of the energy consumption (15.73 J vs. 7.8 J). As with DR, the runtime incurs a little overhead (39 ms and 0.02 J) when comparing CPU to RCPU and GPU to RGPU.

Unlike DR, tasks in BS have no dependencies; thus, the runtime can exploit the parallelism and use the four cores of the CPU at a time speeding up the execution of the kernels up to 2.72x (2,939 ms). The reduction of the CPU frequency to control the temperature of the processor and the thread oversubscribing with the runtime threads separates the obtained performance from the optimal. These measures increase the energy consumption of the tasks which grows from 15.74 J to 19.65 J. Since BS tasks have no dependencies, they never read values generated by other tasks; therefore, the runtime cannot reuse values already transferred for preceding tasks. However, the computation of one task can overlap with the transfers of output/input values of the preceding and succeeding ones. This optimization allows the runtime to reduce the time spent on memory transfers from 337 ms to 3 ms on the RGPUO scenario. On the RGPUO scenario, BS lasts 2,714 ms and consumes 7.68 J.

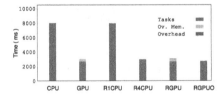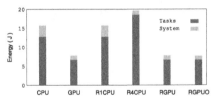

Fig. 7. Execution time (left) and energy consumption (right) obtained from the Bézier Surface runs

Canny Edge Detection. In this case, the GPU device processes the 30 frames in 420 ms, 11.95x faster than the CPU; and again, the data transfers worsen the application performance adding a 324 ms overhead. In overall, the application takes 5,020 ms to run in the CPU scenario and consumes 9.39 J; while for the GPU case, it needs 744 ms and 1.33 J respectively. The runtime adds an overhead of 34 ms and 0.02 J slightly noticeable when comparing CPU and GPU to R1CPU and RGPU, respectively.

In this case, the application presents task-level parallelism and dependencies among tasks; thus, the GPU can apply both optimizations. The GPU reuses the output of some tasks as the input of its successors; thus, the runtime reduces the number of transfers. Besides, the remaining transfers can overlap with the computation of other dependency-free tasks. Enabling these optimizations allows the runtime to reduce the 324 ms overhead caused by memory transfers to 1 ms. On the RGPUO scenario, the application lowers the execution time to 455 ms and its energy consumption to 1.22 J (Fig. 8).

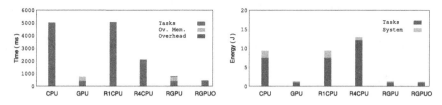

Fig. 8. Execution time (left) and energy consumption (right) obtained from the Canny Edge Detection runs

5.2 Load Balancing Policies

The second experiment studies the impact of extending the resource-assignment policies on the execution time and energy consumption of the application. For that purpose, we run the COMPSs-Mobile version of each application with different task granularity using every possible combination of resources. For the heterogeneous scenarios - i.e., using both computing platforms -, we compare the results of three different policies: Static, DynPerf and DynEn. Static is a predetermined load distribution that mimics what application developers could easily devise to minimize the execution time. The load arrangement employed on each execution depends on the application workflow, the number of tasks and the time they require to run on each device; further details on the division applied on each application are provided on the corresponding subsection. With the same purpose, the DynPerf policy automatically decides which computing platform executes the task according to the earliest end time forecasted by the platforms. Conversely, DynEn aims to find a balance between reducing the execution time and the additional energy that it incurs. For that purpose, the policy takes into account not only the end time of the task but also the energy spent on its processing; the policy would pick a later end time if for each sacrificed ms the application can save 5 mJ.

Digits Recognition. DR is an application where a set of images go through a 7-stage process. Each stage is encapsulated in a task; thus, their granularity depends on the number of images to process. In this experiment, we use three different input sets composed of 128, 256 and 512 images. Since DR has no task-level parallelism, we dismiss all those configurations using more than one core of the CPU. All the CEs that compose the application take less time and energy to run on the GPU device than on the CPU; therefore, the Static policy for this application consists of submitting all the tasks to the GPU.

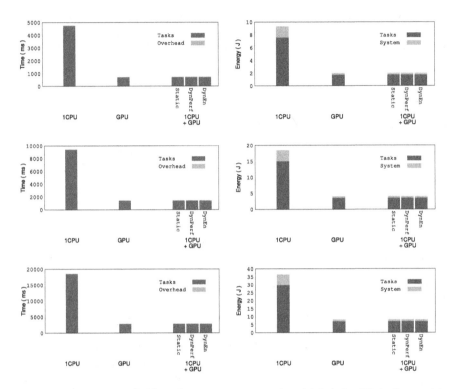

Fig. 9. Execution time (left) and energy consumption (right) for Digit Recognition runs using 128, 256 and 512 images (from top to bottom)

Charts in Fig. 9 show the execution time (left) and energy consumption (right) when processing 128, 256 and 512 images (from top to bottom). Despite the difference in the magnitude of the values, the application behaves alike regardless the input size. As we double it, almost does so the execution time and the energy consumption whether if the application runs on the CPU (4,762 ms and 9.333 J for 128 images; 9,410 ms and 18.490 J for 256 images, and 18,547 ms and 36.493 J for 512 images) or on the GPU (731 ms and 2.015 J, 1,446 ms and 4.065 J, and 2,862 ms and 8.127 J respectively for processing 128, 256 and 512 images). Given that the GPU is faster and less energy-consuming than the CPU and that the application presents no task-level parallelism, submitting all the executions to the GPU is the optimal solution either from the performance or the energy point of view. Hence, both dynamic policies schedule all the executions to the GPU as expected. Despite all the employed configurations use the COMPSs-Mobile runtime which incurs an overhead, it is important to notice that dynamically deciding where to run a task adds no significant overhead compared to those cases where the runtime handles a homogeneous system or the decision is statically set beforehand.

Bézier Surface. BS is an application whose task-granularity and parallelism depends on the partitioning of the output. For this experiment, the application computes a fixed-size surface of 1024×1024 points varying the size of the chunk computed by a task from a 1024×1024 block – 1 task –, through 256×256 – 4 tasks – and 512×512 blocks – 16 tasks –, right up to blocks of 128×128 points – 64 tasks. Figure 10 depicts the execution time (left) and energy consumption (right) of running the application with the four granularities (top to bottom). Considering the number of tasks, the number of CPU cores and the ratio between the time to run a task on a GPU and a CPU – the more CPU cores are used, the higher the speedup is; 3x, 3.4x, 3.9 and 4.3x respectively for using 1, 2, 3 and 4 cores –, it is easy for the application developer to find the number of tasks to assign to each computing device to minimize the application execution time. For instance, in the case of a 128×128 block size output using a single core of the CPU, the speedup is 3.03x; thus, the optimal load balancing from a temporal point of view is to run 48 tasks on the GPU while the CPU core processes 16. For the Static policy in this experiment, we assume the application developer to be fully aware of the number of CPU cores to use, the granularity of the task and the corresponding speedup and code the application to balance the load using this knowledge.

From a temporal point of view, the Static policy balances the load in such a way that the execution time is minimal. As with DR, DynPerf behaves like Static in all executions (as expected) achieving the optimal performance with no significant overhead due to taking the decision dynamically. Regarding energy consumption, running all the tasks on the GPU is the optimal solution in all four cases (7.825 J, 7.741 J, 7.684 J and 7.538 J respectively for 1024, 512, 256 and 128). The cause of this reduction in the energy is the better performance of the GPU when processing smaller chunks – 2,692 ms to compute the surface in one single block vs. 2,621 ms to compute 64 blocks, 40.96 ms each –; the CPU behaves alike – 8,035 ms vs. 7,934 ms.

For those cases with a coarse granularity, the low number of tasks and the big difference in the energy consumption of the computing devices lead the DynEn policy to schedule the execution of all tasks on the GPU. On finer-grained scenarios, the heterogeneous systems and the GPU present a different behavior. In the case of 256×256, 1 task is computed on the CPU; thus allows the application to reduce 167 ms despite an increase of 381 mJ. Using more CPU cores increases both the execution time and the energy consumption of each task run on the CPU (by 72 ms and 116 mJ); DynEn dismisses executing more tasks on

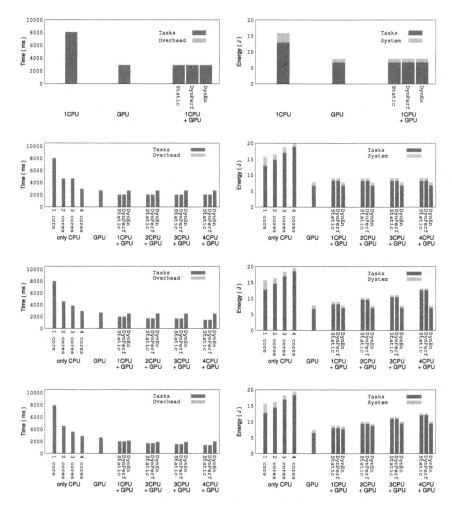

Fig. 10. Execution time (left) and energy consumption (right) for Bézier Surface runs using block sizes of 1024×1024, 512×512, 256×256 and 128×128 (from top to bottom)

the CPU to avoid their growth. Using smaller blocks reduces the difference in time and energy; thus gives more freedom to the *DE* and allows more diverse schedulings as shown by the four heterogeneous cases using 128×128 blocks. With the GPU and one core of the CPU at its disposal, DynEn assigns 12 tasks to the CPU (requiring 2,130 ms and 7.70 mJ to run), while DynPerf assigns 16 tasks to the CPU (1,983 ms and 8.09 mJ). For the heterogeneous case using 2 CPU cores, DynEn assigns 18 tasks to the CPU vs. the 23 assigned by DynPerf. Again the growth on the execution time and energy consumption due to the concurrent exploitation of multiple cores cuts the number of tasks assigned to the CPU; DynEn and DynPerf assign 18 and 27 tasks to the CPU with three available CPU cores. For the same reason, when using all the computing devices of the phone, DynEn reduces the number of tasks assigned to the CPU to 16 while DynPerf assigns 30 to it. Thus, DynEn shrinks the energy consumption from 12.09 J to 9.5 J while DynPerf shortens the execution time 570 ms.

Canny Edge Detection. Instead of using different input sizes, for the third application, we always process a 30-frames video. However, we consider two different workload divisions that the developer could easily implement: Task Partitioning, where the GPU runs the first two tasks of each frame and the CPU the last two; and Data Partitioning, where one device processes the whole frame. Figure 11 shows the execution time (left) and energy consumption (right) obtained when running the application and compares them to the ones obtained with DynPerf and DynEn.

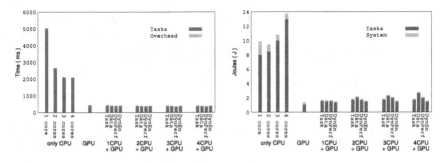

Fig. 11. Execution time (left) and energy consumption (right) obtained from the Canny Edge Detection runs

Task Partitioning achieves lower energy consumptions while Data Partitioning offers better performance. The behavior of Task Partitioning does not change when it has more than one core at its disposal. The time to process the first two tasks of a frame on the GPU – 12 ms – is higher than what it takes to execute the last two – 9 ms and 5 ms respectively, but the executions corresponding to different iterations can overlap. With one CPU core available, the application takes 451 ms and consumes 1.71 J, vs. 412 ms and 1.87 J when using two or more CPU cores.

Data Partitioning assigns the whole processing of a frame to the same computing unit. The problem of this approach is that the number of frames assigned to the CPU does not progress according to the number of available cores – 2, 4, 4, 4 frames, respectively for 1 to 4 cores – due to the performance loss when using multiple cores simultaneously. Using one core, the application takes 427 ms and 1.67 J. When using two or more cores, the execution time shows no improvement – 399 ms with 2 and 4 cores available; indeed, using 3 cores worsens the execution time to 410 ms –; however, the energy consumption reflects the usage of more cores and increases according to the number of used cores – 2.19 J, 2.40 J and 2.79 J.

DynPerf avoids this effect and schedules the executions similarly to Task Partitioning but adjusting the load imbalances. When only one core is available, DynPerf assigns 4 non-maximum suppressions and 1 hysteresis to the GPU to balance the 2 ms difference. Thus, the execution time is reduced to 411 ms consuming only 1.65 J. Conversely, when using more cores, the runtime fills their idle time with Gaussian filter tasks. With two cores at its disposal, the DE decides to run two of them on the CPU reducing the execution time to 395 ms with an energy consumption of 1.84 J; with more cores available, it assigns 6 Gaussian filter tasks to the CPU achieving a 379 ms execution time (79 FPS) with an energy consumption of 2.12 J.

DynEn tends to schedule more tasks on the GPU to avoid the higher consumption of the CPU. Hence, with one available core, the DE submits only 14 non-maximum suppressions and 27 hystereses to the GPU; thus obtaining an execution time of 422 ms and an energy consumption of 1.51 J – the GPU alone achieves 455 ms and 1.22 J. From two cores on, the number of non-maximum suppressions assigned to the CPU raises to 24 to shrink the execution time to 409 ms (73 FPS) with an energy consumption of 1.61 J.

6 Conclusions and Future Work

COMPSs-Mobile is a framework to develop applications targetted to Mobile-Cloud environments. Its programming model, COMPSs, allows developers to parallelize their applications automatically with no need of modifying the code. Through an annotated interface, programmers select the methods whose invocations are replaced by asynchronous tasks. A runtime toolkit executed along with the application detects the data dependencies among these tasks and orchestrates their execution on the underlying infrastructure to exploit the application parallelism while guaranteeing the sequential consistency of the application.

This article introduces an extension to the COMPSs programming model to allow the implementation of these tasks as OpenCL kernels to run on GPUs, FPGAs or any other accelerator. Thus, applications following the model could make the most of the heterogeneous systems composing the infrastructure and use all the available computing devices collaboratively. Beyond inherent parallelism exploitation, the proposed extension helps COMPSs to ease the development of applications by hiding away from the developer all the details related to the handling of the OpenCL platform – managing the content of the device memory and kernels submission – and the load balancing.

Section 4.2 describes the required developments on the runtime toolkit to support the execution of OpenCL kernels on the mobile device as well as the optimizations implemented to maximize the performance of the application automatically. The results presented in Sect. 5 for the three applications using only one core of the CPU or offloading all the computation to the GPU illustrate the potential benefits of using the accelerators embedded on the device instead of a CPU core to compute a task either from the temporal or energetic point of view. For the CED application, the GPU is ~12x faster and consumes an 87% less energy; for BS, GPU is ~3x faster and 54% less energy consuming.

Accelerators may also be part of the remote nodes to which COMPSs-Mobile offloads computation. Although the proposed extension of the programming model already allows developers to write applications that use them, the described runtime system does not support OpenCL code offloading yet. We believe that a natural step forward in our research is to enable this feature to improve the performance of those application taking benefit of computation offloading.

Delegating the load balancing to the runtime system improves the portability of applications. The execution time of a task and its energy consumption depends on the characteristics of the hardware running the task; therefore, the task scheduling is different for each computing infrastructure. The optimal scheduling may not be evident nor easy to implement; dynamic policies can achieve the desired behavior with no strain for the developer, as shown in the CED test case. Besides, they allow the application user to decide whether if the application should aim for the best performance, the lowest energy consumption or finding a balanced solution with no additional cost for the developer.

Another aspect that we would like to work on is dynamic, adaptative computing platform assignment. Currently, upon the task detection, the runtime picks a platform considering the end time, energy consumption and cost forecasts of running the task on each platform based on the profiling data from previous executions. Hence, the runtime makes the decision considering only task-scoped information instead of considering the impact on the execution as a whole. This makes some scheduling decisions hard to explain. For instance, if the runtime has to pick between option A, where the task ends at ms 50 consuming 0.1 J, and B, finishing at ms 250 with 0.07 J consumed; it would choose the former. However, if we contextualize this decision on an execution that finishes at ms 300 regardless the chosen option, the latter would be better. Besides, the forecasts are based on the profiling data from previous executions. If the characteristics of the workload do not meet those of previous workloads, the runtime makes decisions that harm the application performance. We envisage to enhance the platform selection by enabling a mechanism to correct the current scheduling by re-assigning the execution of pending tasks to another platform.

Acknowledgments. This work is partially supported by the Joint-Laboratory on Extreme Scale Computing (JLESC), by the European Union through the Horizon 2020 research and innovation programme under contract 687584 (TANGO Project), by the Spanish Goverment (TIN2015-65316-P, BES-2013-067167, EEBB-2016-11272, SEV-2011-00067) and the Generalitat de Catalunya (2014-SGR-1051).

References

1. Java programming assistant (javassist). http://www.javassist.org
2. Android Developers: Renderscript. https://developer.android.com/guide/topics/renderscript/compute.html
3. Augonnet, C., Thibault, S., Namyst, R., Wacrenier, P.A.: StarPU: a unified platform for task scheduling on heterogeneous multicore architectures. Concurrency Comput. Pract. Experience **23**(2), 187–198 (2011). https://doi.org/10.1002/cpe.1631/full/5Cndoi.wiley.com/10.1002/cpe.1631

4. Bosilca, G., Bouteiller, A., Danalis, A., Herault, T., Lemarinier, P., Dongarra, J.: DAGuE: a generic distributed DAG engine for high performance computing. Parallel Comput. **38**(1–2), 37–51 (2012)

5. Chun, B.G., et al.: CloneCloud: elastic execution between mobile device and cloud. In: Proceedings of the Sixth Conference on Computer Systems (EuroSys 2011), pp. 301–314. ACM, New York (2011). https://doi.org/10.1145/1966445.1966473

6. Cuervo, E., et al.: MAUI: making smartphones last longer with code offload. In: Proceedings of the 8th International Conference on Mobile Systems, Applications, and Services (MobiSys 2010), pp. 49–62. ACM, New York (2010). https://doi.org/10.1145/1814433.1814441

7. Duran, A., Ayguadé, E., Badia, R.M., Labarta, J., Martinell, L., Martorell, X., Planas, J.: OmpSs: a proposal for programming heterogeneous multi-core architectures. Parallel Process. Lett. **21**(2), 173–193 (2011)

8. Kemp, R., Palmer, N., Kielmann, T., Bal, H.: Cuckoo: a computation offloading framework for smartphones. In: Gris, M., Yang, G. (eds.) MobiCASE 2010. LNICSSITE, vol. 76, pp. 59–79. Springer, Heidelberg (2012). https://doi.org/10.1007/978-3-642-29336-8_4

9. Khronos OpenCL Working Group, et al.: The OpenCL specification. Version 1(29), 8 (2008)

10. Kosta, S., et al.: Unleashing the power of mobile cloud computing using ThinkAir. CoRR abs/1105.3 (2011). http://arxiv.org/abs/1105.3232

11. Lordan, F., Badia, R.M.: COMPSs-mobile: parallel programming for mobile cloud computing. J. Grid Comput. **15**(3), 357–378 (2017). https://doi.org/10.1007/s10723-017-9409-z

12. Lordan, F., et al.: Servicess: an interoperable programming framework for the cloud. J. Grid Comput. **12**(1), 67–91 (2014). https://doi.org/10.1007/s10723-013-9272-5

13. Montella, R., Ferraro, C., Kosta, S., Pelliccia, V., Giunta, G.: Enabling android-based devices to high-end GPGPUs. In: Carretero, J., Garcia-Blas, J., Ko, R.K.L., Mueller, P., Nakano, K. (eds.) ICA3PP 2016. LNCS, vol. 10048, pp. 118–125. Springer, Cham (2016). https://doi.org/10.1007/978-3-319-49583-5_9

14. Nvidia: Compute unified device architecture programming guide (2007)

15. Ratering, R., Hoppe, H.C.: Accelerating openCL applications by utilizing a virtual OpenCL device as interface to compute clouds (2011). https://www.google.ch/patents/US20110161495

16. Rellermeyer, J.S., Riva, O., Alonso, G.: AlfredO: an architecture for flexible interaction with electronic devices. In: Issarny, V., Schantz, R. (eds.) Middleware 2008. LNCS, vol. 5346, pp. 22–41. Springer, Heidelberg (2008). https://doi.org/10.1007/978-3-540-89856-6_2

17. Silla, F., et al.: Remote GPU virtualization: is it useful? In: 2016 2nd IEEE International Workshop on High-Performance Interconnection Networks in the Exascale and Big-Data Era (HiPINEB), pp. 41–48. IEEE (2016)

Concurrent Parallel Processing on Graphics and Multicore Processors with OpenACC and OpenMP

Christopher P. Stone[1]([✉]), Roger L. Davis[2], and Daryl Y. Lee[2]

[1] Computational Science and Engineering, LLC, Athens, GA 30605, USA
chris.stone@computational-science.com
[2] Department of Mechanical and Aerospace Engineering, University of California Davis,
Davis, CA 95616, USA
{davisrl,dywlee}@ucdavis.edu

Abstract. Hierarchical parallel computing is rapidly becoming ubiquitous in high performance computing (HPC) systems. Programming models used commonly in turbomachinery and other engineering simulation codes have traditionally relied upon distributed memory parallelism with MPI and have ignored thread and data parallelism. This paper presents methods for programming multi-block codes for concurrent computational on host multicore CPUs and many-core accelerators such as graphics processing units. Portable and standardized methods are language directives that are used to expose data and thread parallelism within the hybrid shared and distributed-memory simulation system. A single-source/multiple-object strategy is used to simplify code management and allow for heterogeneous computing. Automated load balancing is implemented to determine what portions of the domain are computed by the multi-core CPUs and GPUs. Preliminary results indicate that a moderate overall speed-up is possible by taking advantage of all processors and accelerators on a given HPC node.

Keywords: High-performance computing · Heterogeneous · Accelerators

1 Introduction

High performance computing (HPC) is undergoing a significant paradigm shift as the parallelism of computing systems increases. Most HPC systems relevant to computational fluid dynamics (CFD), and other computational science and engineering disciplines, consist of clusters of networked servers. The parallelism within these HPC systems is hierarchical and multifaceted: multiple servers with distributed memory interconnected via a network fabric; one or more CPUs per server sharing the main server memory; multiple cores per CPU sharing one or more levels of cache memory; and multiple single-instruction, multiple-data (SIMD) lanes within each CPU core (i.e., vector processing). Some systems also incorporate many-core accelerator devices such as graphics processing units (GPUs) that significantly increase the system parallelism and add a second layer of heterogeneous, hierarchical parallelism.

Clusters of servers with multiple CPUs have been a common HPC system design for nearly 20 years. Parallel CFD applications commonly use a distributed memory programming model supported by the message passing interface (MPI) with a flat

© Springer International Publishing AG, part of Springer Nature 2018
S. Chandrasekaran and G. Juckeland (Eds.): WACCPD 2017, LNCS 10732, pp. 103–122, 2018.
https://doi.org/10.1007/978-3-319-74896-2_6

parallel topology. This design is well suited for a cluster environment with little hierarchical parallelism. However, the level of parallelism within each server has increased significantly in recent years. For example, the number of cores per CPU has increased significantly over the past decade. Data parallelism, i.e., vector parallelism, within HPC CPU cores has increased fourfold in five years from SSE to AVX-512. Many-core accelerator devices, such as graphical processing units (GPUs), have hundreds or thousands of lightweight cores and have become common in HPC systems. The increased parallelism at all levels is intended to increase the total computational capability of the devices without increasing the total power consumption. That is, increasing parallelism has replaced increasing clock speeds (i.e., frequency) in subsequent hardware generations in the post-Moore and post-Dennard scaling [1] era.

Harnessing the rapidly increasing and heterogeneous parallelism on these systems usually requires significant refactoring for a wide range of CFD applications that were optimized for many years for single-threaded CPU environments using a flat MPI topology. Extending the existing bulk synchronous and flat MPI paradigm to systems with many cores and/or heterogeneous accelerators becomes ever more inefficient due to the increasing communication overheads. For example, parallel domain partitions need to shrink to fit within the smaller CPU cores increasing the communication-to-computational overhead. Incorporating a multi-threaded model across the shared-memory cores within the larger MPI environment is a common approach to reducing this overhead. This hybrid approach, often implemented with OpenMP threads and MPI processes, is a promising strategy to efficiently use the hierarchical parallelism in modern multi-core-based HPC systems.

Data parallelism, or vector parallelism, uses a SIMD parallel processing paradigm to apply the same instruction (e.g., add, multiply) to multiple data elements at once. This is most commonly applied to innermost do- or for-loops with simple data arrays and can theoretically accelerate the throughput by approximately eight times[1] over non-vectorized loops using double-precision arithmetic on the latest HPC platforms (e.g., Intel Xeon CPUs or Xeon Phi accelerators with AVX-512 capabilities). Efficient use of data parallelism requires proper nested loop structures and array memory layouts that are, at times, in conflict with optimizations targeting older HPC systems. For example, array-of-structure data layouts are often more efficient on older SSE-based CPUs (i.e., narrower SIMD systems) due to data locality cache efficiencies but a structure-of-arrays layout may perform faster on newer, wider SIMD systems due to more efficient use of the SIMD hardware tuned to process contiguous elements of an array.

GPUs contain hundreds of cores and are designed for high throughput through massive parallelism. They are efficient at SIMD operations and their effective vector width is several times wider than the latest HPC CPU core. As with multi-core CPUs with SIMD processing capabilities, algorithms must be adapted to efficiently fit into the massively parallel, multi-threaded environment of the GPUs. For NVIDIA-based GPUs, blocks of 10's or 100's of threads are mapped to each multiprocessor. The threads within these thread-blocks execute in a *single-instruction, multiple-thread* (SIMT) paradigm,

---

[1] This assumes that all operations can be computed within a vector logic unit capable of processing eight values simultaneously compared to a scalar logic unit.

similar to the SIMD paradigm of vector processors. Large vector operations can be efficiently implemented by mapping thousands of these thread-blocks to the hundreds of cores concurrently. In addition to supporting basic parallel vector operations out of the GPU main memory, thread-blocks have access to a shared and addressable cache as well as efficient synchronization mechanisms. These two features facilitate complex iterative and hierarchal algorithms within thread blocks that can significantly increase the computational throughput. Many of the parallel processing features of GPUs are becoming more common on CPUs (e.g., wider vectorization). Algorithms redesigned for these novel GPU architectures frequently provide improved CPU performance when reapplied by exposing greater parallelism. Programming GPU parallelism traditionally required expertise in C/C++ programming and posed a challenge for legacy CFD applications written in Fortran. The OpenACC standard [2] directly supports Fortran and can produce similar performance as native GPU programming [3] (e.g., CUDA). OpenACC provides a syntax similar to OpenMP [4] which has been used in the CFD environment for more than a decade and has been used successfully to offload CFD applications to many-core accelerators in previous studies (e.g., [5, 6]).

Historically, parallel simulation codes have largely relied upon distributed-memory parallelism via the message passing interface (MPI) regardless of the underlying system topology. That is, while most HPC systems are large collections of shared-memory, multicore nodes, many application codes do not utilize the available multilevel parallelism. The most common approach for mixing distributed- and shared-memory parallelism is to use OpenMP threading across shared-memory cores and one or more distributed-memory processes across each cluster node.

A similar multilevel parallel paradigm can be applied when nodes also have attached HPC accelerator devices such as GPUs. In this context, the computational workload must be partitioned between the host CPU cores and the accelerator to maximize the net computational throughput. Offloading to GPU accelerators is complicated by the fact that their memory is, in general, distinct and separate from the host CPU cores. In this case, data transfer overhead must be taken into account when partitioning the workload between the CPU and GPU compute devices.

This paper presents the computational performance improvements and refactoring technics of a multiblock, structured-grid, multidisciplinary fluid dynamic and conjugate heat transfer solver refactored to run efficiently on heterogeneous CPU/GPU systems. The refactoring techniques using OpenMP and OpenACC presented here will be useful for other CFD developers and practitioners as HPC systems continue to increase the required application parallelism and device heterogeneity.

2   MBFLO3 Application

This study examines the computational performance of MBFLO3, a multidisciplinary computational fluid dynamics and thermal analysis application used primarily to model the complicated turbulent flow and heat transfer occurring through turbomachinery devices such as compressors and turbines.

2.1 Mathematical Formulation

MBFLO3 solves the unsteady, Favre- and Reynolds-averaged mass, momentum, and energy conservation equations for an ideal, compressible gas in the right-handed, Cartesian coordinate system using relative-frame primary variables that can be written as:

$$\frac{\partial \rho}{\partial t} + \frac{\partial (\rho u_i)}{\partial x_i} = 0 \tag{1}$$

$$\frac{\partial (\rho u_i)}{\partial t} + \frac{\partial (\rho u_j u_i)}{\partial x_j} + \frac{\partial p}{\partial x_i} = \frac{\partial \tau_{ji}}{\partial x_j} - \overline{Sm_i} \tag{2}$$

$$\frac{\partial E}{\partial t} + \frac{\partial (\rho u_j I)}{\partial x_j} = \frac{\partial}{\partial x_j} \left[u_i \tau_{ij} + \left(\frac{\mu}{Pr} + \frac{\mu_t}{Pr_t} \right) \frac{\partial h}{\partial x_j} \right] \tag{3}$$

where ρ, u_i, p, E, I, h, τ_{ij}, and μ are the density, velocity vector, pressure, energy, rothalpy, enthalpy, stress tensor, and viscosity, respectively. The turbulent viscosity, μ_t, is determined by the RANS model assuming a constant Prandtl (Pr) number. The body-force vector, Sm_i, in the momentum equation, Eq. (2), represents all body forces per unit volume such as those due to rotation (Coriolis and centripetal):

$$\overline{Sm_i} = 2\rho \left(\bar{\Omega} \times \overline{V} \right) + \rho \bar{\Omega} \times \left(\bar{\Omega} \times \bar{R} \right) \tag{4}$$

where Ω, V, and R are the rotation, total velocity, and radius vectors. Additional equations as developed by Wilcox [7] for the transport of turbulent kinetic energy and turbulence dissipation rate in regions of the flow where the computational grid or global time-step size cannot resolve the turbulent eddies can be written as:

$$\frac{\partial (\rho k)}{\partial t} + \frac{\partial (\rho u_j k)}{\partial x_j} =$$
$$\left(\tau_{ij} - \frac{2}{3} \rho k \delta_{ij} \right) \frac{\partial u_i}{\partial x_j} - \beta^* \rho k \omega + \frac{\partial}{\partial x_j} \left[\left(\mu + \sigma^* \frac{\rho k}{\omega} \right) \frac{\partial k}{\partial x_j} \right] \tag{5}$$

$$\frac{\partial (\rho \omega)}{\partial t} + \frac{\partial (\rho u_j \omega)}{\partial x_j} = \alpha \frac{\omega}{k} \left(\tau_{ij} - \frac{2}{3} \rho k \delta_{ij} \right) \frac{\partial u_i}{\partial x_j} - \beta^* \rho \omega^2$$
$$+ \sigma_d \frac{\rho}{\omega} \frac{\partial k}{\partial x_j} \frac{\partial \omega}{\partial x_j} + \frac{\partial}{\partial x_j} \left[\left(\mu + \sigma \frac{\rho k}{\omega} \right) \frac{\partial \omega}{\partial x_j} \right] \tag{6}$$

where β, α, and σ are modeling parameters [7].

In regions of the flow where the larger-scale eddies can be resolved with the computational grid, techniques borrowed from large-eddy simulation are used to represent the viscous shear and turbulent viscosity. The large-eddy sub-grid model described by Smagorinsky [8] is modified according to the detached-eddy considerations described by Strelets [9] and Bush and Mani [10] in which the turbulent viscosity is determined with

$$\mu_t = \rho \, l_{le} \sqrt{k} \qquad (7)$$

where l_{le} is an eddy length scale proportional to the grid/time-step filter width, Δ, and is modeled as:

$$l_{le} = \min(\frac{\sqrt{k}}{\omega}, \beta^* C_{des} \Delta) \qquad (8)$$

In addition, the dissipation term, $\beta^* \rho k \omega$, of the turbulent kinetic energy transport equation in Eq. (5) is limited by the eddy length scale, l_{le}, according to:

$$\beta^* \rho k \omega \Rightarrow \beta^* \rho k \max\left(\omega, \frac{\sqrt{k}}{\beta^* C_{des} \Delta} \right) \qquad (9)$$

where C_{des} is a proportionality coefficient usually given a value of 0.65.

The physics governing the flow of heat through a solid body can be represented by a simple relationship. This transient heat conduction equation can be written as

$$\rho_s c_{p_s} \frac{\partial T_s}{\partial t} = k_s \left[\frac{\partial^2 T_s}{\partial x_i^2} \right] \qquad (10)$$

where T_s is the temperature of the solid, ρ_s is the solid density, Cp_s is the solid specific heat, and k_s is the solid thermal conductivity.

Equation (10) is a first-order ordinary differential equation in time that is similar in form to the fluid governing equations, Eqs. (1)–(3), (5) and (6). These equations can be integrated over the cells that make up the solid to ultimately give the change in temperature at the nodes of the solid.

2.2 Numerical Method

The flow field conservation equations given in Eqs. (1)–(3), (5), (6), and (10) are solved using a Lax-Wendroff control-volume, explicit time-marching scheme developed by Bozinoski and Davis [11] which is based on the work of Ni [12], Dannenhoffer [13], and Davis [14]. Unsteady flows are integrated using a dual time-stepping scheme [15]. These techniques are second-order accurate in both time and space. Multigrid convergence acceleration [12] is used for both steady Reynolds-averaged solutions and within the inner convergence loop of unsteady simulations using the dual time-stepping scheme. The dual time-stepping scheme permits larger time-step sizes than otherwise allowed by the explicit scheme and allows for convergence acceleration techniques common for steady flows to be exploited (e.g., local time-stepping and multigrid). The number of inner iterations used in the dual-timestep scheme can differ between the fluid and thermal solvers to account for differences in convergence rates.

MBFLO3 uses a multiblock, structured grid approach with point-matched blocks whenever possible. Overset grids are incorporated where flexibility in geometry creation and placement is required (e.g., for film-cooling holes or leakage slots). Each block face may have an arbitrary number of sub-faces allowing arbitrary block-to-block connectivity and any combination of physical boundary conditions. Block connectivity and boundary condition information is defined by a global connectivity file that is automatically produced for turbomachinery configurations by the grid generation preprocessor, STAGE3 [16].

The fluid and thermal blocks are coupled through heat transfer boundary conditions that conserve energy. That is, a unified heat flux on the fluid-solid interface is enforced as well as ensuring the temperature at this boundary is the same for both the fluid and solid components.

Fluid and solid (thermal) regions of the domain are separated into unique mesh blocks so that only one multidisciplinary solver is used within a given block. Blocks exchange shared data along adjoining faces using standard MPI-1 non-blocking point-to-point communication routines.

3   Heterogeneous Multiblock Computing Strategy

In this section, several techniques are described to enable concurrent, parallel computing on GPU accelerators and multicore CPUs. Major considerations for the heterogeneous computing framework are code portability and maintainability as well as raw computational performance. For this reason, the implementation methodology is given in detail here. Performance benchmark results and analysis are presented in the following section. The overall strategy used here is to use combine OpenMP multithreading for the host CPU cores with OpenACC parallelism targeting the available GPU accelerator devices. MPI-based distributed-memory parallelism was already available in MBFLO3; therefore, only the two multithreading compiler directives were added.

MBFLO3 is designed to handle an arbitrary number of mesh blocks and each MPI process will have at least one block. In the case of heterogeneous computing with GPUs, each MPI process will have at least one block per CPU and one block per GPU device. Note, that the computational cost per block is not uniform since the blocks can be of varying size and solid blocks (i.e., heat transport blocks) have a lower cost per-cell compared to the fluid blocks due to the different number of equations. The distribution of blocks to available compute devices is discussed later.

Figure 1 shows a flow chart of the MBFLO3 code. The elements highlighted in yellow denote the routines that were ported to GPUs using OpenACC. These routines constitute the time-consuming components of the MBFLO3 application. Routines responsible for inter-block communication, physical boundary conditions, and multigrid acceleration were not refactored with OpenACC due to the low data volume and computational cost associated with these parts of the algorithm. All routines, including those controlling boundary conditions and block interfaces, were refactored using OpenMP for host-side multicore parallelism.

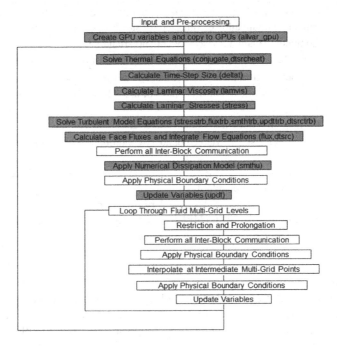

Fig. 1. MBFLO3 flowchart. Blocks in yellow are routines implemented for GPUs. (Color figure online)

Table 1 gives a listing of all fine-grid solver routines along with a functional description of each. These routines constitute all routines ported to the GPU identified in Fig. 1. Note that CONJUGATE and TRBVIS are full solution methods and employ the same sequence of routines as the core flow solver. That is, the heat and turbulence transport solvers contain the similar sequence of routines from STRESS through UPDT themselves but are not described here for brevity.

3.1 Multicore Host Parallelism

Multithreaded and vector (SIMD) parallelism targeting the host multicore CPUs were controlled through OpenMP directives. MBFLO3 uses triply nested loops within each block computational kernel. The MBFLO3 data structures are designed to allow unit-stride array access across the innermost loop to encourage efficient vectorization. Most loops are simple enough that optimizing compilers can automatically vectorize the inner loop. However, some complex loops required compiler directives to ensure inner loop vectorization.

Table 1. Fine-grid solver routines that were multithreaded, vectorized, and GPU enabled.

Function	Description
DELTAT	Compute the minimum and maximum timestep over all cells and compute each cell's maximum allowed timestep for steady-state convergence
LAMVIS	Compute the laminar viscosity via Sutherland's Law
CONJUGATE	Solve the conjugate heat conduction equation through the solid blocks
TRBVIS	Compute the turbulent stress tensor and advance the k-ω RANS equations
STRESS	Compute the stress and strain rates of the velocity vector and form the viscous stress tensor
FLUX	Compute the Euler and viscous fluxes across the cell faces
BLKBND	Set the block state variable boundary conditions on block-to-block interfaces with MPI point-to-point communication
SMTHU	Compute the smoothing flux to maintain stability near shocks and avoid odd-even decoupling of solution
BCOND	Set the block state variable boundary conditions on physical boundary faces using local data (i.e., no MPI communication)
UPDT	Update the primary state variables after each timestep

OpenMP multithreading was employed in two scenarios: for loop-level data parallelism targeting the outer two loops of the common triply nested loops and for task parallelism in which different single-threaded functions are computed concurrently. A third thread parallelism strategy in which smaller mesh blocks are computed by unique threads (i.e., similar to the MPI block-level decomposition), was not implemented since the number of blocks per MPI process can become small when strongly scaled in parallel. Also, MBFLO3 does not have the capability to automatically subdivide mesh blocks beyond what the STAGE3 mesh generator produces. That is, the maximum number of MPI ranks is limited to a fixed number of mesh blocks. For this reason, multithreading is a key performance enabler as it allows more compute resources to be applied to the problem than if only MPI distributed-memory parallelism was used.

In the current framework, there exists a loop over the number of blocks per MPI process followed by a call to a per-block computational kernel (e.g., search for the maximum allowed timestep on the given block). An OpenMP parallel section is created before the block-level loop to avoid repeated thread team spawning.

OpenMP provides a straightforward mechanism for controlling nested loop parallelism. The OpenMP `parallel do` directives were applied to the outer two loops of the nested `ijk` loop structures; that is, both the `j` and `k` loops are threaded. The outer two loops were threaded to increase the total thread parallelism in order to scale to hundreds of cores. This was facilitated using the `collapse` clause which causes the `j` and `k` loops to be combined into a single iteration space and distributed across the available cores. This increases the total potential thread parallelism from `Kmax` to `Jmax*Kmax`. Loop collapsing incurs additional overhead (relative to nested loops) since the unique `ijk` indices must be recomputed from the collapsed iteration index. This involves integer division and (or) moduli operations which can be costly. It was observed that collapsing the innermost loop (i.e., `collapse(3)`) also interfered with compiler auto-vectorization in select conditions reducing overall throughput. In general, collapsing only the outer two loops avoided conflict with compiler vectorization while also providing sufficient thread parallelism for modern multicore and manycore devices (e.g., Intel Xeon Phi). This also created a natural two-level parallel hierarchy well suited for these thread- and data-parallel platforms. Static scheduling, the default, was used for all parallel loops. Static scheduling was appropriate for the common nested loops as the cost per-iteration was constant. Based upon these considerations, all ijk nested loops used the OpenMP collapse(2) statement for loop-level thread parallelism and, where necessary, OpenMP SIMD (v4) directives[2] to ensure efficient inner loop vectorization. An example code segment highlighting the OpenMP directives for triply nested loops is shown in Listing 1.

Listing 1. Parallel directives example for triply nested Fortran loops.

```
!$omp parallel do collapse(2) private( xvel,… )
!$acc parallel loop gang collapse(2) vector_length(64)
!$acc&    async( block_idx ) pcopyin( x,u … ) pcopy( du, … )
      Do k = 1, kmax
        Do j = 1, jmax
!$omp       simd safelen(8)
!$acc       loop vector
        Do i = 1, imax
          xvel = u(i,j,k,2) / u(i,j,k,1)
          …
          du(i,j,k,1) = du(i,j,k,1) + xvel**2
```

Task parallelism was employed in scenarios were there was not sufficient computational work within the nested loops and when the per-iteration workload was variable. Both of these scenarios commonly occurred in the boundary condition and block interface routines which deal primarily with two-dimensional data along sub-faces of the blocks. These small doubly nested loops do not have sufficient work to overcome thread scheduling costs. Furthermore, each block can have an arbitrary number of boundary conditions and block interfaces and the cost can vary significantly between different boundary condition computations. Task-based parallelism with the OpenMP task directive was employed for these operations. In the current framework, an OpenMP task is created for each boundary condition sub-face computation or block-interface update (i.e., unpack a received MPI_Recv buffer) for all blocks. A single OpenMP thread enqueues the various tasks and then the OpenMP task scheduler assigns the threads to available asynchronous tasks to extract concurrency. Note that boundary conditions are applied to non-overlapping sub-face sections so all tasks are fully independent. Furthermore, within each boundary condition or block interface, inner loop vectorization (of the doubly nested loop) is enabled when appropriate to increase the single-threaded throughput. An example of the OpenMP task directive applied to a sub-face boundary condition and block-interface update loop is shown in Listing 2.

---

[2] The legacy !dir$ ivdep directive can often be used where OpenMP v4 is not supported.

3.2 Manycore Accelerator Parallelism

A similar strategy was employed with the OpenACC implementation targeting the GPU accelerators. As noted above, the block interface and boundary condition routines were not implemented with OpenACC. Instead, those operations are handled exclusively on the host using the OpenMP implementation. This, therefore, requires that the relevant host data be updated with the latest device data before the operations can begin. Likewise, the device data is then updated with the modified host data. This strategy can incur significant overhead due to the host-device data transfer costs. Whenever possible, these transfers are overlapped with host- and device-side computations to minimize the realized transfer overhead. The multiblock framework provides a ready means of overlapping communication and computation. For example, if more than one block is allocated to a given GPU, it is then possible to transfer block 1's data while block 2 is executing a computational kernel. That is, the block-level data structures can be used to form a parallel pipeline to reduce the incurred latency.

Listing 2. Task-based parallelism example for updating block boundary data.

```
!$omp parallel private (n,blkid,f,p) shared (irecv,buf)
!$omp single
! -- Loop over all blocks, faces, and subface patches.
      Do n = 1, n_blocks
         blkid = block_list(n)
         Do f = 1, 6
            Do p = 1, n_face_patches(blkid, f)
               If (has_remote_neighbor( blkid,f,p )) Then
! -- Enqueue task to unpack shared buffer filled by MPI_Recv.
                  irecv = irecv + 1
!$omp             task firstprivate( irecv,blkid,f,p )
                  call unpack_recv_buf( buf(irecv),blkid,f,p,…)
!$omp             end task
               Else
! -- Enqueue task to set conditions on a subface patch
!$omp             task firstprivate( blkid,f,p )
                  call set_phys_bc( blkid,f,p,…)
!$omp             end task
               Endif
            Enddo
         Enddo
      Enddo
!$omp end single nowait
!$omp end parallel
```

As with OpenMP, the same collapse(2) clause was used to join the outer two loops into one parallel work-sharing iteration space. Each collapsed jk loop iteration is mapped to an OpenACC gang, equivalent to a thread-block in CUDA. The inner i loops were specified as vector loops with the vector length defined as a compile-time constant (e.g., 64). The unit-stride data layout described earlier for SIMD vectorization also encourages efficient data usage on the GPU. That is, *coalesced* data reads and writes are enabled on the NVIDIA GPU systems. Listing 1 includes the OpenACC loop directives used for the triply nested loops in addition to the OpenMP directives.

3.3 Heterogeneous Host-Device Parallelism

When a GPU and CPU compute resource is available, both are used concurrently. In the current framework, one MPI process is assigned to each GPU device and mapped to all or a subset of the CPU cores depending upon the number of CPUs and GPUs on the system. For example, a two-socket CPU system with two GPUs will map one MPI process per CPU and use all of the CPU cores within the same CPU. This is done to optimize the CPU multithreaded performance by localizing memory access to the same CPU memory device (i.e., within the same NUMA node).

The key to concurrently using both the CPU and GPU resources is to launch independent work on both devices. This is accomplished by assigning one or more mesh blocks to both devices. The workload is partitioned based upon the relative performance of the two compute devices. For example, if the CPU has twice the overall throughput as the GPU, the CPU will be assigned approximately two-thirds of the workload and the GPU one-third. The OpenACC kernels for the GPU-allocated blocks are initiated first and placed in separate OpenACC asynchronous streams. Once all GPU blocks are enqueued, the remaining CPU-allocated blocks are computed. By launching the OpenACC kernels in unique streams, one or more GPU blocks can be scheduled simultaneously on the GPU, and the GPU work can proceed concurrently to the CPU workload.

The OpenACC run-time consumes CPU resources. To prevent this from impeding the CPU computational workload, the number of OpenMP threads used for the work-sharing parallel sections is one less than the available CPU cores. The process affinity is specified such that all CPU cores are exclusively reserved to the parent MPI process.

The parallel loop compiler directives are very similar with OpenMP and OpenACC which eases code maintenance. OpenMP and OpenACC compiler directives can exist in the same source code (see Listing 1). However, both OpenMP and OpenACC parallel loop kernels cannot be compiled at the same time. That is, a loop with both `!$omp parallel` and `!$acc parallel` cannot be compiled with both directives enabled.

To avoid maintaining two, unique OpenMP and OpenACC versions of the source code, a three-stage compilation strategy was devised. The source code structure was divided so that block-loop driver codes were stored separately from the kernel source (with the `ijk` nested loop structures). The kernel source is compiled twice, once with OpenMP and once with OpenACC. Simple compiler pre-processor macros were used to create unique OpenMP and OpenACC function names from the same source. The driver code is compiled with both OpenACC and OpenMP since, by design, there are no conflicting compiler directives. This compilation and linking process is easily automated (e.g., GNU *make*) allowing the same source code to be used for both OpenMP and OpenACC. Huismann et al. [17] also used a single-source approach with OpenMP and OpenACC; however, they exploited both directives through MPI's multiple program multiple data (MPMD) paradigm.

4   Performance Results and Analysis

The benchmark results using the heterogeneous MBFLO3 CFD code are presented here. All benchmark results are based on a steady-state RANS simulation of a first stage turbine vane model typical of modern high-pressure turbines. The multiblock mesh system contains 16 blocks with 1.6 million mesh points in total. Fourteen of the blocks model the turbulent fluid flow using body-conforming grids and the remaining two blocks model the thermal transport (i.e., conjugate heat conduction) within the vane (i.e., the solid). Figures 2a and b show the geometry and standard computational grid for the test case.

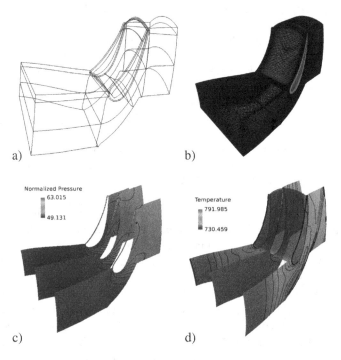

Fig. 2. Geometry, configuration, and flow/temperature results for turbomachinery test case; (a) mesh blocks; (b) computational mesh with fluid regions in black and solid (thermal) regions in red/blue; (c) pressure; and (d) temperature contours at three spanwise locations. (Color figure online)

MBFLO3 contains many pre- and post-processing routines as well as core solver functions and multigrid acceleration routines (see Fig. 1 and Table 1). Typical simulations consist of 1,000's of timesteps with nearly all of the computational time spent in the solver routines alone. For this reason, we have limited the current benchmark analysis to only the core solver loop routines involved in the steady-state RANS simulation. Benchmark results are based on the wallclock time per-timestep averaged over the final 30 timesteps of the steady-state simulation and excluding file I/O.

The current benchmark grid model was selected so that single-core and single-node benchmarks could be performed. Large-scale benchmarks with 100's of cluster nodes stress the MPI point-to-point communication methodology, not necessarily the vectorization and multithreaded approach of interest here.

Benchmark results were obtained on three systems: (i) *Thunder*, an SGI ICE-X cluster at the Air Force Research Laboratory (AFRL); (ii), *ARL-KNL*, an Intel Xeon Phi *Knights Landing* (KNL) development system at the Army Research Laboratory (ARL); and (iii) the *Hokule'a* cluster at the Maui HPC Center. Thunder has over 3,216 CPU-only multicore nodes and 356 accelerator nodes that include either two NVIDIA K40 m Kepler GPUs or two Intel Xeon Phi *Knights Corner* (KNC) 7120P co-processors along with multicore CPUs. The CPU-only nodes have two Intel Xeon E5-2699v3 (Haswell) CPUs with 18 cores per CPU. The accelerator nodes have two Xeon E5-2697v3 CPUs with 14 cores per CPU in addition to the accelerator devices. All nodes have 128 GB of main memory. All single-core, multicore, and heterogeneous benchmarks with OpenMP and OpenACC were run on the accelerator nodes on Thunder. The PGI v16.10 compiler was used to build all benchmark application binaries on Thunder using default optimization (–O2).

ARL-KNL is a development system with 28 KNL nodes. Each node contains one Intel Xeon Phi 7230 processor with 64 cores and 96 GB of DDR4 memory and 16 GB of high-bandwidth multi-channel DRAM (MCDRAM). All tests on the KNL operated in *quadrant-flat* mode meaning that the 16 GB MCDRAM and the 96 GB DDR4 DRAM are separately addressable. All data was allocated in MCDRAM for these benchmarks using the *numactl* Linux utility. MCDRAM has approximately four times higher bandwidth than DDR4 if accessed in parallel; however, the latency from MCDRAM is higher than DDR4. For the current structured-mesh benchmarks, MCDRAM was found to always be beneficial due to the regular memory access patterns associated with the unit-stride data layout. All benchmarks on the ARL-KNL cluster used the Intel v17.0 compiler.

Hokule'a is a 32-node cluster with two IBM Power8 10-core CPUs per node and four NVIDIA P100 GPUs per node. All executables on Hokule'a were compiled using the PGI 17.10 compiler with –O2 optimization.

Before presenting the heterogeneous CPU-GPU results, the performance using OpenMP on the multicore and manycore systems and OpenACC on the GPU accelerators shall first be examined. Figure 3 shows the single-core and OpenMP multithreaded routine run-times on a single 14-core Thunder Haswell CPU socket. The parallel speed-up is defined as

$$S_p = \frac{T_{serial}}{T_{Parallel}} \tag{11}$$

where T_{serial} is the single-core (single-threaded) run-time and $T_{parallel}$ is the multithreaded run-time. Both the Navier-Stokes and turbulence equations routines are given in detail but only the net cost of the conjugate heat solver is given for space considerations. The speed-up for the costliest kernels (e.g., flux, stress, stresstrb) all have S_p well above 7 times (or 50% efficiency) and the net S_p over the single-threaded performance is 8 times (57% efficiency). The task-based parallel routines (e.g., blkbnd and bcond) have lower parallel S_p but are still above 2 times indicating that the task parallelism is providing positive S_p for these complex routines.

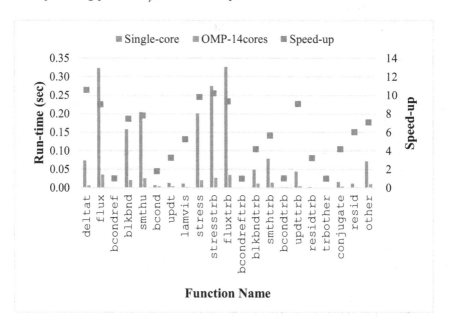

Fig. 3. MBFLO3 parallel performance for core solver functions using OpenMP multithreading on Thunder using 14-core Haswell CPU. Parallel speed-up relative to single-core run-times. Routines not explicitly named are included in other.

Figure 4 presents the same benchmark on an Intel Xeon Phi Knights Landing 7230 many-core device using 64 threads (i.e., one thread per core). As with the Haswell host benchmark, significant speed-up is observed for the computationally expensive routines. What's most important though is the higher speed-up observed for the task parallel routines. The higher realized performance (compared to the 14-core host) is critical to achieving acceptable overall speed-up on the KNL. Otherwise, those nominally low-cost routines, executing serially, would dramatically limit the overall speed-up due to Amdahl's law. Overall, the OpenMP speed-up compared to single-threaded execution on the KNL was 29x incorporating the task-based parallelism.

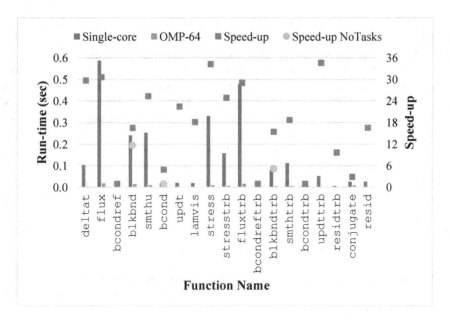

Fig. 4. OpenMP performance on the Intel Xeon Phi Knights Landing 7230 many-core processor with 64 threads. Speed-up shown with and without (NoTasks) task-based parallelism.

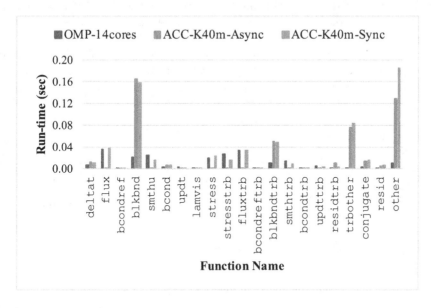

Fig. 5. Comparison of multicore OpenMP performance on the Haswell CPU and the NVIDIA Kepler K40 m GPU with OpenACC. Synchronous and asynchronous OpenACC kernel launches and transfers were tested; transfer and synchronization costs are included in `trbother` and `other` functions.

Figure 5 shows the function profile of the OpenACC implementation on the NVIDIA Kepler K40 m GPU as measured on the host. The previous OpenMP profile (with 14-threads) is shown for comparison. The OpenACC implementation uses asynchronous kernel launches and data transfers throughout (i.e., kernels and data for separate blocks are launched in unique *streams*); therefore, the host wallclock time is very small for routines without any transfer or synchronization points. As noted earlier, inter-block communication and boundary condition routines run on the host (serially here) requiring transfers to/from the host and device. Host ↔ device data transfers occur only in the main *driver* routines for each solver (i.e., flow, turbulence, and heat transfer). Those transfer and synchronization costs have been isolated into the `other` and `trbother` function profiles. The net overhead for the one-device benchmark is 43% of the total run-time. This same case was repeated with synchronous kernels and data transfers (i.e., ACC-K40 m-Sync). The total time in the transfer routines was 40% in this scenario though the overall runtime was 40% higher indicating that the asynchronous operation does improve the throughput though the net transfer overhead is substantial in this application.

The above results show that the OpenMP multithreaded implementation is capable of scaling across multiple cores within a single MPI process domain. Figure 6 shows the parallel speed-up of the average time per timestep using multiple MPI processes. Recall that the maximum number of MPI processes is limited to the number of mesh blocks, 16 in this benchmark. The speed-up in this case was relative to the MPI-only scenario which was run on a single multicore Haswell node. Two different OpenMP cases were run: 7 OpenMP threads per process and 14 OpenMP threads per process. In the former case, 4 total compute nodes were used with 4 MPI ranks per node. In the later, twice the number of nodes (and cores) were used. And finally, in the case of MPI+OpenACC, one MPI process per GPU was run across up to 8 nodes.

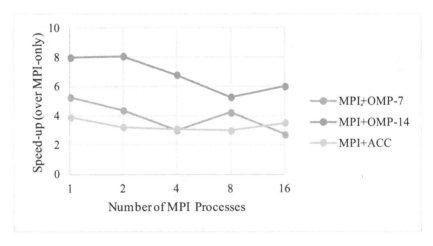

Fig. 6. Multiprocess speed-up of MPI+OpenMP and MPI+OpenACC methods relative to MPI-only. Seven and 14 threads per MPI process were used with OpenMP.

The one MPI process scenario in Fig. 6 gives the single-device performance comparison of the various methods. For seven threads per process, the net speed-up is 5.3 times over the single-threaded run-time which is 75% parallel efficiency. As noted earlier, the net speed-up with 14 threads was 8 times. As the number of MPI processes increases, the difference between the 7 and 14 thread cases remains largely the same until 8 MPI processes. This level of distributed parallelism is anomalous with MPI+OpenMP: S_p with 7 thread increases while it decreases with 14 threads. Recall that the 7-thread case is using half the number of nodes and there may be a difference in the effective inter-process bandwidth since more neighboring processes may be on the same node (i.e., more lower cost intra-node point-to-point transfers may occur). At 16 processes, the difference between 7 and 14 threads returns to approximately twice.

Figure 6 also shows the MPI+OpenACC performance. The 1 MPI processes case shows the single GPU performance. Overall, the GPU run-time is 3.9 times faster the single-core run-time. As more GPUs are used, the speed-up remains at or above 3 times. Comparing the OpenACC performance to the 14-thread OpenMP performance, the accelerator achieves 48% of the 14-core CPU. This would suggest that the GPU should be assigned approximately one-third of the total workload in a heterogeneous case.

Figure 7 shows the average time per timestep using multiple GPUs and CPUs in a heterogeneous fashion for several GPU-to-CPU workload ratios, including the most performant (i.e., 0.4). The host-only MPI+OpenMP runtime is also given for comparison. The workload ratio is defined as the weighted number of mesh points assigned to each device. The weighting takes into account the block type (i.e., fluid or solid) and the cost difference between the two types is 7 (fluid) to 1 (solid) based upon the number of equations solved respectively. The final workload distribution within each MPI process will not necessarily be the specified ratio since the partitioning is done by allocating entire blocks but instead represents the lower bound on the GPU workload. Note that a GPU will always be assigned at least one block.

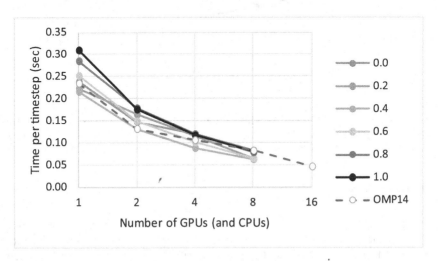

Fig. 7. Heterogeneous CPU+GPU benchmark showing performance versus the GPU-to-CPU workload ratio. MPI+OpenMP (14 threads/process) is also shown for comparison.

For 1 MPI rank, we see that fastest time is achieved with workload of 0.4, close to the predicted value of one-third. At this workload, the net performance using the CPU and GPU is 8% higher than using the CPU alone. For two or more GPU-CPU pairs, the heterogeneous run-time matches or is lower than the CPU-only though the benefit fluctuates. Using eight CPU-GPU pairs, the maximum number possible with 1 block per device, the heterogeneous system run-time was 20% faster than with the CPU only.

Figure 8 presents the same heterogeneous CPU-GPU benchmark executed on the Hokule'a system using the Power8 CPU and P100 GPU. There are two GPUs per CPU in this system; therefore, half of the cores per CPU (i.e., 5) are assigned to each MPI rank. Four OpenMP threads per core was found to be most performant for a total of 20 threads per MPI rank. The P100 GPU was found to be 2.0x faster than the K40 m GPU on single-GPU benchmarks showing the performance evolution with the newer GPU technology. The P100 was also found to be 1.6x faster than OpenMP on the five CPU cores suggesting 60% of the workload should reside on the GPU. However, the heterogeneous benchmark indicates that the most performant configuration is to perform all of the computations on the GPU (i.e., a workload of 1.0).

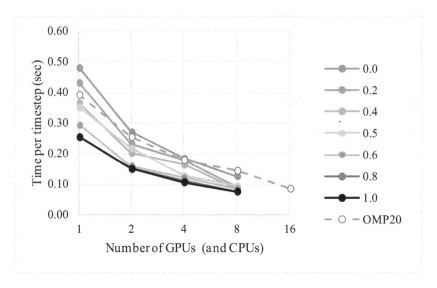

Fig. 8. Heterogeneous CPU+GPU benchmark showing performance versus the GPU-to-CPU workload ratio on the Hokule'a cluster using 20 OpenMP threads and 1 P100 GPU per MPI rank. MPI+OpenMP is also shown for comparison.

5   Conclusions

This work presented an approach for simultaneously using multicore CPUs and attached GPU accelerators. Multithreaded parallelism was implemented with compiler directives: OpenMP for the CPUs and OpenACC for the GPUs. Multicore and manycore CPU benchmarks showed promising speed-up when combining MPI and OpenMP.

Parallel efficiency of 75% was observed when using two MPI ranks per multicore Haswell CPU device and more than 8 times speed-up when using 14 threads per CPU (i.e., one MPI rank per CPU). Single device benchmarks were also reported on the Intel Xeon Phi Knights Landing manycore device that showed the benefit of combining loop-level parallelism for the common nested loops within the kernels with task-level parallelism to accelerate the complicated boundary condition and block interface operations. Using multiple GPUs with OpenACC resulted in a speed-up of over more than 3 times over the MPI-only scenario. Combining multicore and accelerator parallelism in a heterogeneous fashion resulted in a net 20% speed-up compared to only using the CPU or the GPU alone on the Thunder system. On dense GPU systems, such as Hokule'a, it was shown that it may be more efficient to use only the GPUs.

Acknowledgements. This material is based upon work supported by, or in part by, the Department of Defense High Performance Computing Modernization Program (HPCMP) under User Productivity, Technology Transfer and Training (PETTT) contract number GS04T09DBC0017.

US Department of Defense (DoD) Distribution Statement A: Approved for public release. Distribution is unlimited.

References

1. Martin, C.: Multicore processors: challenges, opportunities, emerging trends. In: Proceedings of Embedded World Conference 2014, Nuremberg, Germany (2014)
2. OpenACC Specification Page. http://www.openacc.org/specification. Accessed 31 July 2017
3. Stone, C., Davis, R.: High-performance 3D multi-disciplinary fluid/thermal prediction using combined multi-core/multi-GPGPU computer systems. In: 22nd AIAA Computational Fluid Dynamics Conference, Dallas, Texas, USA (2015). https://doi.org/10.2514/6.2015-3058
4. OpenMP Specification Page. http://www.openmp.org/specifications. Accessed 31 July 2017
5. Pickering, B.P., Jackson, C.W., Scogland, T.R.W., Feng, W.-C., Roy, C.J.: Directive-based GPU programming for computational fluid dynamics. Comput. Fluids **114**, 242–253 (2015)
6. Kraus, J., Schlottke, M., Adinetz, A., Pleiter, D.: Accelerating a C++ CFD code with OpenACC. In: 1st Workshop on Accelerator Programming Using Directives, pp. 47–54. IEEE (2014). https://doi.org/10.1109/WACCPD.2014.11
7. Wilcox, D.C.: Turbulence Modeling for CFD. DCW Industries, La Cannada (1998)
8. Smagorinsky, J.: General circulation experiments with the primitive equations. Mon. Weather Rev. **91**, 99–164 (1963)
9. Strelets, M.: Detached eddy simulation of massively separated flows. In: 39th Aerospace Sciences Meeting and Exhibit, Reno, Nevada (2001). https://doi.org/10.2514/6.2001-879
10. Bush, R.H., Mani, M.: A two-equation large eddy stress model for high sub-grid shear. In: 15th AIAA Computational Fluid Dynamics Conference, Anaheim, CA (2001). https://doi.org/10.2514/6.2001-2561
11. Bozinoski, R., Davis, R.L.: General three-dimensional, multi-block, parallel turbulent Navier-Stokes procedure. In: AIAA Aerospace Sciences Meeting. Reno, Nevada (2008). https://doi.org/10.2514/6.2008-756
12. Ni, R.H.: A multiple grid scheme for solving the Euler equations. AIAA J. **20**(11), 1565–1571 (1982). https://doi.org/10.2514/3.51220

13. Dannenhoffer, J.F.: Grid Adaptation for Complex Two-Dimensional Transonic Flows. Technical report CFDL-TR-87-10, Institute of Technology, Massachusetts (1987)
14. Davis, R.L., Ni, R.H., Carter, J.E.: Cascade viscous flow analysis using the Navier-Stokes equations. J. Propul. Power **3**, 406–414 (1987). https://doi.org/10.2514/3.23005
15. Jameson, A.: Time dependent calculations using multi-grid, with applications to unsteady flows past airfoils and wings. In: 10th AIAA Computational Fluid Dynamics Conference, Honolulu, HI (1991). https://doi.org/10.2514/6.1991-1596
16. Davis, R.L., Clark, J.P.: Geometry-grid generation for three-dimensional multidisciplinary simulations in multistage turbomachinery. J. Propul. Power **30**, 1502–1509 (2014). https://doi.org/10.2514/1.B35168
17. Huismann, I., Stiller, J., Frohlich, J.: Two-level parallelization of a fluid mechanics algorithm exploiting hardware heterogeneity. Comput. Fluids **117**, 114–124 (2015). https://doi.org/10.1016/j.compfluid.2015.05.012

Program Evaluation

Exploration of Supervised Machine Learning Techniques for Runtime Selection of CPU vs. GPU Execution in Java Programs

Gloria Y. K. Kim[1]([⊠]) [iD], Akihiro Hayashi[1] [iD], and Vivek Sarkar[2]

[1] Rice University, Houston, USA
gloria.kim@ricealumni.net, ahayashi@rice.edu
[2] Georgia Institute of Technology, Atlanta, USA
vsarkar@gatech.edu

Abstract. While multi-core CPUs and many-core GPUs are both viable platforms for parallel computing, programming models for them can impose large burdens upon programmers due to their complex and low-level APIs. Since managed languages like Java are designed to be run on multiple platforms, parallel language constructs and APIs such as Java 8 Parallel Stream APIs can enable high-level parallel programming with the promise of performance portability for mainstream ("non-ninja") programmers. To achieve this goal, it is important for the selection of the hardware device to be automated rather than be specified by the programmer, as is done in current programming models. Due to a variety of factors affecting performance, predicting a preferable device for faster performance of individual kernels remains a difficult problem. While a prior approach uses machine learning to address this challenge, there is no comparable study on good supervised machine learning algorithms and good program features to track. In this paper, we explore (1) program features to be extracted by a compiler and (2) various machine learning techniques that improve accuracy in prediction, thereby improving performance. The results show that an appropriate selection of program features and machine learning algorithm can further improve accuracy. In particular, support vector machines (SVMs), logistic regression, and J48 decision tree are found to be reliable techniques for building accurate prediction models from just two, three, or four program features, achieving accuracies of 99.66%, 98.63%, and 98.28% respectively from 5-fold-cross-validation.

Keywords: Java · Runtime · GPU · Performance heuristics
Supervised machine-learning

1 Introduction

Multi-core CPUs and many-core GPUs are both widely used parallel computing platforms but have different advantages and disadvantages that make it difficult to say that one is comprehensively better than the other. In a multi-core

© Springer International Publishing AG, part of Springer Nature 2018
S. Chandrasekaran and G. Juckeland (Eds.): WACCPD 2017, LNCS 10732, pp. 125–144, 2018.
https://doi.org/10.1007/978-3-319-74896-2_7

CPU, since threads exclusively occupy each core, each core can handle the execution of completely *different* tasks at once. On the other hand, in a many-core GPU, hundreds or thousands of cores can run hundreds or thousands of threads simultaneously. Since each workgroup of threads in each GPU core is executed together, all threads belonging to the same workgroup must be synchronized for coordinated data processing. Because of the differences between the two platforms, parallelism can vary drastically based on the selection of multi-core CPU or many-core GPU for a particular program.

Many prior approaches explore a good mix of productivity advantages and performance benefits from CPUs and GPUs. Many of them are capable of generating both CPU and GPU code from high-level languages. For example, from OpenMP 4.0 onwards [24], GPU platforms are supported by extending OpenMP's high-level parallel abstractions with accelerator programming. Lime [2] and Habanero-Java [8] accept user-specified parallel language constructs and directives. In addition, IBM's Java compiler [14] supports Java 8 parallel stream APIs, which enables programmers to express parallelism in a high level and machine-independent manner in a widely-used industry standard programming language.

Unfortunately, programmers still have to make the important decision of which hardware device to run their programs on. This method not only relies on programmers to understand low-level issues to make a thoughtful selection, but the nature of non-data-driven prediction also does not guarantee that the full capability of the underlying hardware is utilized. In recent work, the possibility of using supervised machine learning to automate the selection of the more optimal hardware device as a capability in IBM's Java 8 just-in-time (JIT) compiler was explored with success [10]. In [10], a set of program features such as the number of arithmetic/memory instructions is extracted at JIT compilation time, and then a binary prediction model that chooses either the CPU or GPU is generated using LIBSVM (a library of support vector machines) after obtaining training data by running different applications with different data sets.

However, to the best of our knowledge, there is no comparable study on (1) good machine learning algorithms and (2) good program features to track. The focus of this paper is to improve the prediction heuristic in accuracy and time overhead by exploring a variety of supervised machine learning techniques and different sets of program features. Finding the ideal set of features and algorithm can allow us to achieve better accuracy, which can also improve overall performance, and using fewer features to achieve high accuracy can reduce overheads of feature extraction and runtime prediction.

We collected 291 samples from 11 Java applications, each containing ten program features to serve as training data. However, instead of using this information as one training data to build a single binary prediction model, we generated separate training data sets for every possible subset of the original ten features to explore good program features, resulting in a 10^3 order of training data sets. Distinct binary prediction models were trained on these data for every unique

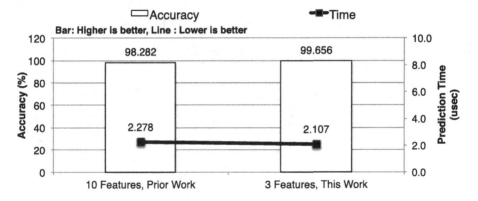

Fig. 1. The impact of changing a set of program features that is fed into LIBSVM on an IBM POWER8 and NVIDIA Tesla platform.

supervised machine learning technique: decision stump, J48 decision tree, k nearest neighbors, LIBSVM, logistic regression, multi-layer perceptron, and naive bayes.

This paper makes the following contributions:

- Exploration of supervised machine learning based binary prediction models with various program features for runtime selection of CPU vs. GPU execution.
- Quantitative evaluation of performance heuristics with 5-fold-cross-validation.
- Detailed discussion on implementing prediction models into runtime systems.

The rest of the paper is organized as follows. Section 2 summarizes the background on runtime CPU/GPU selection. Section 3 describes our compilation framework for Java 8 programs. Section 4 discusses how we explore different supervised machine learning algorithms and various program features. Section 5 presents an experimental evaluation. Section 6 discusses related work and Sect. 7 concludes.

2   Motivation

While optimal hardware selection for heterogeneous platforms is a challenging problem because a wide variety of factors affect performance, it is the programmer's responsibility to select a preferable device even in well-established programming models. We believe that automating the process of runtime CPU/GPU selection can greatly improve productivity and performance portability.

One approach is to build a cost/prediction model to predict a device that could run faster. In this regards, analytical cost models [12, 20] can be very accurate, assuming deep understandings of target programs and underlying architectures, but are often device-specific. Another direction is to build cost/prediction

Listing 1.1. An example of a parallel stream.

```
1 IntStream.range(0, 100).parallel().forEach(i -> a[i] = i);
```

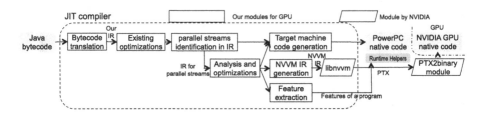

Fig. 2. JIT compiler overview.

models empirically [7,10,16–19,29]. Since empirical cost/prediction models are often based on historical performance data, they are platform neutral and can be built without device-specific knowledge.

Prior empirical approaches demonstrated that the use of machine learning algorithms (e.g., linear regression and support vector machines) is a promising way to empirically build prediction models. However, to the best of our knowledge, there is no comparable study on (1) good machine learning algorithms and (2) good program features to use for runtime CPU/GPU selection.

Figure 1 shows the impact of changing a set of program features that is fed into support vector machines (SVMs) on an IBM POWER8 and NVIDIA Tesla platform. Detailed information on the platform can be found in Sect. 5. The results show that a set of program features can improve the accuracy by 1.374% and the overhead of making a prediction by 8.116% compared to our prior work. Hence, an appropriate selection of program features and a machine learning algorithm can further improve the accuracy and the overheads of prediction models. This motivates us to explore various different machine learning algorithms with different sets of features.

3   Compiling Java to GPUs

This section explains an overview of a parallel loop in Java and compilation of the parallel loop that is used in our framework.

3.1   Java Parallel Stream API

From Java 8 onwards, *Stream* APIs are available for manipulating a sequence of elements. Elements can be passed to a lambda expression to support functional-style operations such as `filter`, `map`, and `reduce`. This sequence can also be used to express loop parallelisms at a high level. If a programmer explicitly specifies `parallel()` to a stream, a Java runtime can process each element with the lambda expression in this sequence of the stream in parallel.

Listing 1.1 shows an example of a program using a parallel stream. In this case, a sequence of integer elements i = 0,1,2,...,99 is firstly generated. Then, the sequence is passed with `parallel()` to a lambda parameter i in the lambda expression in `forEach()`. The lambda body `a[i]` = i in the lambda expression can be executed with each parameter value in parallel. While this lambda expression can be executed in parallel by multiple threads on CPUs (e.g., by using Java fork/join framework), the specification of the *Stream* API does not explicitly specify any hardware device or runtime framework for parallel execution. This allows the JIT compiler to generate a GPU version of the parallel loop and execute it on GPUs at runtime.

In general, the performance of this parallel execution can be accelerated only when a Java runtime appropriately select one of the available hardware devices.

3.2   JIT Compilation for GPUs

Our framework is built on top of the production version of the IBM Java 8 runtime environment [13] that consists of the J9 Virtual machine and Testarossa JIT compiler [5]. Figure 2 shows an overview of our JIT compiler.

First, the Java runtime environment identifies a method to be compiled based on runtime profiling information. The JIT compiler transforms Java bytecode of the compilation target method to an intermediate representation (IR), and then applies state-of-the-art optimizations to the IR. The JIT compiler reuses existing optimization modules such as dead code elimination, copy propagation, and partial redundancy elimination.

The JIT compiler looks for a call to the `java.util.Stream.IntStream.forEach()` method with `parallel()` in the IR. If it finds the method call, the IR for a lambda expression in `forEach()` with a pair of lower and upper bounds is extracted. After this extraction, the JIT compiler transforms this parallel `forEach` into a regular loop in the IR. Then, the JIT compiler analyzes the IR and applies optimizations to the parallel loop.

The optimized IR is divided into two parts. One is translated into an NVVM IR [21], which is fed into a GPU code generation library (libNVVM) for GPU execution. Features are extracted from the corresponding IR from this part. The other part is translated into a PowerPC binary, which includes calls to make a decision on selecting a faster device from available devices and to CUDA Drive APIs. The latter includes memory allocation on GPUs, data transfer between the host and the GPU, and a call to GPU binary translator with PTX instructions [22]. When the former call decides to use the GPU, the PowerPC binary calls a CUDA Driver API to compile PTX instructions to an NVIDIA GPU's binary, then the GPU binary is executed.

Currently, the JIT compiler can generate GPU code from the following two styles of an innermost parallel stream code to express data parallelism:

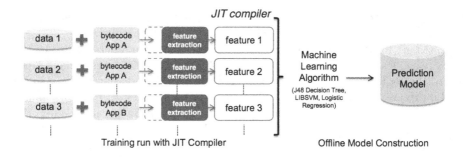

Fig. 3. Supervised machine learning based binary prediction model construction.

Listing 1.2. Supported parallel streams.

```
1 IntStream.range(low, up).parallel().forEach(i -> <lambda>)
2 IntStream.rangeClosed(low, up).parallel().forEach(i -> <lambda>)
```

The function `rangeClosed(low, up)` generates a sequence within the range of $low \leq i \leq up$, where i is an induction variable, up is upper inclusion limit and low is lower inclusion limit. $\langle lambda \rangle$ represents a valid Java lambda body with a lambda parameter i whose input is a sequence of integer values. In the current implementation, only the following constructs are allowed in $\langle lambda \rangle$:

- **types**: all of the Java primitive types
- **variable**: local, parameters, one-dimensional array whose references are a loop invariant, and a field in an instance
- **expression**: all of the Java expressions for Java primitive types
- **statements**: all of the Java statements except all of the following: `try-catch-finally` and `throw`, `synchronized`, a `interface` method call, and other aggregate operations of the stream such as `reduce()`
- **exceptions**: `ArrayIndexOutOfBoundsException`, `NullPointerException`, and `ArithmeticException` (only division by zero).

4   Exploring Supervised Machine Learning Algorithms

This section discusses the supervised machine learning algorithms and various program features explored. We provide descriptions of the algorithms and features, then give an overview of the work flow for constructing models on various subsets of features using each algorithm.

4.1   Supervised Machine Learning

Supervised machine learning is a technique of inferring a function using labeled training data. Typically, *regression* algorithms are used for inferring a real number value (e.g., predicting housing prices) and *classification* algorithms are used

Table 1. Description of program features

Kind	Feature	Description
Size	*range*	Size of parallel loop
Instruction	*arithmetic*	ALU instructions such as addition and multiplication
	branch	Unconditional/conditional branch instructions
	math	Math methods in `java.lang.Math`
	memory	Load and store instructions to and from memory
	other1	Other types of instructions
Array Access	*coalesced*	Aligned array access with zero offset
	offset	Misaligned array access with non-zero offset
	stride	Misaligned array access with stride
	other2	Other types of array accesses

for inferring a boolean value (e.g., zero or one). In this paper, we explore classification algorithms to infer a preferable device for a given parallel loop - i.e. CPUs or GPUs.

Figure 3 summarizes our approach to build a binary prediction model. In constructing supervised machine learning based performance heuristics, program features served as the predictors on which the binary prediction models were trained on. Program features were dynamically extracted in the JIT compiler.

4.2 Generating Subsets of Features

Table 1 summarizes program features extracted by the JIT compiler. These features are essentially the dynamic numbers of our IR instructions, which have a strong relationship with execution time. More details on the feature extraction part can be found in our prior work [10]. Every possible subset of features from the union of the sets {*range*}, {*arithmetic, branch, math, memory, other1*} and {*coalesced, offset, stride, other2*} - where the first set with just *range* refers to the number of iterations of a parallel loop, the second set of features refers to the number of such instructions per iteration, and the third set of features refers to the number of such array accesses per parallel loop - was used to create a separate prediction model. Subsets of features (1024 combinations) - as opposed to only the full set of features - were explored to determine which program features more critically contributed to an accurate prediction model.

4.3 Constructing Prediction Models

Algorithms Used. Supervised machine learning with each of decision stump, J48 decision tree, k nearest neighbors, LIBSVM, logistic regression, multi-layer perceptron, and naive bayes, was performed to obtain multiple binary prediction models:

- **Decision Stump:** Divide data points into two groups (CPU vs GPU) based on one feature to create the most distinct groups as possible. Results in a single-level decision tree where the root node represents the feature and the leaf nodes represent either CPU or GPU.
- **J48 Decision Tree:** For each feature, divide data points into two groups (CPU vs GPU) to create the most distinct groups as possible. Results in a multilevel *pruned* decision tree where non-leaf nodes represent features and the leaf nodes represent either CPU or GPU.
- **K-nearest Neighbors:** Map each data point in relation to one another using a distance function. Classify a new data point by assigning it to the class (CPU vs GPU) that is most common amongst its k nearest neighbors.
- **LIBSVM/SVM (Support Vector Machines):** Plot data as points in an n-dimensional space where n is the number of features, then find an optimal hyperplane that splits the data for classification (CPU vs GPU). Prediction on new data is based on which side of the hyperplane it lands when plotted.
- **Logistic Regression:** Predict the probability of an outcome (CPU vs GPU) by fitting data to a logit function. The log odds of binary prediction are modeled as a linear combination of features, which serve as predictor variables.
- **Multi-layer Perceptron:** Build a network of sigmoid nodes and classify instances (CPU vs GPU) using backpropagation.
- **Naive Bayes:** Compute the posterior probability of a class (CPU vs GPU) given features using Bayes' theorem.

These algorithms were deemed appropriate for our context of binary selection (GPU vs CPU) using supervised machine learning (training data includes both predictors as well as the outcomes), and were explored to determine the best algorithm for our model. All prediction models except for those from LIBSVM were built using the Weka software [28] offline. Afterwards, the models were used to make predictions for unseen programs.

Detailed Steps. The following steps explain the basic workflow for each model construction:

Step 1: Formatting training data

Training data was formatted for proper processing. In the case of Weka, an ARFF file was formatted as an array of attribute values (features and outcome) for each data sample like such:

$$\langle value1 \rangle, \langle value2 \rangle, ..., \langle outcome \rangle$$

where every value is an integer representing the number of times a feature appears in the sample program, and $\langle outcome \rangle$ is a string ('GPU' or 'CPU') representing which hardware device was the better choice for this particular program.

Step 2: Training

Supervised machine learning was performed with the training data to generate a binary prediction model.

Step 3: Cross Validation

5-fold-cross-validation was used to evaluate the accuracy of the prediction model. In n-fold-cross-validation, data is divided into n sections, then n-1 sections are used as data to train the model while the remaining section is used as new data to test the accuracy of the model.

Step 4: Additional Testing

The prediction model was used on other testing data to evaluate the accuracy of the model on data unrelated to what was used to build the model.

4.4 Integrating Prediction Models

To integrate a prediction model into the JVM runtime, we first prepare an equivalent C function that takes features and returns a boolean value (CPU or GPU). For example, we put a sequence of if-then-else statements for doing J48 decision tree predictions and put some library calls (e.g., LIBSVM). The JIT compiler generates both CPU and GPU versions of a parallel loop and the runtime selects an appropriate one on the output of the prediction function.

5   Experimental Results

5.1 Experimental Protocol

Purpose: The goal of this experiment is to study how program features and supervised machine learning algorithms affect the accuracy of runtime CPU/GPU selection. For that purpose, we constructed binary prediction models on various subsets of features using the following algorithms: decision stump, J48 decision tree, k nearest neighbors, LIBSVM, logistic regression, multi-layer perceptron, and naive bayes.

Datasets: We used a training dataset from our previous work [10] and an additional dataset obtained on IBM POWER8 and NVIDIA Tesla platform with Ubuntu 14.10 operating system. The platform has two 10-core IBM POWER8 CPUs at 3.69 GHz with 256 GB of RAM. Each core is capable of running eight SMT threads, resulting in 160-threads per platform. One NVIDIA Tesla K40m GPU at 876 MHz with 12 GB of global memory is connected over PCI-Express Gen 3. Error-correcting code (ECC) feature was turned off at the time to evaluate this work. The option was either 160 workers on IBM POWER8 or NVIDIA Tesla K40m GPU. The training dataset from [10] was obtained by running the eleven benchmarks shown in Table 2 with different data sets. The additional dataset consisting of 41 samples was obtained by running Bitonic Sort, KMeans, and an IBM's confidential application. In the following, the training dataset from [10] is referred to as *the original dataset* and the additional dataset is referred to as *the unknown testing dataset*. Each sample has the class label showing a faster configuration (160 workers threads on CPU vs. GPU).

Table 2. A list of benchmarks used to create the dataset from [10].

Benchmark	Summary	Maximum data size	Data type
Blackscholes	Financial application which calculates the price of European put and call options	4,194,304 virtual options	double
Crypt	Cryptographic application from the Java Grande Benchmarks [15]	Size C with N = 50,000,000	byte
SpMM	Sparse matrix multiplication from the Java Grande Benchmarks [15]	Size C with N = 500,000	double
MRIQ	Three-dimensional medical benchmark from Parboil [25], ported to Java	large size ($64 \times 64 \times 64$)	float
Gemm	Matrix multiplication: $C = \alpha.A.B + \beta.C$ from PolyBench [26], ported to Java	$2,048 \times 2,048$	int
Gesummv	Scalar, Vector and Matrix Multiplication from PolyBench [26], ported to Java	$2,048 \times 2,048$	int
Doitgen	Multiresolution analysis kernel from PolyBench [26], ported to Java	$256 \times 256 \times 256$	int
Jacobi-1D	1-D Jacobi stencil computation from Polybench [26], ported to Java	N = 4,194,304 T = 1	int
MM	A standard dense matrix multiplication: $C = A.B$	$2,048 \times 2,048$	double
MT	A standard dense matrix transpose: $B = A^{\mathrm{T}}$	$2,048 \times 2,048$	double
VA	A standard 1-D vector addition $C = A + B$	4,194,304	double

5.2 Overall Summary

The binary prediction models were evaluated based on three measures of accuracy: (1) accuracy from 5-fold-cross-validation with the original dataset, (2) accuracy on prediction of the original dataset, and (3) accuracy on prediction of the unknown testing dataset.

Table 3. Accuracies achieved by binary prediction models generated using each ML algorithm from full set of features

	LIBSVM	J48 tree	Logistic regression	Multilayer perceptron	k nearest neighbors	Decision Stump	Naive Bayes
Accuracy from 5-fold-CV	98.282%	98.282%	97.595%	88.660%	88.316%	88.316%	42.268%
Accuracy on original training data	99.656%	98.969%	98.969%	96.220%	90.034%	88.316%	42.268%
Accuracy on other testing data	98.282%	92.683%	80.488%	92.683%	92.683%	82.927%	2.439%

Table 4. Highest 5-fold-cross-validation accuracies achieved by binary prediction models generated using each ML algorithm

LIBSVM	Logistic regression	J48 tree	Multilayer perceptron	k nearest neighbors	Naive Bayes	Decision Stump
99.656%	98.625%	98.282%	96.907%	95.876%	91.753%	88.316%

The rest of this section is organized as follows: we first present and discuss accuracies on the full set of features in Sect. 5.3. Then, in Sect. 5.4, we present and discuss accuracies on subsets of features. Through deeper analysis and comparison of models, we see how the features included and the algorithm used affect the accuracy of runtime CPU/GPU selection.

5.3   Accuracies on the Full Set of Features

Models trained on the full set of features yielded very different accuracies across different algorithms. The Naive Bayes-trained model performed the worst with a 42.268% accuracy from 5-fold-cross-validation, while LIBSVM and J48 Tree-trained models performed the best with 98.282%, followed by the Logistic Regression-trained model with 97.595% accuracy. The other models achieved accuracies in the 88.3–88.7% range. A summary of the accuracy results are shown in Table 3 and visually represented in Fig. 4.

5.4   Exploring ML Algorithms by Feature Subsetting

Models were also trained on different subsets of features to determine the features that most significantly contribute to high accuracy - the ideal case being the smallest subset of features resulting in the highest accuracy possible. We compared the important features for each algorithm from (1) the subsets achieving highest accuracy and (2) the full set of features. By subsetting, we were able to build models that achieved higher accuracy than those built from the full set of features.

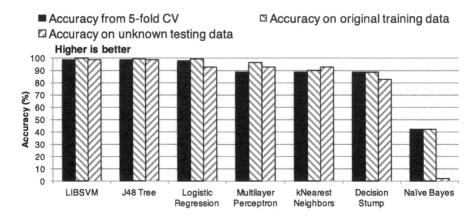

Fig. 4. Accuracies of models with full set of features

Subsets Achieving Highest Accuracy. A summary of the accuracy results are shown in Table 4. Here, each of the accuracies refers to the prediction model(s) - based on some subset of features - that achieved the highest accuracy among all other models built using the same algorithm. The result suggests that the top three algorithms are LIBSVM, logistic regression, and J48 tree, all of which achieved highest accuracies of ≥98.282% from 5-fold-cross-validation.

99 models built using LIBSVM, 30 models built using logistic regression, and 256 models built using J48 tree achieved highest accuracies of 99.656%, 98.969%, and 98.969% respectively. For each of these top three algorithms, we further analyzed the models based on the smallest subset of features that achieved highest accuracy. For LIBSVM, the smallest subset size was three, for logistic regression four, and for J48 tree two. The results are shown in Table 5 and visually represented in Fig. 5.

Comparison of important features and accuracies of models generated using these algorithms led to several key findings. First, the features identified as important were inconsistent across algorithms and slightly differed between subset and full set models for the same algorithm. Second, including more features in the prediction model did not correlate to a higher accuracy.

Table 5. Analysis of binary prediction models with smallest subset of features that achieved highest 5-fold-cross-validation accuracies

	LIBSVM	Logistic regression	J48 tree
# of features included in model	3	4	2
Accuracy from 5-fold-cross-validation	99.656%	98.625%	98.282%
Accuracy on original training data	99.656%	98.969%	98.282%
Accuracy on other testing data	99.656%	82.927%	92.683%

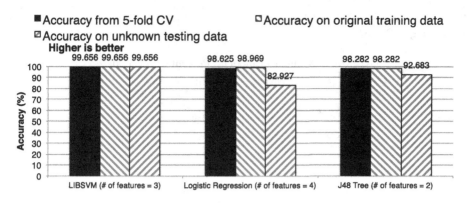

Fig. 5. Accuracies of models with smallest subset size that achieved highest 5-fold-cross-validation accuracies

Comparison of Important Features. The models that achieved highest accuracy using LIBSVM, logistic regression, and J48 tree were not built from the same subset of features. To determine which features were important for each algorithm, we analyzed the features of models that achieved the highest accuracy from 5-fold-cross-validation. Although models of various combinations of features achieved the same level of accuracy, for each algorithm, there was at least one feature that was necessarily present in all models. For LIBSVM, this feature is *parallel loop range*; for logistic regression, *coalesced array accesses* and *other array accesses*; for J48 decision tree, *parallel loop range* and *other array accesses*. Tables 6, 7, and 8 detail the number of these models respective to each algorithm that incorporated each feature.

To identify the important features from models trained on the full set of features, the odds ratio of features in logistic regression and the branches representing features in the J48 tree were analyzed. In logistic regression, *offset* was the most important feature; in the J48 tree, *math*, *range*, and *other2* were the most important features. Our analyses indicate that important features identified by subsetting did not exactly match features suggested by the model (e.g., weight vectors) trained on the full set of features. Analyzing the model from LIBSVM was difficult as the model trained on the full set of features produced a (non-)linear hyperplane in a 10-dimensional space.

Comparison of Accuracy. As mentioned in Sect. 5.4, the smallest subset size of the highest accuracy achieved was three for LIBSVM, four for logistic regression, and two for J48 tree. On the other hand, models built from the full set of features at best achieved equivalent accuracy as those built from these subsets. These accuracies are visually represented in Fig. 6. A comparison of accuracies between the subset-trained and full-set-trained models suggests that including more features in the prediction model not only fails to improve accuracy, but in fact decreases the accuracy of the model. This is because as the complexity of a model increases, the risk of overfitting and curse of dimensionality

Table 6. Feature analysis on highest accuracy (5-fold-cross-validation) subset models built using LIBSVM.

Feature	Number of models with feature	Percentage of models with feature
range	99	100.0%
stride	96	97.0%
arithmetic	65	65.7%
other2	56	56.6%
memory	56	56.6%
offset	55	55.6%
branch	54	54.5%
math	46	46.5%
other1	43	43.4%
coalesced	0	0.0%

Table 7. Feature analysis on highest accuracy (5-fold-cross-validation) subset models built using Logistic Regression.

Feature	Number of models with feature	Percentage of models with feature
other2	30	100.0%
coalesced	30	100.0%
offset	25	83.3%
arithmetic	20	66.7%
stride	18	60.0%
range	16	53.3%
memory	16	53.3%
branch	9	30.0%
math	9	30.0%
other1	6	20.0%

potentially increases. Specifically for LIBSVM, with fewer features (assuming the ideal/appropriate combination of them), the smaller the dimension of space and constraints imposed by each additional dimension as the algorithm searches for an optimal non-linear hyperplane that has the largest separation between two classes.

Analysis of Runtime Prediction Overheads. The relationship between subset size and runtime prediction overheads is shown in Table 9. The results show that a smaller subset size can reduce runtime prediction overheads and improve

Table 8. Feature analysis on highest accuracy (5-fold-cross-validation) subset models built using J48 Decision Tree.

Feature	Number of models with feature	Percentage of models with feature
other2	256	100.0%
range	256	100.0%
arithmetic	128	50.0%
memory	128	50.0%
branch	128	50.0%
math	128	50.0%
coalesced	128	50.0%
other1	128	50.0%
stride	128	50.0%
offset	128	50.0%

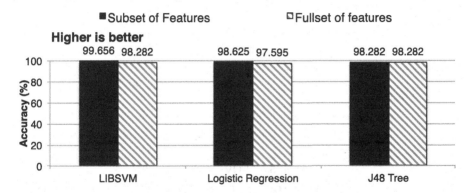

Fig. 6. The impact of feature subsetting

accuracy in general. For J48 decision tree, there was no significant difference in runtime overheads by subsetting because the algorithm does not fully consider all the given features. Also, it is worth noting that each kernel takes at least several milliseconds, which is several orders of magnitude larger than the prediction overhead shown in Table 9.

5.5 Lessons Learned

Results show that an appropriate selection of program features and machine learning algorithm can improve accuracy and reduce runtime overheads. Based on our analysis, our suggestions for utilizing machine learning techniques for runtime CPU/GPU selection are as follows:

1. LIBSVM, Logistic Regression, and J48 Decision Tree are machine learning techniques that produce models with best accuracies.
2. *Range, coalesced, and other2* are particularly important features. In particular, since *range* is a good metric to measure the amount of work, which in general significantly correlates to execution time, it is an important feature to incorporate in the prediction models. *range* was present in all models built with LIBSVM or J48 Decision Tree that achieved highest accuracy; *coalesced* was present in all models built with Logistic Regression that achieved highest accuracy; *other2* was present in all models built with Logistic Regression or J48 Decision Tree that achieved highest accuracy. Additionally, *arithmetic* was present in most of the models built with LIBSVM, J48 Decision Tree, or Logistic Regression that achieved highest accuracy.
3. While LIBSVM shows excellent accuracy in prediction, runtime prediction overheads are relatively large compared to other algorithms.
4. J48 Decision Tree shows comparable accuracy to LIBSVM. Also, compared to other approaches, the output of the J48 Decision Tree is more human-readable and fine-tunable because it is a sequence of if-then-else statements.

Table 9. Overheads of runtime prediction

		LIBSVM	Logistic regression	J48 tree
Fullset of features	nFeatures	10	10	10
	Accuracy from 5-fold-CV	98.282%	97.595%	98.282%
	Prediction overheads	2.278 us	0.158 us	0.020 us
Subset of features	nFeatures	3	4	2
	Accuracy from 5-fold-CV	99.656%	98.625%	98.282%
	Prediction overheads (usec)	2.107 us	0.106 us	0.020 us

6 Related Work

6.1 GPU Code Generation from High-Level Languages

GPU code generation is supported by several JVM-compatible language compilation systems.

Many previous studies support *explicit parallel programming* by programmers on GPU. JCUDA [30] provides a special interface that allows programmers to write Java code that calls user-written CUDA kernels. The JCUDA compiler automatically generates the JNI glue code between the JVM and CUDA runtime by using this interface. Some other tools like JaBEE [31], RootBeer [27], and Aparapi [1] perform runtime generation of CUDA or OpenCL code from a code region within a method declared inside a specific class/interface (e.g. run() method of `Kernel` class/interface).

Other previous work provide higher-level programming models for ease of parallel programming. Hadoop-CL and Hadoop-CL2 [6,7] are built on top of Aparapi and integrates OpenCL into the Hadoop system. Lime [2] is a Java-compatible language that supports map/reduce operations on CPU/GPU through OpenCL. Firepile [23] translates JVM bytecode from Scala programs to OpenCL kernels at runtime. HJ-OpenCL [8,9] generates OpenCL from Habanero-Java language, which provides high-level language constructs such as parallel loop (`forall`), barrier synchronization (`next`), and high-level multi-dimensional array (`ArrayView`). Some other work (e.g. [3,4]) has proposed the use of high-level array programming models for heterogeneous computing that can also be built on top of the Java 8 parallel stream API.

These approaches leave the burden of selecting the preferred hardware device on the programmer. While they also provide impressive support for making the development of Java programs for GPU execution more productive, these programming models lack the portability and standardization of the Java 8 parallel stream APIs.

6.2   Offline Model Construction

OSCAR [11] is an automatic parallelizing compiler that takes user-provided cost information for heterogeneous scheduling. Some approaches automate this process by constructing performance prediction models offline (e.g., when the JIT compiler is installed on the machine) and making decisions at runtime. For example, Qilin [19] empirically builds a cost model offline for the hybrid execution between CPUs and GPUs. In the context of managed languages like in [18], the runtime predicts absolute performance numbers for CPUs and GPUs with linear models constructed by running micro-benchmarks with different datasets beforehand. Similarly, in [10], the JIT compiler extracts a set of features of a parallel loop (e.g., the number of arithmetic instructions, memory instructions, etc.) at JIT compilation time and the runtime selects the faster device based on a binary prediction model trained on applications with different datasets using support vector machines.

Some of the prior approaches utilize hardware counter information [17,29] for offline performance model construction, but such information is not usually available.

7   Conclusions

Due to a variety of factors affecting performance, selecting the optimal platform for parallel computing (multi-core CPU vs many-core GPU) for faster performance of individual kernels is a difficult problem. To automate this process and remove the burden from programmers to make the decision between CPU and GPU, we built prediction heuristics from different combinations of program features using a variety of supervised machine learning techniques. Our models achieved accuracies of 99.656% with LIBSVM from three features, 98.625%

with logistic regression from four features, and 98.282% with J48 tree from two features. These prediction models can be incorporated into runtime systems to accurately predict, on behalf of the programmers, the more optimal platform to run their parallel programs on, thereby improving performance.

In subsequent work, we plan to increase the training and test data set, then use our prediction-model-based automated selection of CPU vs GPU to compare improvements in runtime performance. In the future, we plan to apply our technique to AOT-compiled programs like OpenMP and OpenACC programs. One challenging problem is how to accurately collect performance metrics since feature extraction is done statically. Another direction of this work is to build prediction models for the systems that have recent GPUs such as Tesla K80, P100, and V100.

A   Appendix

- **Backpropagation:** In a Multilayer Perceptron (an artificial neural net), the repeated process of adjusting the weight of each neuron node in order to minimize error.
- **Logit function:** In Logistic Regression, the cumulative distribution function of the logistic distribution.
- **Overfitting:** In machine learning, an undesired occurrence when noise in the training data is learned by the model as concepts, negatively impacting the model's ability to make predictions on new data.
- **Sigmoid node:** In a Multilayer Perceptron (an artificial neural net), a node that is activated based on the Sigmoid function, a special kind of logistic function.

References

1. APARAPI: API for Data Parallel Java (2011). http://code.google.com/p/aparapi/. Accessed 20 June 2017
2. Dubach, C., Cheng, P., Rabbah, R., Bacon, D.F., Fink, S.J.: Compiling a high-level language for gpus: (via language support for architectures and compilers). In: Proceedings of the 33rd ACM SIGPLAN Conference on Programming Language Design and Implementation, PLDI 2012, pp. 1–12. ACM, New York (2012). http://doi.acm.org/10.1145/2254064.2254066
3. Fumero, J.J., Remmelg, T., Steuwer, M., Dubach, C.: Runtime code generation and data management for heterogeneous computing in Java. In: Proceedings of the Principles and Practices of Programming on the Java Platform, PPPJ 2015, pp. 16–26. ACM, New York (2015). http://doi.acm.org/10.1145/2807426.2807428
4. Fumero, J.J., Steuwer, M., Dubach, C.: A composable array function interface for heterogeneous computing in Java. In: Proceedings of ACM SIGPLAN International Workshop on Libraries, Languages, and Compilers for Array Programming, ARRAY 2014, pp. 44:44–44:49. ACM, New York (2014). http://doi.acm.org/10.1145/2627373.2627381

5. Grcevski, N., Kielstra, A., Stoodley, K., Stoodley, M., Sundaresan, V.: JavaTM just-in-time compiler and virtual machine improvements for server and middleware applications. In: Proceedings of the 3rd Conference on Virtual Machine Research And Technology Symposium, VM 2004, vol. 3. p. 12. USENIX Association, Berkeley (2004). http://dl.acm.org/citation.cfm?id=1267242.1267254

6. Grossman, M., Breternitz, M., Sarkar, V.: HadoopCL: MapReduce on Distributed heterogeneous platforms through seamless integration of Hadoop and OpenCL. In: Proceedings of the 2013 IEEE 27th International Symposium on Parallel and Distributed Processing Workshops and PhD Forum, IPDPSW 2013, pp. 1918–1927. IEEE Computer Society, Washington, DC (2013). https://doi.org/10.1109/IPDPSW.2013.246

7. Grossman, M., Breternitz, M., Sarkar, V.: Hadoopcl2: motivating the design of a distributed, heterogeneous programming system with machine-learning applications. IEEE Trans. Parallel Distrib. Syst. **27**(3), 762–775 (2016)

8. Hayashi, A., Grossman, M., Zhao, J., Shirako, J., Sarkar, V.: Accelerating Habanero-Java programs with OpenCL generation. In: Proceedings of the 2013 International Conference on Principles and Practices of Programming on the Java Platform: Virtual Machines, Languages, and Tools, PPPJ 2013, pp. 124–134 (2013)

9. Hayashi, A., Grossman, M., Zhao, J., Shirako, J., Sarkar, V.: Speculative execution of parallel programs with precise exception semantics on GPUs. In: Caşcaval, C., Montesinos, P. (eds.) LCPC 2013. LNCS, vol. 8664, pp. 342–356. Springer, Cham (2014). https://doi.org/10.1007/978-3-319-09967-5_20

10. Hayashi, A., Ishizaki, K., Koblents, G., Sarkar, V.: Machine-learning-based performance heuristics for runtime CPU/GPU selection. In: Proceedings of the Principles and Practices of Programming on the Java Platform, PPPJ 2015, pp. 27–36. ACM, New York (2015). http://doi.acm.org/10.1145/2807426.2807429

11. Hayashi, A., et al.: Parallelizing compiler framework and API for power reduction and software productivity of real-time heterogeneous multicores. In: Cooper, K., Mellor-Crummey, J., Sarkar, V. (eds.) LCPC 2010. LNCS, vol. 6548, pp. 184–198. Springer, Heidelberg (2011). https://doi.org/10.1007/978-3-642-19595-2_13

12. Hong, S., Kim, H.: An analytical model for a GPU architecture with memory-level and thread-level parallelism awareness. In: Proceedings of the 36th Annual International Symposium on Computer Architecture, ISCA 2009, pp. 152–163. ACM, New York (2009). http://doi.acm.org/10.1145/1555754.1555775

13. IBM Corporation: IBM SDK, Java Technology Edition, Version 8 (2015). https://developer.ibm.com/javasdk/downloads/. Accessed 20 June 2017

14. Ishizaki, K., Hayashi, A., Koblents, G., Sarkar, V.: Compiling and optimizing java 8 programs for GPU execution. In: 2015 International Conference on Parallel Architecture and Compilation (PACT), pp. 419–431, October 2015

15. JGF: The Java Grande Forum benchmark suite. https://www.epcc.ed.ac.uk/research/computing/performance-characterisation-and-benchmarking/java-grande-benchmark-suite

16. Kaleem, R., Barik, R., Shpeisman, T., Lewis, B.T., Hu, C., Pingali, K.: Adaptive heterogeneous scheduling for integrated GPUs. In: Proceedings of the 23rd International Conference on Parallel Architectures and Compilation, PACT 2014, pp. 151–162. ACM, New York (2014). http://doi.acm.org/10.1145/2628071.2628088

17. Karami, A., Mirsoleimani, S.A., Khunjush, F.: A statistical performance prediction model for OpenCL kernels on NVIDIA GPUs. In: The 17th CSI International Symposium on Computer Architecture Digital Systems (CADS 2013), pp. 15–22, October 2013

18. Leung, A., Lhoták, O., Lashari, G.: Automatic parallelization for graphics processing units. In: Proceedings of the 7th International Conference on Principles and Practice of Programming in Java, PPPJ 2009, pp. 91–100 (2009)
19. Luk, C.K., Hong, S., Kim, H.: Qilin: exploiting parallelism on heterogeneous multiprocessors with adaptive mapping. In: Proceedings of the 42nd Annual IEEE/ACM International Symposium on Microarchitecture, MICRO 42, pp. 45–55. ACM, New York (2009). http://doi.acm.org/10.1145/1669112.1669121
20. Luo, C., Suda, R.: A performance and energy consumption analytical model for GPU. In: 2011 IEEE Ninth International Conference on Dependable, Autonomic and Secure Computing, pp. 658–665, December 2011
21. NVIDIA: NVVM IR specification 1.3 (2017). http://docs.nvidia.com/cuda/pdf/NVVM_IR_Specification.pdf. Accessed 20 June 2017
22. NVIDIA: Parallel Thread Execution ISA v5.0 (2017). http://docs.nvidia.com/cuda/pdf/ptx_isa_5.0.pdf. Accessed 20 June 2017
23. Nystrom, N., White, D., Das, K.: Firepile: run-time compilation for GPUs in scala. SIGPLAN Not. **47**(3), 107–116 (2011). http://doi.acm.org/10.1145/2189751.2047883
24. OpenMP: OpenMP Application Program Interface, version 4.5 (2015). http://www.openmp.org/wp-content/uploads/openmp-4.5.pdf. Accessed 20 June 2017
25. Parboil: Parboil benchmarks. http://impact.crhc.illinois.edu/parboil/parboil.aspx
26. PolyBench: The polyhedral benchmark suite. http://www.cse.ohio-state.edu/~pouchet/software/polybench
27. Pratt-Szeliga, P., Fawcett, J., Welch, R.: Rootbeer: seamlessly using GPUs from Java. In: 14th IEEE International Conference on High Performance Computing and Communication and 9th IEEE International Conference on Embedded Software and Systems, HPCC-ICESS 2012, Liverpool, United Kingdom, June 25–27, 2012, pp. 375–380, June 2012
28. Machine Learning Group at the University of Waikato: Weka3: data mining software in Java (2017). http://www.cs.waikato.ac.nz/ml/weka/. Accessed 20 June 2017
29. Wu, G., Greathouse, J.L., Lyashevsky, A., Jayasena, N., Chiou, D.: GPGPU performance and power estimation using machine learning. In: 2015 IEEE 21st International Symposium on High Performance Computer Architecture (HPCA), pp. 564–576, February 2015
30. Yan, Y., Grossman, M., Sarkar, V.: JCUDA: a programmer-friendly interface for accelerating Java programs with CUDA. In: Sips, H., Epema, D., Lin, H.-X. (eds.) Euro-Par 2009. LNCS, vol. 5704, pp. 887–899. Springer, Heidelberg (2009). https://doi.org/10.1007/978-3-642-03869-3_82
31. Zaremba, W., Lin, Y., Grover, V.: JaBEE: framework for object-oriented Java bytecode compilation and execution on Graphics Processor Units. In: Proceedings of the 5th Annual Workshop on General Purpose Processing with Graphics Processing Units, GPGPU-5, pp. 74–83. ACM, New York (2012). http://doi.acm.org/10.1145/2159430.2159439

Automatic Testing of OpenACC Applications

Khalid Ahmad[1]([✉])[ID] and Michael Wolfe[2]

[1] University of Utah, Salt Lake City, UT, USA
Khalid@cs.utah.edu
[2] NVIDIA/PGI, Beaverton, OR, USA
mwolfe@nvidia.com

Abstract. PCAST (PGI Compiler-Assisted Software Testing) is a feature being developed in the PGI compilers and runtime to help users automate testing high performance numerical programs. PCAST normally works by running a known working version of a program and saving intermediate results to a reference file, then running a test version of a program and comparing the intermediate results against the reference file. Here, we describe the special case of using PCAST on OpenACC programs running on a GPU-accelerated system. Instead of saving to and comparing against a reference file, the compiler generates code to run each compute region on both the host CPU and the GPU. The values computed on the host and GPU are then compared, using OpenACC data directives and clauses to decide what data to compare.

Keywords: Program testing · Relative debugging · Reproducibility
OpenACC · GPU

1 Introduction

Porting an application to another processor, or adding parallel algorithms, or even enabling new optimizations can create challenges for testing. The goal may be to get higher performance, but the programmer must also test that the computed answers are still accurate. While essentially all processors use the same IEEE floating point representation, not all will support the same features, such as FMA (fused multiple-add) operations. Different processors, different algorithms, different programs implementing the same algorithm, or different compiler optimizations on the same program can generate a different sequence of operations, producing different floating point roundoff behavior. To validate an updated program may require identifying at which point in the program the results start to diverge and determining if the divergence is significant. We are developing a feature in the PGI compilers and runtime called PGI Compiler-Assisted Software Testing or PCAST. The programmer adds PCAST runtime calls or directives to a working program to save a sequence of intermediate results to a reference file. The same runtime calls or directives in the updated or ported program will then compare the sequence of intermediate results to those in the reference file.

© Springer International Publishing AG, part of Springer Nature 2018
S. Chandrasekaran and G. Juckeland (Eds.): WACCPD 2017, LNCS 10732, pp. 145–159, 2018.
https://doi.org/10.1007/978-3-319-74896-2_8

Porting an application to an accelerator, like a GPU, has even more challenges for testing. With an accelerator, some (perhaps most) of the computations are done on a processor with a different instruction set, a different set of floating point units, and different numerical libraries. It's enough of a problem to test that a port of an application to a new processor is correct, or that enabling a new optimization still produces correct answers, but adding the complexity of using an accelerator for part of the computation exacerbates that even more. Here, we describe the *OpenACC autocompare* feature of PCAST for the special case of testing an OpenACC [1] program that targets GPU parallel execution. The goal is to determine just where the computation starts to go bad. A difference may be due to the same problems that arise when porting to any new processor, or changing optimizations, or running in parallel. However, the difference may also be due to the unique behavior of accelerated applications, such as stale data on the device because of missing data *update* operations.

Our PCAST autocompare implementation executes the parallel kernels on the CPU as well as on the GPU in a single run, and then compares the two results. The user can set options such as floating point tolerances, choosing what to report, and how to proceed if there are differences. For instance, the user can choose to stop the program after n differences or to replace the bad results with the known good values and continue.

The next section describes some of the problems that arise when porting or optimizing an application, the specific problems of testing application ports to a GPU, and the usage cases that the OpenACC autocompare feature is intended to support. Section 3 describes the OpenACC autocompare feature in more detail, including how to use it and other details. Section 4 gives some details of the implementation. Section 5 gives measurements of the overhead of the autocompare feature. Section 6 describes related work. Section 7 describes work in progress, and the final section summarizes the motivation behind the autocompare feature.

2   Testing a GPU Port of a Numerical Application

The general problem is to test whether changes to a numerical application generate different answers. Since these are typically floating point applications, the meaning of *different* depends on the precision needed. Since all processors now use IEEE floating point arithmetic [2], many programmers expect that moving a program to another processor or changing optimizations should produce exactly the same answer. Even with the same floating point representation, different compilers and libraries (even on the same processor) can give different results, for many well-known reasons, including:

- Different optimizations (changing a/5.0 into a*0.2), or
- Presence or absence of FMA operations on the original or new processor, or different FMA association $((a * b) + (c * d)$ treated as $fma(a, b, c * d)$ or $fma(c, d, a * b))$.
- Different transcendentals (different implementations of exp, sin, sqrt), or
- For parallel programs, different order of operations, specifically for reductions (sums).

A good testing scheme must test for significant differences, but allow for and ignore insignificant differences, as long as the final result is accurate.

The test should determine not only that there are differences, but also identify where the differences are introduced. Thus, the testing process should compare intermediate results as well as the final result. There is also the problem of what to do when an error is found. It could be treated the same as a floating point exception, giving an error message and terminating the program. Another option is to report the error and continue, perhaps allowing identification of more errors, with perhaps a limit on the number of errors reported. A third option is to replace the erroneous values with the known correct values before continuing.

The specific problem addressed here is to test whether porting a numerical application to a GPU-accelerated system generates different answers than the host execution. When debugging OpenACC programs targeting GPUs, we have additional problems as well as an important advantage. The problems include using two different processors in the same application, and managing data traffic and coherence between the system memory and the GPU device memory. The important advantage is that we have two processors, so we can create the reference values on the CPU while the GPU is executing, and we have separate memories for the CPU and GPU, so we have a place to store the reference values and the test values.

3   Autocompare with OpenACC

The PCAST OpenACC autocompare feature works by executing each OpenACC compute kernel on both the GPU and the host CPU. This keeps the values in system memory in sync with the values in GPU device memory, assuming the same computation is done correctly on each. Figure 1 illustrates the flow of regular OpenACC program with and without turning on the PCAST autocompare option. The computationally intensive part of the illustration can consist of more than one single kernel.

The next, equally important step is to compare the computed values on the CPU with those on the GPU. We assume that the CPU values are the reference values, and the GPU values are the ones being tested. Ideally, we would compare only the data that was changed in a compute construct. In small sample programs, this is easy to automatically determine, but in general this is not feasible. Instead, we studied several options for choosing what values to compare between host and device, and at what point to do the compare.

1. The runtime could compare all the data in GPU memory to the corresponding CPU memory after each kernel launch. This is feasible, but likely to be prohibitively expensive. Large applications can fill the 16 GB device memory (on an NVIDIA Pascal GPU), and bringing that much data back and comparing it after each kernel launch would be very expensive. However, it would certainly be able to identify the specific kernel where results start to diverge.

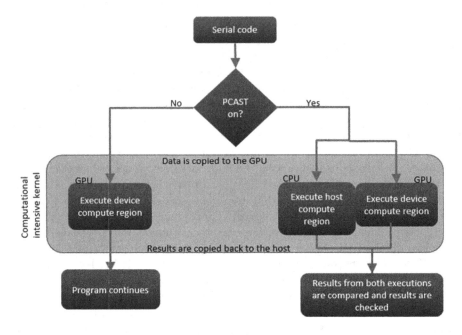

Fig. 1. An overview of the autocompare functionality.

2. The runtime could compare data only at the end of a compute construct, and only data that is either in an explicit data clause or is explicitly referenced in the construct. This is less costly than comparing all data, but it could miss updated global data that is modified only in routines called from the compute construct.

3. The runtime could compare data only at the end of a compute construct, and only that data in an explicit data clause on that compute construct (not data implicitly copied to the GPU, or in a clause for an outer data construct). This is even less costly, and only compares data that the programmer thought important enough to include in a data clause.

4. The runtime could compare data only at the end of a data region, and only the data in explicit data clauses. This is likely to be less costly because a data region typically contains many compute constructs, such as an outer loop that contains a compute construct. However it is less precise about identifying which particular compute construct caused the divergence.

5. The runtime could compare data when it would otherwise be copied back to the host. This would be at the end of a compute or data construct, or at an OpenACC *update* directive. Since the data is already being copied to the host, the only overhead is the actual compare. This method would be even less precise about identifying where the divergent computations occurred.

6. Finally, the runtime could leave the choice to the user. This would allow the user to insert a runtime call or a directive that tells the runtime when to compare data, and what data to compare. We considered two options: one

where the user chose one or more variables or arrays to compare, and a second where the user asks the runtime to compare all variables and arrays present in device memory to the corresponding host memory locations.

In all cases, since the same computations are done on the CPU as well as the GPU, the OpenACC runtime must allow for this and not do any actual data downloads from the device memory to host memory. This means *update host* directives and *copyout* actions from data directives should not update the host values.

There are errors that the PCAST OpenACC autocompare feature can not detect. In particular, since the compare point requires synchronization with the device, any errors due to misplaced or erroneous *async* clauses, or missing *wait* directives or clauses may be hidden. Also, OpenACC has features that allow different computations on the host as on the device, to allow for different algorithmic formulations that are more appropriate for each processor. Such a feature can allow for programming mistakes that are hard to detect. Again, the goal is to detect numeric computational differences between two executions, not to find all errors.

4 Autocompare Implementation

The PCAST OpenACC autocompare feature is enabled with a command line option. When enabled, the compiler generates code for each parallel construct for both the CPU and the GPU. During execution, the program launches the compute region onto the GPU; while the GPU code is running the program executes the corresponding code on the CPU. OpenACC programs have directives to tell the compiler what loops to run in parallel on the GPU (*compute constructs*), and what data to copy to the device and when to update data between device and host (*data constructs*). The PCAST OpenACC autocompare feature uses these directives, along with a table in the OpenACC runtime that keeps track of the correspondence between host and device data, to select what data to compare.

The implementation of OpenACC autocompare is split between our OpenACC compiler and the OpenACC runtime. Most of the compiler work was to enable redundant execution of compute constructs on both the host and device. Our implementation already had the capability of generating code for both host and device and selecting which to execute. We modified that capability so that instead of selecting whether to launch a device kernel or run the host code, it would do both. Currently, the CPU code runs sequentially on one CPU thread.

The compiler already inserted runtime calls for any explicit and implicit data clauses. In the example program shown in Listing 1, these calls are inserted at entry to the data construct at line 4 and the exit from that construct at line 11. In redundant execution mode, these runtime calls follow both the device kernel launch and the host redundant execution. That allowed us to repurpose those runtime calls to do the data compare. The compiler sets two flags in the runtime call, one to tell the runtime that it is in redundant mode and should not actually update host values, and a second to tell the runtime to compare values.

```
void vectorSinGPU(double *A, double *C, uint32_t N)
{
    // Ensure the data is available on the device
    #pragma acc data copyin(A[0:N]) copyout(C[0:N])
    {
        // Compute construct
        #pragma acc kernels loop independent \
                            present(A[0:N],C[0:N])
        for (int i = 0; i < N; i++) {
            C[i] = fsin(A[i]);
        }
    }
}
```

Listing 1. Sample OpenACC loop.

By default, our initial implementation will compare values that appear in a *copy* or *copyout* data clauses (explicitly or implicitly), or an *update host* directive. For the code in Listing 1, the values for **C** would be compared at the exit of the data construct at line 11, but not the values for **A** because **A** is **copyin** only. We have also implemented two runtime routines that will compare host and device values for specific variables or arrays, or for all data present on the device. We have an option to enable redundant execution but disable the automatic comparisons, for when the user adds those runtime routine calls.

Our OpenACC autocompare implementation uses essentially six routines in the OpenACC runtime. The runtime routines use the *present table* [3] maintained by the OpenACC runtime. Our implementation of the *present table* saves the variable or array name, its host address, the corresponding device address, the data type, and its length.

- The **uacc_compare_contiguous** routine is given a host array section descriptor. This descriptor is generated by the compiler for the data directives. This routine finds contiguous blocks of memory in the array section and calls the **uacc_compare** routine on each.
- The **uacc_compare** routine is given the start and end address of a block of host memory. This is the workhorse of the autocompare feature:
  - It finds that block of memory in the *present table*, which gives the corresponding device address and the data type.
  - It allocates temporary host memory for that data.
  - It downloads the data from device memory to the temporary memory.
  - It calls the **pgi_compare** routine to do the actual compare operation.
- The **pgi_compare** routine is part of the more general PCAST runtime. For each block of memory, it first does a fast **memcmp** to see if the two blocks are exactly the same. If not, it does a type-specific compare operation for each element, using the appropriate tolerances.

- The user-callable **acc_compare** routine is passed the host address of one array that is also present on the device. This routine calls **uacc_compare** routine for that block of memory.
- The user-callable **acc_compare_all** routine has no arguments. It walks the entire *present table* to find all blocks of memory that are also present on the device, and calls **uacc_compare** on each block.
- The **pgi_compare_error** routine is called when **pgi_compare** detects an untolerated difference. This is merely a convenient place for the user to set a breakpoint in a debugger, when trying to find what is going wrong.

Table 1. Options that can appear in the **PGI_COMPARE** environment variable.

Option	Description
abs=r	Use 10^{-r} as an absolute tolerance
rel=r	Use 10^{-r} as a relative tolerance
report=n	Report first n differences
skip=n	Skip the first n differences
patch	Patch erroneous values with correct values
stop	Stop after **report=** differences
summary	Print a summary of the comparisons and differences found at program exit

The user can set various options using the **PGI_COMPARE** environment variable. The user can set an *absolute tolerance* or *relative tolerance* for floating point comparisons. The user can select report options, such as to only report the first n differences, or to skip the first n differences. Finally, the user can select the action to take when the report limit is exceeded: to stop execution, continue execution, or to patch the bad results and then continue. In our implementation, patching the values means updating the device locations with the host values. The **PGI_COMPARE** environment variable contains a comma-separated list of options; see Table 1 for details.

An example of the **summary** option is shown in Listing 2. This feature was used to generate the results in the next section.

```
compared 202 blocks, 3388997632 elements, 13555990528 bytes
1488912980 errors tolerated in 201 blocks
  relative tolerance = 0.000100, rel=4
```

Listing 2. Summary option output for one of the benchmark programs.

Some of the advantages of our implementation, or any similar implementation, are:

- The autocompare feature could be used on any OpenACC target device that has separate memory, such as AMD GPUs. The only GPU supported by the current PGI compilers are NVIDIA GPUs, so that is what we report on in the next section.
- If the OpenACC compute constructs are being run on multiple CPUs with MPI parallelism, the autocompare feature will work independently on each CPU. Each CPU will launch its compute construct to the GPU and run that compute on the CPU as well, and do its comparisons independently. The current implementation does not try to separate the reports from different MPI ranks or combine the summaries.
- If the OpenACC compute constructs are being run on multiple cores with OpenMP parallelism, the autocompare feature will work independently on each thread, as with MPI. The difference is that when two OpenMP threads launch work to the same GPU, they share data on that GPU as well. There can be data races on the GPU due to the OpenMP parallelism, which may be exposed with the autocompare feature, but we make no claims to be able to identify or isolate such data races.
- The normal PCAST feature uses extra API calls or directives to designate what data to compare. The autocompare feature uses already-existing OpenACC data directives and clauses, so no extra programming work is needed.
- The normal PCAST feature saves the data to be compared in a file, then rereads that file when doing the compare step. Those files can grow quite large. The autocompare feature doesn't save the data, it generates the data during execution. This makes it feasible to compare more data more frequently.

Some of the disadvantages are:

- The CPU code is run sequentially on a single core. Ideally, this code could be parallelized as well. The biggest difference between parallelized and unparallelized code has to do with different order of reduction operations, which will produce different results that might not be within the acceptable tolerance specified by the application developer.
- This implementation requires separate memories for the accelerator device. Some accelerators share memory with the CPU, and NVIDIA GPUs in particular are moving in that direction. Supporting an autocompare feature with shared memory would require:
  - Identifying all data that might be modified in the compute region, including global data.
  - Saving the original values of data that might be modified.
  - Running the compute region on one target (the GPU, say).
  - Saving the potentially modified data in separate space, and restoring the original values of the modified data. A clever implementation could reuse the same memory for both purposes, and swap the values.
  - Running the compute region on the other target (the CPU, say).
  - Comparing the two modified copies of the data.
  The first step is critical and must be conservative. If the first target modifies some data and it is not restored before the second target executes, the second

target is starting with bad data and could give bad results. Unfortunately, the first step is also extremely difficult in general, and beyond the capability of a commercial product compiler. Because of this, doing an autocompare implementation between a sequential and parallel execution of the same compute region on the same processor is difficult. The normal PCAST feature can be used to handle such a problem.

- The autocompare feature may find where the GPU computes a different value, but it doesn't identify or isolate why the value is different. The user would like to know, for instance, whether the GPU is using a different implementation of an math routine, or if the compiler applied some optimization to one target and not the other. In particular, the user would like to know if there are program changes or command-line options to select or force the results to be the same. Currently, we have no solution for these questions.
- Our current implementation handles variables and arrays of basic data types (integer, floating point, complex), but not C++ structs or Fortran derived types; this is left for future work.

5   Experiments

We have measured the overhead of the PCAST OpenACC autocompare implementation to demonstrate its usability. We used ten of the SPEC ACCEL v1.2 benchmarks, using the *test* dataset. In each case, the program has an outer time step loop containing the main computation. The times shown are in seconds, and these are officially SPEC *estimates*, since they were not run in the SPEC harness. The host machine was a dual socket 16-core Intel Haswell (E5-2698 Xeon, 32-cores total) with a 2.30 GHz clock, with an NVIDIA Tesla Pascal P100 GPU. We used the default autocompare options, but set a relative tolerance. The execution times are in seconds, measured with /usr/bin/time. The values shown in Table 2 are:

- Time to run the test data set sequentially on the CPU.
- Time to run the test data set in parallel on the GPU.
- Time to run the test data set redundantly on both CPU and GPU without the autocompare feature enabled.
- Time to copy the data from GPU to CPU before comparing, measured by nvprof.
- Time to run the test data set redundantly on both CPU and GPU using the autocompare feature.

Figure 2 breaks down the time spent in the autocompare run into:

- Compute Time: the max of the CPU time and GPU time from Table 2.
- Redundancy Overhead: the difference between the redundant execution time from Table 2 and Compute Time.
- Download Time: the time spent downloading data as measured using nvprof.

Table 2. Results showing overhead of the PCAST OpenACC autocompare feature.

Benchmark	CPU time (sequential)	GPU time	Redundant execution on CPU and GPU	CPU to GPU data copy time	Autocompare time
ostencil	3.51 s	1.82 s	4.22 s	1.03 s	17.19 s
olbm	2.19 s	1.30 s	3.03 s	0.96 s	19.09 s
omriq	1.49 s	0.88 s	2.05 s	0.03 s	2.08 s
palm	2.75 s	1.45 s	3.75 s	0.50 s	15.75 s
ep	2.50 s	0.98 s	3.19 s	0.11 s	3.21 s
miniGhost	0.87 s	1.07 s	1.69 s	1.23 s	13.17 s
cg	62.98 s	28.74 s	64.86 s	0.28 s	68.43 s
csp	2.78 s	1.20 s	3.64 s	26.69 s	309.99 s
ilbdc	160.62 s	2.10 s	160.39 s	27.41 s	615.26 s
bt	5.92 s	1.27 s	7.27 s	9.13 s	119.28 s

- Compare Time: the difference between autocompare time from Table 2 and the sum of the above three times.

The costs of the autocompare feature are running the compute region on both CPU and GPU, and downloading and comparing the values. The cost of redundant execution is less than the sum of the CPU and GPU times, because the GPU code executes asynchronously while the CPU executes the corresponding code. Since this is a feature used during code development and debugging, we consider this to be relatively low overhead. The cost of doing the many floating

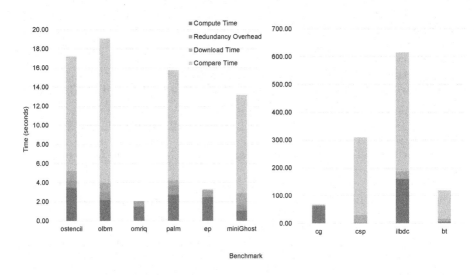

Fig. 2. Results showing overhead of the PCAST OpenACC autocompare feature.

point comparisons is significant, and appears to be directly related to the number of data items compared, and unrelated to the number of arrays or variables being compared. However, using this feature to find where a GPU computation diverges moves the cost from the programmer to the computer, so it could be invaluable regardless of the overhead.

In Table 3 we show some statistics about the benchmarks we used, such as:

- Number of variables or arrays compared.
- Number of data values compared.
- Number of variables or arrays that had some differences.
- Number of data values that were different.

Table 3. Results showing number of variables and values processed by the PCAST OpenACC autocompare.

Benchmark	Variables and arrays compared	Values compared	Variables and arrays with differences	Differences tolerated
ostencil	202	3388997632	0	0
olbm	61	586800000	59	520634266
omriq	3	68608	2	53240
palm	31244	1532482935	14784	374679922
ep	4	13	2	2
miniGhost	2506	1844059545	175	175
cg	186	621600195	168	4858272
csp	4057	40132155677	3897	5693059
ilbdc	3001	53818895200	2000	35305830600
bt	5036	15041440200	4798	38931891

An interesting observation we came across was that on all benchmarks we tested it roughly took one second to compare a gigabyte of data as can be seen in Fig. 3. This can be used as a rough estimate of how long it will take to test a code for correctness as long as the user knows the size of the data set being used.

One side note: the *test* datasets used here are relatively small. Even so, we had to set the relative tolerance to avoid the comparisons detecting differences, mostly due to different summation accumulation order. Surprisingly, those differences propagated to about $\frac{1}{3}$ of the results in two of the ten benchmarks that we show here. This implies that the naive approach to reduce the number of values being compared and therefore reducing the runtime cost by computing and comparing a quick checksum or signature before downloading and comparing all the data would frequently have little or no benefit.

6   Related Work

The PCAST OpenACC autocompare feature is similar in some respects to redundant execution strategies, which are typically used to detect failing hardware or erroneous software. The Tandem NonStop computers [4] implemented redundant execution on identical hardware with automatic checking; the system could detect faulty hardware and fail-over to another processor. The NASA Space Shuttle carried five computers [5]; four of these comprised the primary system and ran identical software with a voting protocol to detect a failing computer. If the four primary system computers could not determine a correct result, the fifth backup system was enabled for ascent and landing. The major difference is the autocompare feature assumes that the CPU execution is correct, and it compares the GPU computations to those assumed correct results.

Following in similar footsteps NASA Ames researchers in 2003 developed a debugging tool that utilizes the relative debugging paradigm proposed by Abramson et al. [6,7] to compare between serial and parallel programs generated by tools such as computer aided parallelization tools CAPTools [8], and also compare the results produced from a parallel program generated by openMP and run using different number of threads [9]. Their main goal is finding if there are any inconsistencies between the different executions and finding where the computations begin to diverge. Their approach requires the user to indicate which variable is wrong and where it is wrong in the program. Then the debugger probes the parallelization tool to locate which routines modify the specified variable. Using that information, the debugger inserts comparison calls at the start and end points of the routines. By running the serial and parallel programs

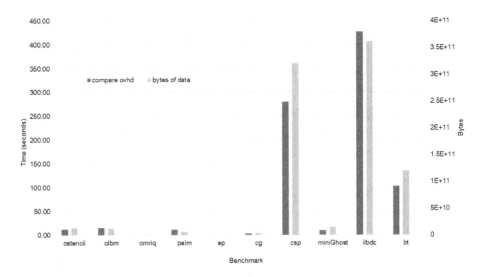

Fig. 3. Results showing amount of data the autocompare feature process per unit time.

side by side, the debugger will be able to locate the cause of the difference to a single subroutine.

The Cray Comparative Debugger (CCDB) [10] which is also based on the relative debugging paradigm which allows a programmer to launch two versions of a program, such as a CPU-only version and a GPU-accelerated version, and to inspect and compare values between the two versions. The programmer can also add breakpoints and have the debugger compare specific values between the two program versions when each reaches the breakpoint. This is perhaps the most aggressive approach to allow value comparisons between two running executions and allows a user to inspect the program when the values diverge, although the comparisons themselves are not performed automatically.

Research using the OpenARC compiler framework [11] has explored several strategies for debugging OpenACC programs [12]. One mechanism is very much like the PCAST autocompare feature, where the compiler generates device code and host sequential code for specific compute regions. The user selects specific compute regions to verify, and the rest of the program is executed sequentially by the host CPU, including other compute regions. All the data is copied from the system memory to the GPU before those selected kernels, and all modified data is copied back and compared afterward. That work allows more fine grain control of which compute regions to compare, but does not allow for a unified framework to run the whole program and compare data after each compute region.

7 Future Work

We are considering future work on the autocompare feature, including:

- Optimizing the comparison operation, since this seems to be the bottleneck for the autocompare feature.
- Ways to reduce the number of values being compared, to reduce the runtime cost.
- Running the compare itself in parallel, and perhaps running the compare code on the GPU itself.
- Some way to isolate regions of the program that are being tested, so as to not require redundant execution and data compares throughout the whole execution.
- Running the host code in parallel as well, for performance, though this assumes that host parallel execution is as accurate and precise as the host sequential execution.
- Adding support for arrays of structs or arrays of derived types, where each field would have a type-specific compare.
- Adding support for nested data structures, where a struct memory is a pointer to another array. The compare function would recurse to compare the nested structure as well.
- Similar to the idea of record and replay [13] we might add support to allow comparisons across runs of the same autocompare and observe if there are any differences between different runs. This reveals if the bug is reproducible or

not, and could potentially help determine whether the problem is more than just a round off error.

- Specifying an arbitrary numerical tolerance through the relative or the absolute tolerance environment variable options may result in missed bugs or spurious false bugs reported, especially when the values are very small. Furthermore, some applications require bitwise equivalent which is a strong requirement and might not be possible especially in non-deterministic applications. A solution would be adding a third environment variable option to the tolerance options suite which would take into account the magnitude of the values and perform the comparisons in a normalized fashion.

8   Conclusion

While directive based GPU programming models improve the productivity of GPU programming, they do not ensure correctness or the absence of logical errors. These programming models usually consist of several compiler optimizations and transformations that are hidden from the programmer. These models improve productivity but unfortunately present challenges to users who must debug and verify program correctness. This work, part of the PCAST feature, can automatically detect numerical differences that can occur due to computational differences on different OpenACC devices. Hence, PCAST can automatically check the correctness of an OpenACC implementation and it can also help to identify bugs in OpenACC data management and computation and support programmers in the development of OpenACC applications.

The overhead incurred due to redundant execution is dominated by the slower execution unit and is relatively small, while the overhead of the compare operation is significant. However, automatic debuggers and correctness checkers always introduce some overhead, and in most cases the total cost is much less than manual investigation.

References

1. The OpenACC Application Programming Interface, Version 2.5 (2016). https://www.openacc.org/sites/default/files/inline-files/OpenACC_2pt5.pdf
2. Goldberg, D.: What every computer scientist should know about floating-point arithmetic. ACM Comput. Surv. **23**(1), 5–47 (1991)
3. Wolfe, M., Lee, S., Kim, J., Tian, X., Xu, R., Chandrasekaran, S., Chapman, B.: Implementing the OpenACC data model. In: Parallel and Distributed Processing Symposium Workshops, Lake Buena Vista, Fla., pp. 662–672, May 2017
4. Bartlett, J., Gray, J., Horst, B.: Fault Tolerance in Tandem Computer Systems, Tandem Computers, Cal., Technical report 86.2, March 1986
5. Fraser, D.C., Felleman, P.G.: Digital fly-by-wire computers lead the way. Astronaut. Aeronaut. **12**, 24–32 (1974)
6. Abramson, D.A., Sosic, R.: Relative debugging: a new debugging paradigm. School of Computing and Information Technology, Faculty of Science and Technology, Griffith University (1994)

7. Abramson, D., Foster, I., Michalakes, J., Sosič, R.: Relative debugging: a new methodology for debugging scientific applications. Commun. ACM **39**(11), 69–77 (1996)
8. Jost, G., Hood, R.: Relative debugging of automatically parallelized programs. Autom. Softw. Eng. **10**(1), 75–101 (2003)
9. Matthews, G., Hood, R., Jin, H., Johnson, S., Ierotheou, C., et al.: Automatic relative debugging of OpenMP programs. In: Proceedings of EWOMP, Aachen, Germany (2003)
10. DeRose, L., Gontarek, A., Vose, A., Moench, R., Abramson, D., Dinh, M.N., Jin, C.: Relative debugging for a highly parallel hybrid computer system. In: Proceedings of the International Conference for High Performance Computing, Networking, Storage and Analysis, SC 2015, November 2015
11. Lee, S., Vetter, J.S.: OpenARC: open accelerator research compiler for directive-based, efficient heterogeneous computing. In: Proceedings of the 23rd International Symposium on High-performance Parallel and Distributed Computing, pp. 115–120, June 2014
12. Lee, S., Le, D., Vetter, J.S.: Interactive programming debugging and optimization for directive-based, efficient GPU computing. In: Proceedings of the 28th International Parallel and Distributed Processing Symposium, May 2014
13. Sato, K., Ahn, D.H., Laguna, I., Lee, G.L., Schulz, M.: Clock delta compression for scalable order-replay of non-deterministic parallel applications. In: International Conference for High Performance Computing, Networking, Storage and Analysis, SC 2015, pp. 1–12. IEEE (2015)

Evaluation of Asynchronous Offloading Capabilities of Accelerator Programming Models for Multiple Devices

Jonas Hahnfeld[1,2(✉)], Christian Terboven[1,2(✉)], James Price[3],
Hans Joachim Pflug[2], and Matthias S. Müller[1,2]

[1] JARA–HPC, Chair for High Performance Computing, RWTH Aachen University,
52074 Aachen, Germany
[2] IT Center, RWTH Aachen University, 52074 Aachen, Germany
{hahnfeld,terboven,pflug,mueller}@itc.rwth-aachen.de
[3] Department of Computer Science, University of Bristol, Bristol, UK
j.price@bristol.ac.uk

Abstract. Accelerator devices are increasingly used to build large supercomputers and current installations usually include more than one accelerator per system node. To keep all devices busy, kernels have to be executed concurrently which can be achieved via asynchronous kernel launches. This work compares the performance for an implementation of the Conjugate Gradient method with CUDA, OpenCL, and OpenACC on NVIDIA Pascal GPUs. Furthermore, it takes a look at Intel Xeon Phi coprocessors when programmed with OpenCL and OpenMP. In doing so, it tries to answer the question of whether the higher abstraction level of directive based models is inferior to lower level paradigms in terms of performance.

1 Introduction

The community of high performance computing has a constant demand for larger supercomputers. At the same time, data centers need to limit their power consumption which has become a significant cost factor. To fulfill these conflicting requirements, new installations often make use of specialized accelerators. They promise high computing power for certain important tasks, for example in the field of linear algebra. This is paired with a high performance per watt ratio.

However, this advantage comes at the cost of programmability which differs for heterogeneous systems. Because the accelerators evaluated in this work are part of a host system, they require some form of offloading. This adds the necessity to explicitly transfer data and launch kernels on the device. Multiple programming models currently compete to ease the programmability and increase the developer's productivity.

The first programming models for accelerators such as CUDA and OpenCL are based on API functions. They require the kernel functions to be rewritten with extensions of the C or C++ programming language. More recently, directive

© Springer International Publishing AG, part of Springer Nature 2018
S. Chandrasekaran and G. Juckeland (Eds.): WACCPD 2017, LNCS 10732, pp. 160–182, 2018.
https://doi.org/10.1007/978-3-319-74896-2_9

based models enable offloading to be achieved by annotating the serial source code. Based on the information given by the user, the compiler takes the task to transform the code. For use with accelerators, offloading capabilities are offered by OpenACC and OpenMP since version 4.0.

Recent systems typically include multiple accelerators per node. This requires the host to distribute the work to the accelerators and synchronize their computations. For performance reasons, developers might employ asynchronous offloading on such setups. This means that the host thread is not blocked while an operation is running on the device. As a first step, this permits computations to start concurrently on multiple accelerators from a single (application) thread. However, it may also be used to overlap computation with the communication. This promises to lower the overhead of transferring data between the devices or with the host.

Asynchronous execution of kernels and data transfers can be used in many of the available programming models. However, the achievable performance differs and depends on the quality of implementation. For example, the operations in the background have to be scheduled efficiently. This implies some overhead that may degrade the overall performance of an application.

The remainder of this paper is structured as follows: Sect. 2 will look at related work for comparing programming models. We give an overview on the evaluated accelerator programming models and the used CG implementation in Sects. 3 and 4. In Sect. 5, we discuss the performance results on NVIDIA GPUs while Sect. 6 focuses on Intel Xeon Phi coprocessors. In the end, we will summarize our findings in Sect. 7. The work presented in this paper has been part of a bachelor thesis [12].

2   Related Work

There has been much research in the field of comparing accelerator programming models. Wienke et al. [29] looked at the Total Cost of Ownership (TCO) when using accelerators. As a key point, the developer has to spend a significant amount of time on porting and tuning. This situation is improved with directive based models such as OpenACC that offer a higher level of abstraction. Another work compares the programmability of the models for common patterns [30].

Hoshino et al. [16] examined the general performance of CUDA and OpenACC on NVIDIA GPUs. A comparison of OpenCL and OpenMP on Intel Xeon Phi coprocessors has been performed by Vinogradov et al. [28]. In contrast, we will evaluate the performance for asynchronous offloading as needed for multiple devices. Early work on support for multiple accelerators has been performed by Yan et al. [33] who proposed extensions to OpenMP. We will focus on the evaluation of multiple programming models and compare the performance of directive-based models with that of low-level standards.

Multiple accelerators can also be programmed by using MPI: In that case, each MPI rank offloads its work to a single GPU. This technique has been used by Meng et al. [22] for Intel Xeon Phi coprocessors on Stampede. Boku et al. [8] have evaluated the CCS QCD Benchmark for multiple nodes with two coprocessors each. Bernaschi et al. [7] have compared the performance of the coprocessors with that of NVIDIA Kepler GPUs.

For GPUs, Jo et al. [18] have presented an MPI-OpenCL implementation of LINPACK. Mu et al. [23] used multiple GPUs with MPI and CUDA to accelerate the discontinuous Galerkin method. The one-sided factorization algorithms of MAGMA have been extended for multiple GPUs by Yamazaki et al. [32]. Abraham et al. [2] describe the performance of GROMACS for heterogeneous systems.

Lawlor proposes CudaMPI with an interface for GPU-to-GPU communication [20] while Stuart et al. implemented DCGN [25]. Later, Stuart et al. [26] proposed an extension of "MPI with Accelerators" (MPIWA). Finally, Aji et al. [3] presented MPI-ACC and integrated it with CUDA and OpenCL. Further research focussed on higher abstraction levels with runtime systems. StarPU by Augonnet et al. [5] and Unicorn by Beri et al. [6] schedule a graph of tasks on nodes to use multiple accelerators. Quintana-Ortí et al. [24] solve dense linear algebra systems using the runtime system SuperMatrix. Krieder et al. [19] implemented GeMTC for many-task computing on GPUs. They use Swift/T [31] to make use of multiple accelerators.

3 Accelerator Programming Models

This section briefly reviews the programming models that were evaluated in this paper and highlights their support for asynchronicity and memory management.

3.1 CUDA

NVIDIA presented their Compute Unified Device Architecture (CUDA) in 2006 as the first programming model fully aimed at running scientific computations on GPUs. In CUDA, kernels are written as functions with extensions to the C++ language and API functions are available to launch the kernels and specify the number of parallel executions. By default, these launches are asynchronous and do not block the host thread.

Asynchronicity in CUDA is built on the concept of so-called streams. Each action is queued to one stream and actions in multiple streams can execute concurrently. The API exposes functions to either synchronize a single stream or all streams associated with a device.

Memory buffers are managed via the functions cudaMalloc and cudaFree, data is transferred by calling cudaMemcpy. Data transfers usually block the host thread until the operation has finished. Thus, another function cudaMemcpyAsync is available which also accepts a stream for the asynchronous transfer.

CUDA also supports the allocation of page-locked memory on the host via the cudaMallocHost function. The performance impact on transfers with the device will be explained in detail in Sect. 5.1.

3.2 OpenCL

The first version of the Open Computing Language (OpenCL) was introduced in December 2008 by the Khronos Group, which is also responsible for OpenGL and Vulkan. As a multi-vendor organization, standards by the Khronos Group are portable across hardware from different vendors.

Asynchronicity in OpenCL is built on the concept of so-called command queues. Similarly to streams in CUDA, operations in different queues can be executed concurrently. Again, the kernels are executed asynchronously by default. The API provides functions to wait until all operations in a queue have finished.

Buffers on the device are handled via opaque `cl_mem` objects. As with the kernels, transfers to the device and back to the host have to be added to a command queue. The argument `blocking_write` determines if the data movement will be executed asynchronously. The function `clEnqueueCopyBuffer` may be used to transfer data between two devices.

Version 2.0 of the OpenCL standard introduced the ability to allocate *shared virtual memory* that is available to the host and its devices. While this work will not focus on sharing pointers, Sect. 5.1 will discuss the impact on the bandwidth of data transfers.

3.3 OpenACC

OpenACC is a directive based programming model used for offloading to accelerator devices. The annotations describe how the compiler shall exploit the parallelism in the code. It was first published in a joint effort by NVIDIA, Cray, PGI, and CAPS in November 2011.

Data transfers are controlled via data clauses that are added to the directives. With this information, the runtime takes care of necessary allocations and mappings of the pointers on host and device. OpenACC also offers so-called `data` regions so that multiple kernel invocations may use the same data without additional transfers. Version 2.0 of OpenACC introduced directives for unstructured data movements.

In OpenACC, by default all operations execute synchronously and block the host thread. However, all constructs except the `data` region accept the `async` clause. Optionally, the programmer may add a nonnegative integer argument which specifies a so-called queue. This concept is once again similar to streams in CUDA so that multiple operations can be executed concurrently. Synchronization can be implemented with the directive `acc wait`. It waits for operations in the queues that may be selected with additional parameters. Otherwise, the directive waits for all queues on the current device.

3.4 OpenMP

The first version of OpenMP (Open Multi-Processing) was released in October 1997. It is maintained by the OpenMP Architecture Review Board that includes representatives from both industry and academia. While it was initially designed for parallel programming on shared memory architectures, OpenMP 4.0 released in June 2013 introduced support for the `target` constructs to program accelerators.

Data transfers in OpenMP are managed with the `map` clause, similar to the data clauses in OpenACC. OpenMP also has constructs to keep data resident on a device, similar to OpenACC: the `target data` region allows multiple `target` constructs to reuse the same data. OpenMP 4.5 added support for unstructured data movements.

Similar to OpenACC, by default all `target` operations block the host thread. Since OpenMP 4.5, kernel invocations with the `target` constructs have been made into implicit tasks, such that blocking the host thread can be circumvented with the optional clause `nowait`. Consequently, asynchronous kernel invocations can be synchronized via the `taskwait` directive in the same way as explicit tasks.

4   Implementing the Conjugate Gradient Method

To evaluate asynchronous offloading, we use an implementation of the Conjugate Gradient (CG) method [15]. It is an iterative solver for linear equation systems $A \cdot \vec{x} = \vec{k}$. The solver is widely used in conjunction with sparse matrices from Partial Differential Equations (PDEs). The concept for multiple devices has been described in previous work [13]. The source code is available on GitHub [11] and a short summary shall be given in the following.

The CG algorithm consists of several vector operations such as `axpy` and `xpay`. In addition, a matrix vector multiplication has to be performed in each iteration. To run on multiple devices, the implementation cuts each vector into parts of equal length. Each device can work on its part independently of the

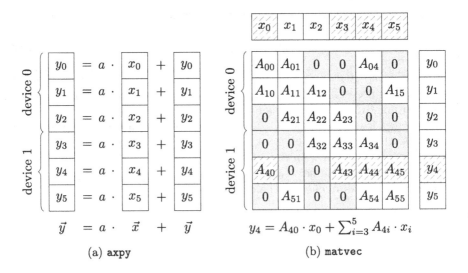

Fig. 1. Concept for executing kernels on multiple devices.

others as seen in Fig. 1a. This is different for the matrix vector multiplication which depends on the full intermediate vector. Figure 1b depicts that x_0 from device 0 is needed for the calculation of y_4 on device 1.

Synchronizing the vector for the matrix vector multiplication creates additional overhead. To limit its impact, we have described how to overlap communication and computation in our previous work [13]: As shown in Fig. 1b, the summation often includes terms that only depend on already local data. In the case of y_4, x_3 to x_5 are the result of previous vector operations on device 1. Therefore, computation with these nonzero elements can be started while the rest of the vector is exchanged with the other devices. This requires an efficient implementation so that the operations execute concurrently.

To obtain correct results when splitting the computation, the implementation needs to ensure that some data transfers have completed before certain kernels can begin executing. The required dependencies are detailed in Fig. 2: Initially, the computation with the local data and the communication can start at the same time. After the intermediate vector $\vec{x}$ has been synchronized, the rest of the computation could start. However, it also needs to wait for the local computation to finish, otherwise it may use values that are still being computed.

If the data is transferred via the host, the implementation needs to order the two phases as seen in Fig. 2a: The data can only be copied to the other device once it has fully arrived on the host. These dependencies are omitted in Fig. 2b as the runtime is responsible for the operation as a whole.

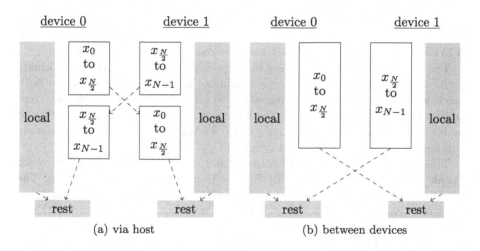

Fig. 2. Dependencies for overlapping the communication with two devices.

For evaluation, we use the Serena matrix from the SuiteSparse Matrix Collection [9]. This matrix has a dimension of 1,391,349 rows by 1,391,349 columns and contains 64,531,701 non-zero elements. The matrix is symmetric and positive definite which fulfills the requirements for the CG method. On the host and on the Intel Xeon Phi coprocessors, the Compressed Row Storage (CRS) format is used to store the sparse matrix. Because only the non-zero elements are stored, the Serena matrix amounts to about 780 MB in memory.

For the GPUs, the matrix is converted to the ELLPACK-R format. As described in [27], this format results in coalesced memory accesses and thus higher performance. Its disadvantage is the increased storage requirement: Each row is padded to the maximum number of non-zero elements in any row. Hence, the Serena matrix consumes roughly 4.16 GB when stored in double precision.

Finally, the right-hand side vector $\vec{k}$ needs to be constructed: In the evaluated implementation, it is chosen so that all elements of the solution vector $\vec{x}$ are equal to 1. This also allows the result to be easily validated once the CG algorithm has terminated. $\vec{k}$ can be obtained by performing the matrix vector multiplication of the original equation $A \cdot \vec{x} = \vec{k}$ with the chosen $\vec{x}$.

5   Performance Results on NVIDIA GPUs

We present performance results for two NVIDIA Tesla P100 GPUs. They are based on the Pascal architecture released in 2016 and consist of 3584 CUDA cores. Each GPU has a theoretical performance of 5.3 TFLOP/s for double precision. Next to each accelerator, there are 16 GB of High Bandwidth Memory 2 (HBM2) with a maximum bandwidth of 732 GB/s. BabelStream [10] measures an achievable bandwidth of 549 GB/s for the `Triad` operation.

The accelerators are plugged into a host with two Intel Xeon E5-2650v4 (Broadwell) processors. PCIe Gen 3 with 16 lanes is used for the communication between the host and the GPUs. This allows for a maximum bandwidth of 15.75 GB/s, out of which 13.19 GB/s can be reached in measurements.

The two GPUs can communicate via a special interconnect, called "NVLink". In the used configuration, it offers a maximum bandwidth of 40 GB/s in both directions. Measurements show that about 37 GB/s can be saturated. The communication between the GPUs is therefore much faster than the connection to the host. This proves to be especially useful for the given algorithm where some data has to be exchanged in each iteration.

The CPUs in the host have 24 cores in total, clocked at 2.20 GHz. They reach a peak performance of 844.8 GFLOP/s for double precision calculations. The four memory controllers have access to 96 GB of main memory. They achieve a memory bandwidth of roughly 120 GB/s as measured with the STREAM benchmark [21].

We will evaluate the programming models CUDA, OpenCL, and OpenACC. In addition to NVIDIA's proprietary OpenCL implementation, we will also present results for the Portable Computing Language (*pocl*) [17]. Table 1 details the software used for the measurements. For all presented performance numbers, the same kernel driver at version 375.39 was used. Each test was executed 10 times and the average runtime is listed. This is not the case for the number of iterations until convergence: That is because it does not vary between multiple runs for the same configuration.

Table 1. Software used for the measurements on NVIDIA GPUs.

Programming model	Software stack
CUDA	GCC 4.8.5 + CUDA 8.0.44
OpenCL	GCC 4.8.5 + CUDA 8.0.44
pocl	LLVM 4.0.1 + development version of *pocl*
OpenACC	PGI Accelerator Compiler 17.4

The "Total Runtime" allows for a fair comparison between the host, a single device and later results where both devices are used. Besides the solve time with the algorithm itself, it consists of other necessary operations: This includes the time to convert the input matrix, its transfer to the device as well as the copy of the solution back to the host.

5.1 Data Transfers with the Host

The time for data transfers with the host will be used later in the performance model. In most cases, the bandwidth is not equal to the maximum that was described above. As one example, the data transfers may be too small to saturate the full bandwidth. Other factors also affect the achievable throughput. Hence, this section examines the bandwidth for the transfer sizes that will be found later in the evaluation of the implemented CG method.

Transferring data over PCIe is implemented using Direct Memory Access (DMA). This means that the hardware directly accesses the main memory via physical addresses. The CPU has to ensure that the data at these physical addresses is not changed in the course of an operation. However, the user space works with virtual addresses that the operating system maps to physical memory. This is why the transfer buffers have to be "page-locked", which is often also called "pinned". With this information, the operating system may not alter the mapping between virtual and physical addresses. This satisfies the aforementioned requirement that the data at a physical address may not change.

In the normal case, this feature is not needed for an application. As a result, memory returned by calls to `malloc` and other functions is "pageable" by default. If such memory shall be used for a data transfer, its content must first be copied to a temporary buffer which is page-locked. This happens transparently by the CUDA software stack that the other programming models also build upon. These copy operations in main memory are responsible for some overhead.

For that reason, the application may choose to explicitly use page-locked memory via special functions. In CUDA, page-locked memory can be allocated with a call to the function `cudaMallocHost`. OpenCL 2.0 introduced `clSVMAlloc` which is implemented in *pocl* to return such memory. With the PGI compiler and OpenACC, there is a command line option `-ta=tesla:pinned` which pins all dynamically allocated memory.

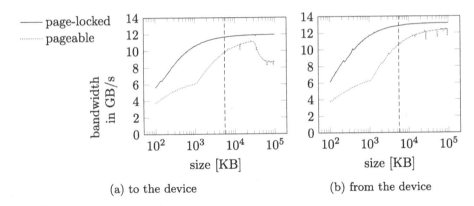

Fig. 3. Bandwidths with page-locked and pageable memory on an NVIDIA Tesla P100.

Figure 3 shows the achieved bandwidths for different sizes on the logarithmically scaled x-axis. The continuous line shows the performance of page-locked memory with CUDA while the dotted one uses pageable memory. As depicted, the page-locked memory is faster for all shown sizes. However, the pageable memory is able to catch up for larger transfers. There is currently no explanation for the drop in bandwidth for transfers to the device for sizes larger than 32 MB. The same behavior can be seen for older GPUs in [4] which does not include a detailed analysis either.

Table 2. Bandwidths and timings for transferring 5.57 MB to and from an NVIDIA Tesla P100.

	To the device		From the device	
	Bandwidth	Time	Bandwidth	Time
Pageable	9.83 GB/s	0.57 ms	10.52 GB/s	0.53 ms
Page-locked	11.68 GB/s	0.48 ms	12.85 GB/s	0.43 ms
pocl	10.97 GB/s	0.51 ms	11.74 GB/s	0.47 ms

In later sections, arrays with a size of $\frac{1391349}{2} \cdot 8\,\mathrm{B} \approx 5.57\,\mathrm{MB}$ are exchanged between the two devices. The corresponding size has been marked with a dashed line in Fig. 3. The extracted bandwidths and timings for CUDA are listed in Table 2. More tests have shown that OpenACC performs similar in the case of pinned memory. *pocl* introduces additional overhead that is accounted for in the last row. If not noted otherwise, we will make use of page-locked memory for the vector that is synchronized in each iteration.

5.2 Single Device

In order to better judge the later results, the following section discusses the performance with only a single device. This also serves as a base comparison between the programming models without the use of asynchronicity. In addition, the performance of the host is presented without any accelerator at all. Here, we use version 17.0.4 of the Intel C++ Compiler and OpenMP on all cores.

Table 3. Measured results on the host and on a single NVIDIA Tesla P100.

	matvec (GFLOP/s)	Vector dot products	Iterations	Total runtime
Host	7.11 s (17.91)	0.24 s	985	9.17 s
CUDA	1.89 s (67.44)	0.20 s	987	5.15 s
OpenCL	2.23 s (57.23)	0.31 s	986	5.72 s
pocl	2.27 s (56.24)	0.32 s	986	5.78 s
OpenACC	2.23 s (57.22)	0.29 s	989	5.69 s

Table 3 shows that `matvec` is faster with all programming models on the GPU when compared with the host. CUDA is the fastest as the compiler generates better code with an added `pragma unroll 1` that we were unable to reproduce with the other programming models. Despite having to transfer the data over PCIe, the total runtimes are lower on the GPU, too. When comparing the total runtimes, CUDA is the fastest of the evaluated programming models. Besides the faster `matvec`, the largest part of the increased runtimes with OpenCL and OpenACC are spent in the vector dot products. In addition, *pocl* is slightly slower for `matvec` than the other programming models.

Table 3 also reveals that the number of iterations until convergence differs. The reason is again found in the implementation of the reductions for the vector dot products: Because each programming model has a slightly different order of summation, they are subject to other rounding-off errors. As a result, a few more iterations might be needed to reach the termination condition.

To summarize, this section has shown that the programming models can be compared on an NVIDIA Tesla P100. All of them are able to reach roughly the same performance for the time consuming `matvec` kernel with synchronous offloading. However, attention has to be paid for some differences in other areas as described above, such as the transfer over PCIe.

5.3   Two Devices

With the results of a single GPU as a baseline, this section will discuss the performance when using both GPUs together. This gives an indication of the overhead when launching asynchronous kernels on multiple devices. As can be seen below, the performance is unsatisfactory when using a naïve implementation. For that reason, the impact of the overlapping presented in our previous work [13] is discussed as well.

CUDA. For the matrix vector multiplication, the intermediate vector has to be exchanged between the devices. There are multiple possible options which can be implemented in CUDA:

via host. The data can be transferred via the host which involves two successive transfers: First the data is collected in a temporary buffer on the host. Afterwards the data can be distributed to the devices. Finally, the computations that use the complete intermediate vector can begin.

between devices. CUDA also supports direct communication between two devices: A call to `cudaMemcpyAsync` with kind `cudaMemcpyDeviceToDevice` initiates a direct copy of data from one device to the other. Without additional setup, this will use PCIe for the transfer. However, the runtime library may optimize the operation, for example by employing double buffering between the two devices. In the discussed case, this leads to a faster exchange of the intermediate vector.

peer to peer (p2p). In order to make use of the fast NVLink, peer access has to be enabled. This can be done by calls to `cudaDeviceEnablePeerAccess`. Because this function only grants access unidirectionally, this has to be done on both devices.

When using `cudaMemcpyDeviceToDevice`, the resulting operation is inserted to streams for both GPUs. To deal with this behavior, a new stream is created for each device and used for this exchange. This allows the concurrent execution of multiple `cudaMemcpyDeviceToDevice` instances for better performance.

Table 4. Measured results on two NVIDIA Tesla P100 using CUDA.

	Naïve (983 iterations)			Overlapping (988 iterations)		
	`matvec` (GFLOP/s)	Solve time	Total	`matvec` (GFLOP/s)	Solve time	Total
Host	1.91 s (66.52)	2.29 s	4.95 s	1.09 s (116.67)	1.48 s	4.62 s
Device	1.74 s (73.01)	2.12 s	4.77 s	1.09 s (116.72)	1.48 s	4.62 s
p2p	1.16 s (109.18)	1.54 s	4.26 s	1.09 s (117.07)	1.47 s	4.70 s

With these considerations, a naïve version can be implemented for multiple devices. The results for two NVIDIA Tesla P100 devices are presented in the left-hand columns of Table 4. In this case, the time for `matvec` also accounts for synchronizing the intermediate vector. The total runtime of the `matvec` kernel has to be compared to 1.89 s from the previous section: When exchanging the data via the host, the runtime actually increases to 1.91 s.

Hence, it is natural to improve performance by overlapping the communication with computation. This aims to hide the overhead of the vector exchange by starting to work with already local data. The overlapping requires an efficient implementation of concurrent computation and communication. It is therefore a promising case for comparing the programming models.

In our previous work [13], we described a performance projection for the over-lapping. The following formula allows us to estimate the maximum optimization that can be achieved:

$$o_{max} \leq \frac{min(t_{comp}, t_{comm})}{t_{exec}} \tag{1}$$

This model does not incorporate overhead and assumes ideal overlapping. Hence, the difference between prediction and measurement quantifies the effectiveness of the implementation. With that, it allows us to draw a conclusion about the asynchronous capabilities.

In the naïve version, 983 iterations have been executed with 984 calls to the `matvec` kernel. Hence, each iteration spent approximately 1.94 ms for the matrix vector multiplication. In each iteration, the intermediate vector has to be synchronized prior to starting the computation. For that, the devices need to transfer their local part to the host which is then copied to the other device. Hence, the data to transfer amounts in both cases to $d = \frac{1391349}{2} \cdot 8\,\text{B} \approx 5.57\,\text{MB}$.

Based on the measured timings in Table 2, this results in an estimation of $t_{comm} = 0.43\,\text{ms} + 0.48\,\text{ms} = 0.91\,\text{ms}$. Hence, $t_{comp} = t_{exec} - t_{comm} \approx 1.03\,\text{ms}$. Based on formula (1), this leads to an estimated maximum optimization of

$$o_{max} \leq \frac{min(t_{comp}, t_{comm})}{t_{exec}} \approx \frac{min(1.03\,\text{ms}, 0.91\,\text{ms})}{1.94\,\text{ms}} \approx 46.91\%.$$

This means that the time in `matvec` can be reduced by at most 46.91% if com-putation and communication are overlapped.

Besides partitioning the matrix, the computations for `matvec` have to be performed in another stream. This allows the concurrent execution of the local computation and the required communication. In addition, the dependencies between the communication and the computation with the exchanged data needs to be modeled. These are put to practice with events in CUDA that allow us to manually synchronize operations in multiple streams.

The results for `matvec` are shown in the right-hand columns of Table 4. While NVLink was the fastest in the naïve version, this optimization leads to roughly the same performance for all configurations. This matches the projection that the runtime of the optimization depends on the maximum of t_{comp} and t_{comm}. As seen above, since the computation takes longer, the communication is com-pletely hidden. Compared to the naïve version, the overlapping led in all cases to an improved performance. When transferring the data via the host, the real improvement is about 42.93%.

Table 4 also compares the time for solving the equation system. The runtime is lower in all cases thanks to the improvement in `matvec` by overlapping the communication. However, the table also shows that the total runtime increases with this optimization when using NVLink: In this particular case it is not beneficial from an overall point of view.

This slowdown can be explained with the other timings that are accumulated in the total runtime: For an efficient implementation of the optimized `matvec`, the matrix has to be partitioned into sub-matrices. As a result the time for converting increases from 2.37 s to 2.79 s. The implementation also needs to transfer two sparse matrices per device instead of one. This increases the time needed for the transfer to the device from 0.27 s to 0.34 s. Nevertheless, the total runtime is still lower than it is for a single device which was 5.15 s with CUDA.

However, the need to convert the matrix is not typical for a real-world application: It arises from the fact that the input matrix is read from a file for evaluation purposes. In simulations the matrix would be constructed in a previous phase, for example from PDEs. This could be implemented in such a way that the matrix is partitioned on the fly. As a result, this would effectively remove the additional overhead for this optimization.

Table 5. Results using NVIDIA's proprietary OpenCL implementation.

	matvec (GFLOP/s)	Solve time	Total time
Single	2.23 s (57.23)	2.84 s	5.72 s
Naïve	3.27 s (38.98)	3.86 s	6.75 s
Overlapping	2.22 s (57.39)	2.81 s	6.29 s

OpenCL. Table 5 shows the results obtained with NVIDIA's proprietary OpenCL implementation. As it only supports OpenCL 1.2 at the time of writing, it does not have `clSVMAlloc` and cannot make use of page-locked memory. That is why the exchange of the vector in the `matvec` is slower than with CUDA. This increases the time for `matvec` from 2.23 s with a single device to 3.27 s in the naïve version. Although the performance is improved when communication and computation are overlapped, two GPUs are still not able to improve on the runtime of a single one. Unfortunately, a performance bug in the driver results in even worse measurements when the vector is exchanged directly between the devices.

Table 6. Results on two NVIDIA Tesla P100 using *pocl*.

	Naïve (985 iterations)			Overlapping (988 iterations)		
	matvec (GFLOP/s)	Solve time	Total	matvec (GFLOP/s)	Solve time	Total
Host	2.18 s (58.34)	2.75 s	5.44 s	1.25 s (102.09)	1.78 s	5.02 s
Device	2.16 s (58.93)	2.68 s	5.38 s	1.26 s (101.33)	1.85 s	5.11 s

This shortcoming can be solved with an implementation of OpenCL 2.0. Hence, we use the CUDA backend of Portable Computing Language (*pocl*), which we have enhanced to perform well for asynchronous offloading across multiple devices. Each OpenCL command queue now has a non-blocking CUDA stream associated with it, along with background CPU threads to handle command submission and finalization. When a data movement or kernel command is enqueued by the application, it is inserted into an internal buffer and control flow is immediately returned to the host code. A background CPU thread services this buffer, and submits commands to the GPU device via the CUDA driver API. This model allows commands that are submitted to different queues to execute concurrently, which satisfies our requirements for overlapping computation with communication, as well as enabling kernel execution across multiple devices simultaneously. Commands submitted to different queues are synchronized with each other where necessary using CUDA events, avoiding the overheads of using the host CPU to do so. We use pthread condition variables inside the background threads to suspend them while they are waiting to receive commands, in order to maximize the CPU resources available to the application code. These changes have been upstreamed to *pocl* and will be available in the next release.

The left-hand columns of Table 6 present the measured results with the naïve version. Compared to the measurements with CUDA above, the runtimes are higher which was also the case for a single GPU: With *pocl*, `matvec` took 2.18 and 2.16 s while the CUDA version spent 1.91 and 1.74 s, respectively. It also has to be noted that *pocl* currently does not make use of the fast NVLink.

We again use Eq. (1) to first project the improvement of the overlapping. According to Sect. 5.1, $t_{comm} = 0.98$ ms while $t_{exec} \approx 2.21$ ms when exchanging the vector via the host. This results in an estimate of

$$o_{max} \leq \frac{min(t_{comp}, t_{comm})}{t_{exec}} \approx \frac{min(1.23\,\text{ms}, 0.98\,\text{ms})}{2.21\,\text{ms}} \approx 44.34\,\%.$$

Analogous to the streams in CUDA, an additional queue is needed for implementing the overlapping. The results are shown in the right-hand columns of Table 6. As expected, the overlapping decreases the time spent in `matvec`. When transferring data via the host, the runtime drops from 2.18 s to 1.25 s which corresponds to a relative improvement of 42.66 %. Correspondingly, the time for the whole solver and the total runtime decreases as well. These measurements have shown that *pocl* currently performs better for asynchronous offloading than the proprietary implementation.

OpenACC. In its current version, OpenACC does not allow transfers between two devices without the host. Both directives and API routines only operate on the (single) device currently being used. Hence, performance results were only obtained when transferring the data via the host. The measured timings for the naïve version are shown in Fig. 4. Compared to the version with a single GPU, the time for `matvec` decreases from 2.23 s to 2.08 s. As a result, the time for the solver is improved from 2.80 s to 2.63 s.

However, the time needed for transferring the data to the device increases from 0.50 s to 0.91 s. This is because PGI's implementation cannot transfer the matrix data from pageable memory asynchronously. In addition, some issues with the OpenACC runtime currently prevent us from using threads in the application to parallelize the transfer. This is why the total runtime of 6.01 s is higher than with a single GPU (5.69 s).

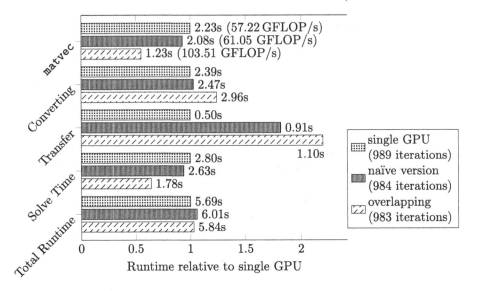

Fig. 4. Results on two NVIDIA Tesla P100 using OpenACC.

To implement the overlapping, the computation has to be launched in a different queue than the communication. Additionally, the dependencies between the operations in the `matvec` kernel must be modeled. Here, the `wait` clause on the `parallel loop` directive seems to be the natural choice: This optional clause specifies queues that the directive should wait on. However, queues are only handled per device and cannot be used to synchronize between multiple devices. Hence, the main thread on the host has to be blocked by one `wait` directive for each device. Afterwards the synchronization is guaranteed and the depending operations can be started.

Analogous to the previous sections, formula (1) allows us to estimate the maximum optimization. Based on the measured timings, it projects an improvement of $o_{max} \leq 43.05\%$. The results are also shown in Fig. 4. The runtime of `matvec` kernel decreases by about 40.87% compared to the naïve version. Hence, the time for the solver is again improved from 2.63 s to 1.78 s while the total runtime is still higher than with a single GPU.

6   Performance Results on Intel Xeon Phi Coprocessors

In this section, we will evaluate two Intel Xeon Phi 5110P coprocessors, code name "Knights Corner". Each coprocessor has 60 cores, clocked at 1.05 GHz, and was released at the end of 2012. With that, it reaches a theoretical performance of roughly 1 TFLOP per second. The coprocessors include 8 GB of memory each which can be accessed at roughly 117 GB/s according to the STREAM benchmark [21].

Each of the two Intel Xeon E5-2650 (SandyBridge) processors in the host has 8 cores which sums up to 16 cores in total. They are clocked at 2.00 GHz and deliver a peak performance of 256 GFLOP/s. The host accesses its 32 GB of main memory at a bandwidth of roughly 65 GB/s, also measured with the STREAM benchmark.

The host and the coprocessors are interconnected via PCIe, generation 2. In measurements, the system saturated roughly 6.53 GB/s when transferring data to or from the device. Compared to the NVIDIA GPUs in the previous section, there is no faster connection between the two accelerators.

Both the host system and the accelerators are significantly older than the setup described in Sect. 5. The presented results should therefore not be directly compared with the previous performance numbers. This section instead provides an evaluation on another architecture with different programming models.

The Intel Xeon Phi coprocessor can be programmed via offloading with OpenCL and OpenMP, amongst others. This section will evaluate the performance of these models as implemented in the Intel C++ Compiler. For OpenCL, we use the latest version 17.0.4. As this version includes a performance regression, we use version 17.0.2 for OpenMP on the coprocessor. The infrastructure is given via the Manycore Platform Software Stack (MPSS) at version 3.8 and the Intel OpenCL SDK, version 14.2. As in the previous section, the average runtime of 10 executions is listed.

6.1   Single Device

In this section, we will first present results for a single device. This allows for a basic comparison between the programming models and their performance without the use of asynchronicity. The achieved performance with the Intel Xeon Phi will also be compared to a version running on the host. We use version 17.0.4 of the Intel C++ Compiler and OpenMP on all cores for the measurement on the CPU.

Table 7. Measured results on the host and on a single Intel Xeon Phi coprocessor.

	matvec (GFLOP/s)	xpay	Vector dot products	Iterations	Total runtime
Host	12.66 s (10.10)	0.22 s	0.48 s	990	15.70 s
OpenCL	12.23 s (10.41)	0.76 s	3.21 s	986	20.77 s
OpenMP	10.34 s (12.27)	1.84 s	5.54 s	983	25.18 s

As seen in Table 7, the coprocessor is faster than the host for the matvec kernel. However, the implementation with OpenMP outperforms the version with OpenCL which is only slightly faster than the host. That is because of the generated instructions in the matvec kernel: In OpenMP, there is the simd directive to assist the compiler in vectorizing the scalar code.

Meanwhile with OpenCL, the developer has to rely fully on the implementation. In the `matvec` kernel, Intel's implementation vectorizes the outer of the two nested loops. This turns out to be even slower than scalar code. We have therefore completely disabled vectorization for the `matvec` kernel for the evaluation of OpenCL.

When looking at the total runtime though, the host defeats the coprocessor with both OpenCL and OpenMP. There are three reasons for this:

1. The data for the computation must be copied to the memory on the coprocessor. This is not necessary for the version running on the host CPUs. The transfer amounts to 0.71 s for OpenCL and 1.01 s with OpenMP.
2. Launching many short kernels creates overhead which is significant in this case. For example, the `xpay` kernel is called once per iteration. The overhead raises the time for all invocations from 0.22 s on the host to 0.76 s with OpenCL. The situation is even worse for OpenMP where 1.84 s are spent for `xpay`.
3. The vector dot product consists of a reduction which requires synchronization. Here, the many cores of the accelerator are slower than the fewer cores in the host CPU. This leads to an increase from 0.48 s to 3.21 s when comparing the host and OpenCL. With OpenMP, the vector dot products take 5.54 s in total.

As in the previous section, the vector dot products are implemented differently for the evaluated programming models. Because of the changed order of summation, the number of iterations until convergence varies for the presented versions. However, this does not account for the increased runtimes explained above. In contrast, the host has to do more iterations than the coprocessor which would suggest a slightly higher runtime.

6.2   Two Devices

This section will discuss the performance when using two coprocessors. The results will be compared to the ones presented above. As in the previous section, we will present the improvement of the overlapping described in our previous work [13]. Together, the achieved performance can be used to draw a conclusion about the overhead for asynchronous offloading.

Table 8. Measured results on two Intel Xeon Phi using OpenCL.

	Naïve (985 iterations)			Overlapping (988 iterations)		
	matvec (GFLOP/s)	Solve time	Total	matvec (GFLOP/s)	Solve time	Total
Host	9.65 s (13.20)	13.99 s	15.28 s	7.08 s (18.06)	11.27 s	13.16 s
Device	9.33 s (13.64)	13.69 s	14.99 s	6.98 s (18.30)	11.18 s	13.08 s

OpenCL. The performance of the naïve version for the `matvec` kernel can be seen in the left-hand columns of Table 8. When employing transfer between the devices, the runtime system improves the data transfer as expected. This results in decreased runtimes as already seen with CUDA for GPUs in the previous section. Compared to a single coprocessor, the runtime drops from 12.23 s to 9.65 and 9.33 s, respectively.

The measured runtime of the `matvec` kernel allows us to project the performance improvement of the described overlapping. The size of the vector that is synchronized amounts to $d = \frac{1391349}{2} \cdot 8\,\mathrm{B} \approx 5.57\,\mathrm{MB}$. For the transfers, we measured 1.12 ms from and 2.38 ms to the device which corresponds to bandwidths lower than the maximum. Based on this, the time for communication for each invocation of the `matvec` kernel is about $t_{comm} = 1.12\,\mathrm{ms} + 2.38\,\mathrm{ms} = 3.50\,\mathrm{ms}$. For 985 iterations, the average time of each invocation is 9.80 ms in total. These values result in the estimation of

$$o_{max} \leq \frac{min(t_{comp}, t_{comm})}{t_{exec}} \approx \frac{min(6.30\,\mathrm{ms}, 3.50\,\mathrm{ms})}{9.80\,\mathrm{ms}} \approx 35.71\,\%$$

when using formula (1).

The right-hand columns of Table 8 show the measurements when overlapping is implemented. As with CUDA above, the advantage of the improved data transfer between the two devices disappears. Again, this results from the overlapped communication which is hidden by the longer computation. In total, the optimization amounts to 26.63 % when transferring the data via the host.

When looking at the algorithm as a whole and the total runtime, the picture remains the same. The measured timings are given in Table 8. This is different to what was observed in Sect. 5: Compared to the Pascal GPUs, the Intel Xeon Phi coprocessors are based on a previous technology generation. As such, the computation of `matvec` with the same matrix takes longer. That is why the converting does not account for as much of the total runtime as with the newer GPUs above.

OpenMP. OpenMP enables direct transfers between two devices via *Device Memory Routines*. In particular, the function `omp_target_memcpy` allows us to specify the source and destination device. However, the current implementation does not yield a higher bandwidth. That is because Intel's *liboffload* does not perform any double buffering. The memory region is fully copied from the source device to a temporary buffer on the host. Afterwards, the data is transferred to the destination device. This is not expected to be faster than the manual transfers via the host.

Hence, measurements are presented only where the data is transferred via the host. Figure 5 shows the results for the naïve version. Compared to the performance on a single coprocessor, the time for the `matvec` kernel improves as expected. However, the improvement is rather low with the decrease from 10.45 s to 9.23 s. That is why both the time for the solver and the total runtime increase.

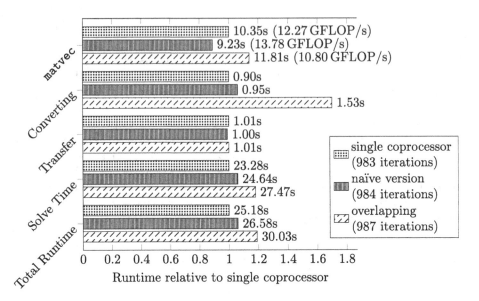

Fig. 5. Results on two Intel Xeon Phi using OpenMP.

The unsatisfactory performance is again the result of the high overhead for launching the kernels. Measurements show that 2.95 s are spent just for launching all kernels for `matvec`. This corresponds to about 31.96 % of the `matvec` runtime (9.23 s). The same effect can be observed for the other kernels that are significantly slower than, for example, with OpenCL.

The high overhead also amortizes the theoretical benefit of the optimization described in our previous work [13]. For the overlapping to happen, an additional kernel has to be launched per device. This increases the overhead by 1.94 s to a total of 4.89 s for the launches in all invocations of `matvec`. Furthermore, the computation with the data that has been transferred from the other device adds additional overhead. As a result, the runtime for the `matvec` kernel increases as depicted in Fig. 5.

Overall, the OpenMP implementation currently does not perform well for multiple Intel Xeon Phi. However, the overhead was also visible for a single device in Sect. 6.1. Because of this, the presented measurements are not necessarily a proof that asynchronous offloading with OpenMP is inferior in general. We are instead expecting that the high launch overhead can be reduced in future updates to the compiler: A small test case shows significantly lower overhead for launching kernels with the older version 16.0. Unfortunately, this older version does not implement all features of OpenMP 4.5 that are required to run the full CG implementation.

7   Summary

In this paper, we have evaluated asynchronous offloading with different programming models. On current NVIDIA GPUs, it was shown that CUDA and OpenACC perform well for the used CG method. An implementation with the OpenCL standard becomes competitive once the newer version 2.0 is used. This enables the usage of page-locked memory for decent performance.

We have revealed some shortcomings with both OpenCL and OpenMP on Intel's Xeon Phi coprocessor: While OpenCL performed well for asynchronous offloading, it suffered from vectorization issues. The current implementation of OpenMP, on the other hand, showed a high overhead for launching kernels. However, we expect that this issue can be solved with an improved runtime library.

Overall, we have shown that multiple accelerators can be used efficiently with asynchronous offloading. The results on NVIDIA GPUs indicate that directive based models are not slower than lower level interfaces. However, the performance varies depending on the programming model and its implementation. In particular, it may not necessarily correlate with the performance on a single device as seen for the Intel Xeon Phi coprocessors.

In the future, it will be interesting to evaluate the Vulkan interface [1] once implementations for scientific accelerators are available. Comparable to OpenCL, kernels are queued and execute asynchronously on the device. This fulfills the prerequisite to use multiple devices as done in this paper.

Furthermore, multiple compilers are currently gaining support for targeting NVIDIA devices with OpenMP. This would complete the set of programming models that were evaluated for this hardware. In particular, the GCC 7 release and the proprietary IBM XLC compiler already allow offloading to GPUs while not yet supporting asynchronicity. Patches for the LLVM/Clang compiler are in the process of being upstreamed. This diversity would also allow the comparison of the same programming model in multiple implementations.

Reproducibility

We have published an archive with the modifications to *liboffload*, all binaries and libraries including their respective commit ids, and the raw data of our measurements [14].

Acknowledgements. The experiments were performed with computing resources granted by JARA-HPC from RWTH Aachen University under project jara0001.

References

1. Vulkan - Industry Forged. https://www.khronos.org/vulkan/. Accessed 6 July 2017
2. Abraham, M.J., Murtola, T., Schulz, R., Pll, S., Smith, J.C., Hess, B., Lindahl, E.: GROMACS: high performance molecular simulations through multi-level parallelism from laptops to supercomputers. SoftwareX **12**, 19–25 (2015). http://www.sciencedirect.com/science/article/pii/S2352711015000059
3. Aji, A.M., Dinan, J., Buntinas, D., Balaji, P., Feng, W.-C., Bisset, K.R., Thakur, R.: MPI-ACC: an integrated and extensible approach to data movement in accelerator-based systems. In: 2012 IEEE 14th International Conference on High Performance Computing and Communication 2012 IEEE 9th International Conference on Embedded Software and Systems, pp. 647–654, June 2012
4. Allada, V., Benjegerdes, T., Bode, B.: Performance analysis of memory transfers and GEMM subroutines on NVIDIA Tesla GPU cluster. In: 2009 IEEE International Conference on Cluster Computing and Workshops, pp. 1–9, August 2009
5. Augonnet, C., Clet-Ortega, J., Thibault, S., Namyst, R.: Data-aware task scheduling on multi-accelerator based platforms. In: 2010 IEEE 16th International Conference on Parallel and Distributed Systems, pp. 291–298 (Dec 2010)
6. Beri, T., Bansal, S., Kumar, S.: A scheduling and runtime framework for a cluster of heterogeneous machines with multiple accelerators. In: 2015 IEEE International Parallel and Distributed Processing Symposium, pp. 146–155, May 2015
7. Bernaschi, M., Salvadore, F.: Multi-Kepler GPU vs. Multi-Intel MIC: a two test case performance study. In: 2014 International Conference on High Performance Computing Simulation (HPCS), pp. 1–8, July 2014
8. Boku, T., Ishikawa, K.I., Kuramashi, Y., Meadows, L., D'Mello, M., Troute, M., Vemuri, R.: A performance evaluation of CCS QCD benchmark on the COMA (Intel(R) Xeon Phi, KNC) system (2016)
9. Davis, T.: The SuiteSparse Matrix Collection (formerly known as the University of Florida Sparse Matrix Collection). https://www.cise.ufl.edu/research/sparse/matrices/. Accessed 30 May 2017
10. Deakin, T., Price, J., Martineau, M., McIntosh-Smith, S.: GPU-STREAM v2.0: benchmarking the achievable memory bandwidth of many-core processors across diverse parallel programming models. In: Taufer, M., Mohr, B., Kunkel, J.M. (eds.) ISC High Performance 2016. LNCS, vol. 9945, pp. 489–507. Springer, Cham (2016). https://doi.org/10.1007/978-3-319-46079-6_34
11. Hahnfeld, J.: CGxx - Object-Oriented Implementation of the Conjugate Gradients Method, August 2017. https://github.com/hahnjo/CGxx
12. Hahnfeld, J.: Evaluation of Asynchronous Offloading Capabilities of Accelerator Programming Models for Multiple Devices, July 2017, Bachelor thesis
13. Hahnfeld, J., Cramer, T., Klemm, M., Terboven, C., Müller, M.S.: A Pattern for Overlapping Communication and Computation with OpenMP Target Directives (2017)
14. Hahnfeld, J., Terboven, C., Price, J., Pflug, H.J., Müller, M.: Measurement data for paper "Evaluation of Asynchronous Offloading Capabilities of Accelerator Programming Models for Multiple Devices" (2017). http://dx.doi.org/10.18154/RWTH-2017-10493
15. Hestenes, M.R., Stiefel, E.: Methods of conjugate gradients for solving linear systems. J. Res. Natl. Bur. Stan. **49**(6), 409–436 (1952)

16. Hoshino, T., Maruyama, N., Matsuoka, S., Takaki, R.: CUDA vs OpenACC: performance case studies with kernel benchmarks and a memory-bound CFD application. In: 2013 13th IEEE/ACM International Symposium on Cluster, Cloud, and Grid Computing, pp. 136–143, May 2013

17. Jääskeläinen, P., de La Lama, C.S., Schnetter, E., Raiskila, K., Takala, J., Berg, H.: pocl: A performance-portable OpenCL Implementation. Int. J. Parallel Program. **43**(5), 752–785 (2015). https://doi.org/10.1007/s10766-014-0320-y

18. Jo, G., Nah, J., Lee, J., Kim, J., Lee, J.: Accelerating LINPACK with MPI-OpenCL on clusters of Multi-GPU nodes. IEEE Trans. Parallel Distrib. Syst. **26**(7), 1814–1825 (2015)

19. Krieder, S.J., Wozniak, J.M., Armstrong, T., Wilde, M., Katz, D.S., Grimmer, B., Foster, I.T., Raicu, I.: Design and evaluation of the GeMTC framework for GPU-enabled many-task computing. In: Proceedings of the 23rd International Symposium on High-performance Parallel and Distributed Computing, HPDC 2014, pp. 153–164. ACM, New York (2014). https://doi.org/10.1145/2600212.2600228

20. Lawlor, O.S.: Message passing for GPGPU clusters: CudaMPI. In: 2009 IEEE International Conference on Cluster Computing and Workshops, pp. 1–8, August 2009

21. McCalpin, J.D.: Memory bandwidth and machine balance in current high performance computers. IEEE Computer Society Technical Committee on Computer Architecture (TCCA) Newsletter, pp. 19–25, December 1995

22. Meng, Q., Humphrey, A., Schmidt, J., Berzins, M.: Preliminary experiences with the Uintah framework on Intel Xeon Phi and Stampede. In: Proceedings of the Conference on Extreme Science and Engineering Discovery Environment: Gateway to Discovery, XSEDE 2013, pp. 48:1–48:8. ACM, New York (2013). https://doi.org/10.1145/2484762.2484779

23. Mu, D., Chen, P., Wang, L.: Accelerating the discontinuous Galerkin method for seismic wave propagation simulations using multiple GPUs with CUDA and MPI. Earthquake Sci. **26**(6), 377–393 (2013). https://doi.org/10.1007/s11589-013-0047-7

24. Quintana-Ortí, G., Igual, F.D., Quintana-Ortí, E.S., van de Geijn, R.A.: Solving dense linear systems on platforms with multiple hardware accelerators. In: Proceedings of the 14th ACM SIGPLAN Symposium on Principles and Practice of Parallel Programming, PPoPP 2009, pp. 121–130. ACM, New York (2009). https://doi.org/10.1145/1504176.1504196

25. Stuart, J.A., Owens, J.D.: Message passing on data-parallel architectures. In: 2009 IEEE International Symposium on Parallel Distributed Processing, pp. 1–12, May 2009

26. Stuart, J.A., Balaji, P., Owens, J.D.: Extending MPI to accelerators. In: Proceedings of the 1st Workshop on Architectures and Systems for Big Data, ASBD 2011, pp. 19–23. ACM, New York (2011). https://doi.org/10.1145/2377978.2377981

27. Vázquez, F., Garzón, E.M.: The sparse matrix vector product on GPUs (2009)

28. Vinogradov, S., Fedorova, J., Curran, D., Cownie, J.: OpenMP 4.0 vs. OpenCL: performance comparison. In: OpenMPCon 2015, October 2015

29. Wienke, S., an Mey, D., Müller, M.S.: Accelerators for technical computing: is it worth the pain? A TCO perspective. In: Kunkel, J.M., Ludwig, T., Meuer, H.W. (eds.) ISC 2013. LNCS, vol. 7905, pp. 330–342. Springer, Heidelberg (2013). https://doi.org/10.1007/978-3-642-38750-0_25

30. Wienke, S., Terboven, C., Beyer, J.C., Müller, M.S.: A pattern-based comparison of OpenACC and OpenMP for accelerator computing. In: Silva, F., Dutra, I., Santos Costa, V. (eds.) Euro-Par 2014. LNCS, vol. 8632, pp. 812–823. Springer, Cham (2014). https://doi.org/10.1007/978-3-319-09873-9_68

31. Wozniak, J.M., Armstrong, T.G., Wilde, M., Katz, D.S., Lusk, E., Foster, I.T.: Swift/T: scalable data flow programming for many-task applications. In: Proceedings of the 18th ACM SIGPLAN Symposium on Principles and Practice of Parallel Programming, PPoPP 2013, pp. 309–310. ACM, New York (2013). https://doi.org/10.1145/2442516.2442559

32. Yamazaki, I., Tomov, S., Dongarra, J.: One-sided dense matrix factorizations on a multicore with multiple GPU accelerators. Procedia Comput. Sci. **9**, 37–46 (2012). http://www.sciencedirect.com/science/article/pii/S1877050912001263. Proceedings of the International Conference on Computational Science, ICCS 2012

33. Yan, Y., Lin, P.H., Liao, C., de Supinski, B.R., Quinlan, D.J.: Supporting multiple accelerators in high-level programming models. In: Proceedings of the Sixth International Workshop on Programming Models and Applications for Multicores and Manycores, PMAM 2015, pp. 170–180. ACM, New York (2015). https://doi.org/10.1145/2712386.2712405

Author Index

Printed in the United States
By Bookmasters